Women and the Second World War in France

WOMEN AND MEN IN HISTORY

This series, published for students, scholars and interested general readers, will tackle themes in gender history from the early medieval period through to the present day. Gender issues are now an integral part of all history courses and yet many traditional texts do not reflect this change. Much exciting work is now being done to redress the gender imbalances of the past, and we hope that these books will make their own substantial contribution to that process. We hope that these will both synthesize and shape future developments in gender studies.

The General Editors of the series are *Patricia Skinner* (University of Southampton) for the medieval period; *Pamela Sharpe* (University of Bristol) for the early modern period; and *Penny Summerfield* (University of Lancaster) for the modern period. *Margaret Walsh* (University of Nottingham) was the Founding Editor of the series.

Published books:

Imperial Women in Byzantium 1025–1204 Power, Patronage and Ideology
Barbara Hill

Masculinity in Medieval Europe *D.M. Hadley (ed.)*

Gender and Society in Renaissance Italy
Judith C. Brown and Robert C. Davis (eds)

Widowhood in Medieval and Early Modern Europe
Sandra Cavallo and Lyndan Warner (eds)

Gender, Church and State in Early Modern Germany:
   Essays by Merry E. Wiesner *Merry E. Wiesner*

Manhood in Early Modern England: Honour, Sex and Marriage
Elizabeth W. Foyster

English Masculinities, 1600–1800
Tim Hitchcock and Michele Cohen (eds)

Disorderly Women in Eighteenth-Century London:
   Prostitution in the Metropolis 1730–1830 *Tony Henderson*

Gender, Power and the Unitarians in England, 1760–1860 *Ruth Watts*

Women and Work in Russia, 1880–1930: A Study in Continuity through
   Change *Jane McDermid and Anna Hillyar*

More than Munitions: Women, Work and the Engineering Industries
   1900–1950 *Clare Wightman*

The Family Story: Blood, Contract and Intimacy, 1830–1960
Leonore Davidoff, Megan Doolittle, Janet Fink and Katherine Holden

Women and the Second World War in France, 1939–48:

Choices and Constraints

HANNA DIAMOND

Longman

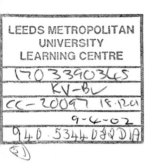
Pearson Education Limited,
Edinburgh Gate,
Harlow,
Essex CM20 2JE,
United Kingdom
and Associated Companies throughout the world

*Published in the United States of America
by Pearson Education Inc. New York*

Visit us on the world wide web at:
http://www.awl-he.com

First published 1999

ISBN 0-582-29910-1 CASED
ISBN 0-582-29909-8 PPR

British Library Cataloguing-in-Publication Data

A catalogue record for this book is available from the British Library

Library of Congress Cataloging-in-Publication Data

Diamond, Hanna, 1962–
Women and the Second World War in France, 1939–1948 : choices and
constraints / Hanna Diamond.
p.   cm. — (Women and men in history)
Includes bibliographical references and index.
ISBN 0-582-29910-1 (hardcover). — ISBN 0-582-29909-8 (paper)
1. World War, 1939–1945—Women—France.   2. Women—France—
History—20th century.   I. Title.   II. Series.
D810.W7D44   1999
940.53′44′082—dc21   99-25044
                                                                        CIP

Set in Baskerville 10/12pt by 35
Produced by Addison Wesley Longman Singapore (Pte) Ltd.
Printed in Singapore

Contents

Acknowledgements

This book owes much to many people who have helped and supported me over the years. I first wish to thank the ESRC and the CNRS for the original Franco-British studentship which was awarded to me in 1986 to finance my 18-month field trip to Toulouse for the original local study for my doctorate. The British Academy awarded me a generous grant in 1996 making it possible for me to conduct the further research in Paris, Chatellerault and the Finistère which has resulted in this book.

I am also grateful to the numerous archivists I met along the way and the fact that I was able to sift through so much information in short visits to Paris, Toulouse and Brittany owes much to their expertise. These include Madame de Tourtier-Bonazzi and her successor Madame René-Bazin at the CARAN (*Centre d'Acceuil et de Recherches des Archives Nationales*). I think I had help from nearly all the team of the *section contemporaine* over the years, but particular thanks to Monsieur Pouessel, Madame Poule and Madame Callu. I shall never forget my days out at Villemoisson at the depot of the Archives Locales de Paris guided by Monsieur Grand and his aide, Monsieur Cousin. Monsieur Daniel Collet arranged for me to see what I needed in a very short space of time in the Archives of the Finistère and I am very grateful to him for that. In Toulouse, Monsieur Christian Cau, Director of the Municipal Archives was most helpful and I will never forget Madame Maillard who was so excited finally to find someone who would be interested in the information she had amassed about women. The staff of the Archives de la Haute-Garonne and the Archives de la Défense in Chatellerault were most helpful. I was also helped by numerous librarians; Lilou Cohen at the Bibliothèque Municipale de Toulouse, Monsieur Astruc at the IHTP, the staff of the Bibliothèque Nationale de Paris, the BDIC at Nanterre, the Bibliothèque Marguerite Durand and the Musée Sociale in Paris. Katy Jordan and especially Pat Ham and her colleagues in inter library loans at the University of Bath library have been terrific and deserve a special mention for their inde-fatiguable patience in acquiring articles and books for me.

I also want to thank my informants for their particular contribu-tion to this study. They welcomed me with enormous generosity and for many, it was to talk of a very painful time. I have decided to list their names here as a measure of my appreciation but they have been changed in the text of the book. In Toulouse my thanks go to Madame Artier, Madame Auba, Madame Augot, Madame Baillaud, Madame and Monsieur Barlangue, Madame Benac, Madame Bourillon, Madame Bord, Madame Bradfer, Madame Bruno, Mon-sieur Carovis, Madame Cau, Madame Cazou, Monsieur Chauvin, Madame Chavant, Madame Cluzon, Madame de Courèges, Mon-sieur Debauges, Madame Dejean, Madame Deleysses, Madame Delpech, Madame Desmoulin, Madame Dopazo, Madame Dou, Madame Farizon, Madame Fontanier, Madame Fontes, Madame Franco, Madame Frouvelle, Madame Garrique, Madame Gineste, Madame Golenia, Madame Guchens, Madame Hercule, Madame Irastorza, Madame Jacquier, Madame Janine, Madame Lafforgue, Madame Lambert, Monsieur Latapie, Madame Linzau, Madame Maries, Madame Marty, Madame Maruzezak, Madame and Mon-sieur Maux, Madame and Docteur Mazelier, Madame Mazet, Mad-ame Metzger, Madame Monde, Madame Panlout, Madame Perie, Madame Pignières, Madame Pinel, Madame Quaranta, Madame Ramos, Docteur Rose, Madame Rioland, Madame Rivals, Madame Rumeau, Madame Ruquet, Monsieur Schintone, Madame Sicard, Madame Silvestre, Madame Strickler, Madame Taupiez, Madame Trempé, Maître Viala and Madame Ybry. In the Finistère, Madame Camus, Madame Derrien, Madame Garrec, Madame Gendron, Madame Gentric, Madame and Monsieur Glehen, Madame Hascoet, Madame Irant, Madame Kerloc'h, Madame Kervarec, Madame Le Berre, and Madame Quillevéré were kind enough to talk to me about their lives.

I have benefited from much academic advice both in the UK and in France. This book would not have existed without Rod Kedward whose undergraduate course on Vichy France awakened my interest in the period and his continuing involvement through-out the project has been invaluable. Siân Reynolds has also been a staunch adviser guiding me through my awakening to various theo-retical approaches and ways of writing history; she kindly also read and commented on parts of the manuscript. Thanks also to Máire Cross for reading the manuscript in its entirety. Ayla Aglan, Laurent Douzou and Olivier Wieviorka kindly gave me access to their oral interviews held at the CARAN. I have respected Olivier Wieviorka's request that his informants remain anonymous and this is why their names do not appear either in the text or references. Luc Capdevila provided me with accommodation in Rennes on a research trip there and offered invaluable advice about the war years in the Britanny context. Madame and Monsieur Jegou invited me to stay on their trout farm in Saint Ségal and arranged for me to meet some of their acquaintances. Christiane and Christian Nedelec put me up in Brest and the Anglas family has become my *deuxième famille* who look after me whenever I am in the South West of France. Intellectual help and support came from Dominique Veillon, Danièle Voldman and Jacqueline Sainclivier. Paula Schwartz has been a *confidante* since the beginning of the project, Simon Kitson alowed me access to unpublished material, Jenny Williams transcribed some of the interviews for me. My editors Hilary Shaw and Penny Summerfield and Verina Pettigrew were patient when the delivery of my manuscript was somewhat delayed by the arrival of my son Samuel, and when they finally received it were full of helpful comments. Claire Gorrara provided unceasing encouragement even in the most difficult times. Thanks also to colleagues in the Department of European Studies and Modern Languages particularly Bill Brooks, Anna Bull, Adalgisa Giorgio, and Steve Wharton for being prepared to listen to me and for passing on helpful material.

Finally, I dedicate this book to my mother and father; to my mother because she died in 1990 and was sadly unable to see this research come to fruition – it was she who instilled in me my interest in history and I think it is telling that I chose to work on her generation of women who lived through the war; to my father for his unstinting support of my work and because he considers himself a feminist.

Abbreviations

Abbreviations used in footnotes

ADBduR	Archives Départementales du Bouches du Rhône
ADF	Archives Départementales du Finistère
ADHG	Archives Départementales de la Haute Garonne
ALP	Archives Locales de Paris
AMT	Archives Municipales de Toulouse
AN	Archives Nationales
IHTP	Institut d'Histoire du Temps Présent
IMT	Institut Marxiste de Toulouse (Marxist Institute of Toulouse)
INED	Institut National des Etudes Démographiques (National Institute of Demographic Studies)
INSEE	Institut National de la Statistique et des Etudes Economiques (National Institute of Statistics and Economic Studies)
RG	Renseignements Généraux

Abbreviations used in text

ACA	*Assemblée des Cardinaux et Archevêques* (Committee of Cardinals and Archbishops).
CDL	*Comités Départementaux de Libération* (Departmental Liberation committees). Local committees nominated often as early as the winter of 1943–44. These committees were set up to formulate local policy and oversee the passage from the Occupation to peace.
CFLN	*Comité Français de Libération Nationale* (French Committee for National Liberation). The governing body established in Algiers under both de Gaulle and Giraud. From the spring of 1944, de Gaulle assumed sole leadership.

CGT   *Confédération Générale du Travail* (General Confederation of Labour). Communist trade union.

CLL   *Comité Local de Libération* (Local Liberation committee). Committees nominated by the Resistance to take the place of the municipal councils at the Liberation until the first postwar local elections of April–May 1945.

CNR   *Conseil National de la Résistance* (National Resistance Council). The main achievement of Jean Moulin, who managed to unite the Resistance under de Gaulle. Its essential role was to give shape to the aims of the Resistance for liberated France.

COSOR   *Comité des Œuvres Sociales de la Résistance.* The Resistance social services which was founded during the Occupation and continued into the postwar period to help those who were victims of the war.

CVR   *Combattant Volontaire de la Résistance.* Card-carrying member of the Resistance.

DF   *Défense de la France.* A Resistance network based in the northern zone which arose from the clandestine newspaper of the same name.

FFI   *Forces Françaises de l'Intérieur* (French Interior Forces). The official and at first largely theoretical merging of all armed Resistance into one military organization. The FFI dated from the end of 1943, but it was not until the spring of 1944 that regional and departmental FFI leaders were in place.

FFL   *Forces Françaises Libres.* Free French Forces based in London.

FN   *Front National* (National Front). The Resistance movement initiated by the communist party in 1941, which operated in both zones and was open to all volunteers whether communist or not.

FTP   *Francs-Tireurs-Partisans.* The military organization of the *Front National.*

GPRF   *Gouvernement Provisoire de la République Française* (Provisional Government of the French Republic). This developed from the CFLN, and, led by de Gaulle, established itself in Paris at the Liberation and continued the war against Germany.

JAC   *Jeunesse Agricole Chrétienne.* Catholic youth agricultural movement.

JOC   *Jeunesse Ouvrière Chrétienne.* Christian youth workers movement.

JOCF   *Jeunesse Ouvrière Chrétienne Féminine.* Women's section of the above.

LVF   *Légion des Volontaires Français contre le Bolchévisme.* Young men who fought for Germany on the Russian front created on 11 July 1941.

MNPGD   *Mouvement National des Prisonniers de Guerre et Déportés.* Clandestine movements of prisoners-of-war and deportees.

MOI   *Main-d'Œuvre Immigrée* (Immigrant Workforce). Prewar organization set up by the PCF to defend the rights of immigrant workers in France. It became a Resistance force and worked with local Resistance leaders, particularly communists, to create *maquis* and FTP groups.

MRP   *Mouvement Républicain Populaire* (Popular Republican Movement). A political grouping which appeared at the Liberation formed by a group of Christian Resisters who wished to reconcile democracy, social progress and Christianity. They benefited from the support of a large part of the moderate electorate, particularly women, and came to be seen as the undeclared Gaullist party.

MUR   *Mouvements Unis de la Résistance* (United Movements of the Resistance). This was created in 1943 by Jean Moulin when the movements *Combat, Libération* and *Franc-Tireur* were joined together; MUR means 'wall' in French.

PCF   *Parti Communist Français* (French Communist Party).

PPF   *Parti Populaire Français.* The prewar party of ex-communist Jacques Doriot which was originally founded in reaction to the Popular Front. Closely involved in acts of collaboration, notably the recruitment of the *Légion des Volontaires Français contre le Bolchévisme* (LVF). Its membership was generally younger than the RNP, and it had its own youth section, the *Jeunesse Françaises Populaires.*

RNP   *Rassemblement National Populaire.* Founded 1 February 1941 by Marcel Déat, like other European fascist groups it recruited essentially from the middle classes.

SFIO   *Section Française de l'Intérnationale Ouvrière* (French section of the International Socialist Movement – Socialist Party).

SNCF   *Société Nationale des Chemins de Fer Français.* The French railway network.

SOL   *Service d'Ordre Légionnaire.* Created on 23 February 1942 as an activist section of the *Légion.* Although its creation led to an overall decline in membership of the *Légion,* the SOL remained strong in the main cities of the south.

SS   *Schutzstaffeln.* Organized by Heinrich Himmler, they made up several armoured divisions within France and were the most determined in their actions against the *maquis.*

STO   *Service de Travail Obligatoire* (Compulsory Labour Draft). A successor to the *Relève* scheme to meet Sauckel's demands for labour in Germany introduced in February 1943. Men aged between 18 and 35 were obliged to work in Germany; women between 21 and 35 were also affected, but were not sent abroad. Departures took place intermittently until June 1944. This measure, more than any other, precipitated opposition to Vichy and the Germans in the French population and many attempted to find ways of escaping it.

TC   *Témoignage Chrétien.* A Catholic-based Resistance group, originally most active in the southern zone.

UFCS   *Union Féminine Civique et Sociale* (Women's Civic and Social Union). A Catholic, conservative women's organization.

UFF   *Union des Femmes Françaises* (Union of French Women). This group was founded during the war as a broad-based Resistance movement but nearly always remained communist-dominated. At the Liberation, many women became members of the CDLs or CLLs as representatives of the UFF.

Map

CHAPTER ONE

Introduction

From one war to another

No history which deals with any aspect of twentieth-century France, and particularly one which is concerned with women, can ignore the devastating impact of the First World War on French society. Most families were directly affected by it, with at least one male member who was killed or maimed. Hardly had the country had time to recover when more upheaval was to come. Although France was not hit as early as other European countries by the world depression, when it did arrive it was longer lasting. One consequence of this economic hardship was a period of social and political upheaval. Fear of Fascism led to unprecedented anti-fascist demonstrations and the election of a left-wing Popular Front government, a coalition of radicals, socialists and communists, from 1936 to 1937, presided over by Leon Blum.

Hitler had come to power in Germany in 1933 and his expansionist aims increased throughout his dictatorship. Most of the population of France, like that of the rest of Europe, refused to allow itself to believe that another war was a serious possibility. French governments between 1933 and 1939 failed to define a clear policy towards Hitler's Germany. The outbreak of the Spanish Civil War in 1936 distracted European attention away from Germany, but French government policy towards it was confused. French Republicans felt bound to support the Spanish Republicans, but the British policy of non-intervention prevailed in French government circles. The French again followed the British lead in their relations with Germany by adopting the approach of appeasing Hitler in order to prevent another war. After the signing of the Munich agreement in 1938, many believed that Hitler's expansionist aims had been satisfied, and it was hoped that war had been postponed, if not completely avoided. However, after the invasion of Poland by German troops on 1 September 1939, Daladier, Prime Minister of France, along with the British government honoured their alliance and declared war on Germany two days later.

The French were not totally unprepared for war, but had concentrated all their efforts on a defensive policy, investing in a fortified border along the eastern frontier, known as the Maginot line, which stopped short of Belgium. After several months of inactivity known as the phoney war, in May 1940 German tanks were able to break through the Ardennes forest in Belgium and into France, thus circumventing the Maginot line. German advance was swift. The Maginot line collapsed, and huge numbers of refugees fled south in the wake of the German army in a phenomenon that has become known as the exodus. What had began as a stream took on massive proportions as people headed south using every conceivable means of transport, many simply on foot. Between 15 May and 20 June at least six million French women and men (perhaps as many as eight million) left their homes. As some towns in the north emptied, others further south filled.[1] Historians have shown that this was an experience that particularly affected women, children and the elderly.[2] Belgian refugees arrived in the southern part of the country, quickly followed by French men and women from the north and east of France and the area around Paris. In an atmosphere of fear and panic, the population of the major towns in the south swelled enormously. Local authorities found it hard to feed and find shelter for all those who needed it. The shops emptied and certain products disappeared altogether. For many, whether they were on the move or witnessing the presence of numerous refugees in the town or village square, this event had a major impact. Despite unpleasant stories that have survived about locals charging refugees for a glass of water, it appears that many families took in and helped people, and for some women this kind of activity served as a consciousness-raising experience, which may in some cases have established a predisposition to later resistance (see Chapter 5).

Paris was declared an open city, and the authorities of Paris surrendered to Germany on 14 June 1940. The defeat was complete. The French government fled south from Paris ahead of the

1. Jean-Pierre Azéma, *De Munich à la Libération* (Paris, 1979), p. 62.
2. Nicole Ann Dombrowski, 'Beyond the Battlefield: The French Civilian Exodus of May–June 1940 (World War II)', unpublished PhD thesis (New York University, 1995); Guylaine Guidez, *Femmes dans la guerre 1939–1945* (Paris, 1989), p. 20.

advancing German forces, stopping first at Tours and then moving on to Bordeaux. On 17 June, Marshal Philippe Pétain offered himself as leader to the French people in a radio broadcast suggesting that the country should agree to an Armistice. A day later, a little-known General Charles de Gaulle, in a speech transmitted from London by the BBC, rejected any thought of Armistice and called for the battle to continue. Few people heard the BBC broadcast. It was Pétain with his entourage who were able to gain full powers on 10 July 1940 when the *députés* of the Third Republic meeting in the casino of the town of Vichy (the only local place able to accommodate them all) almost exclusively voted in his favour. Vichy immediately became the new centre of government.

Pétain's announcement that he was seeking an Armistice was received with some relief in the atmosphere of confusion, overcrowding and general disorientation. Its political significance was often overlooked since for many it appeared to represent the end of a nightmare. According to the terms of the Armistice, Alsace-Lorraine was annexed to Hitler's Reich and ten departments from the Somme to the Doubs were attached to the Brussels command: an area known as the reserved or forbidden zone. The rest of France was divided into two main zones, with a dividing line running from the Pyrénées up to Tours and then across to the Alps just south of Dijon (see map). The northern Occupied zone, covering over half the country, more than half of its population, and the greater part of its resources, was invaded and administered by the Germans. The Non-Occupied zone, south-west of the line, the *zone libre*, otherwise known as the *zone sud*, was placed under the authority of Pétain based in Vichy. Until its suppression in March 1943, the line of demarcation between the two zones functioned as a real territorial frontier. It was manned by German soldiers and special papers were necessary to be able to cross from one zone to the other. The north and east coastal areas had an even more intense German presence, and permits were again required both for travel within and entry into these areas. In 1941, a forbidden coastal zone was created which ran from Dunkerque to Hendaye along the coast and covered the territory 30 km inland.

In the weeks following the Armistice, the authorities urged people to return home, and many did so, hoping to have news of absent relations. Most were relieved to be spared another war like that of 1914–18. The fighting over, demobilized soldiers returned. Women in the Finistère recalled husbands and fathers returning home on foot, some after walking for several days. These households soon readapted to the return of their men, and family life resumed its prewar pattern, but under the changed circumstances of the war. However, not all the men returned. About 92,000 soldiers had been killed[3] and 1,850,000 had become prisoners-of-war in Germany.[4] Of these prisoners, the vast majority were young married men who left wives and young families in France. Their time of absence could vary. Some were able to escape in the course of the war, and Azéma estimates that by 1944 only 940,000 were left in Germany.[5] However, most prisoners who were absent from their homes were away for a full five years, leaving their families to manage without them.

From the summer of 1940, French people set about carrying on with their lives as best they could, but life was strikingly different in the two zones of France. In the northern zone, the population had to learn to live in close proximity with Germans. All information was controlled, and it took some time before they realized that the shortages that they were experiencing were a direct consequence of German requisitioning. The German presence was postponed for two years for those living in the southern zone, where the Vichy government under Pétain took charge. The true impact of the Occupation may have been delayed for those living in the so-called 'free zone', but they were subjected to the National Revolution launched by Vichy which was designed to purge the country of the decadence which had led to its defeat. This involved a desire to return to traditional values. The Republican motto of 'Liberty, Egality, Fraternity' was replaced with that of 'Work, Family and Homeland'. The purification process focused particularly on Jews, and Vichy passed a series of anti-Semitic statutes without being asked to by the Germans. From 1942, 'Jew' had to be stamped on their identity cards and, once identified, they were barred from holding jobs in administration; a 2 per cent quota in medicine, law and teaching meant that many lost their jobs. Foreign Jews (and later French Jews) were rounded up and then handed over to the Germans.

The existence of the southern zone, the domain of the Vichy government, was brought to an abrupt end in November 1942 after the Allied invasion of North Africa, when the Germans marched across the demarcation line, installing themselves across the country from the Pyrénées to the Italian frontier. The introduction of STO (*Service de Travail Obligatoire*) in February 1943, which forcibly drafted French men to work in Germany, after the failure of the

3. Jean-Pierre Rioux, *La France de la Quatrième République* (Paris, 1980), p. 80.
4. Azéma, *De Munich à la Libération*, p. 176.   5. Ibid.

voluntary *Relève* scheme, triggered further hostility towards the Germans. Although most French people had supported Pétain in 1940, perhaps believing that he was playing a 'double game' and working ultimately in the interests of France, the reality of the Vichy government, as no more than a puppet for the Germans, now gradually became apparent.

De Gaulle's speech on 18 June 1940, rejecting the Armistice and calling for the battle to continue, was heard by few people. Gradually his regular broadcasts on the BBC gained a following which grew as the months went by, and he began to become a key figure and rallying point for those who rejected the German presence. Inside France, despite the courageous gestures of some rare individuals, it was more difficult for people to organize opposition, particularly in the Occupied areas. In 1941–42, groups of like-minded people (men and women) began to meet and organize networks and eventually to liaise with de Gaulle in London. Early resistance was often the result of contacts between friends who felt the need to do something. The nature of their efforts depended on where they were. In the north, resistance was predominantly directed against the German presence. The earliest resistance in the south took the form of small groups of refugees who helped Jews and other political refugees to escape from concentration camps and from the country. The crucial date given by most commentators as the time when resistance began to emerge is 1942. For many, the Occupation of the *zone libre* in November 1942 revealed the true link between the Vichy regime and the Germans. The time for *attentisme* was past and people were increasingly having to accept or reject the idea of Vichy and Occupation. Until this time, the worries of daily life prevented many people from taking an interest in political and military events. The realities of 'collaboration' as defined by the Vichy government and the increasing difficulties of daily life, lack of food and shortages of every kind, led some people to withdraw their support from the regime. For those who were prepared to take the risks involved, the Resistance was beginning to offer them an alternative, and by 1942 resistance groups were becoming increasingly established. Networks like *Libération*, *Combat* and *Franc-Tireur* appeared at first in the southern zone and later in the northern zone. Initially, these different organizations were far from being structured: people were rarely formally affiliated to them, but worked with one or two others. A number might have belonged simultaneously to several different groups. At first, their main concern was to create a clandestine press in an attempt to try to convince the public that action was necessary and possible.

Over the next two years, networks of resistance became increasingly organized and liaised with de Gaulle in London and then Algiers. From Christmas 1944, preparations for invasion by the Allies intensified. A provisional government was established in Algiers which organized departmental and local Liberation committees (*Comités Départementaux de Libération*, CDL) to deal with local administration after the departure of the German forces. From May 1944, resistance activities increased, and in some parts of the country the population was drawn into open street battles with the Germans as the *maquis* intensified their guerrilla warfare aimed at disorganizing transport and destabilizing the enemy. The invasion of the Allies in Normandy on 6 June was taken as a signal for resistance groups across the country to increase their activity. This led to a cycle of attacks by the Resistance, often followed by vicious repression by the Germans. The ensuing withdrawal of the German army was unpleasant and often bloody as fighting troops carried out revenge attacks on civil populations.

Events of the Liberation varied across France with different degrees of impact on local populations as different parts of France underwent liberation from the Germans in different ways. Many of those in urban areas experienced bombing as the Allies attacked key industrial targets. In some regions, the liberation was achieved without the help of the Allies (the Alps, the Jura and much of the South-West and the Massif Centrale). By 26 August, de Gaulle was able to march triumphantly down the Champs Elysées. Although in some areas there was drawn-out fighting – pockets of Brittany, for example, remained under the control of Germans until 1945 – most of France was liberated by September 1944.

The Liberation was a painful period of transition for the country, which moved from being an occupied, defeated power under an authoritarian government to a restored Republic somewhat answerable to the Allies. Politically, there were tensions about who was to step into the power vacuum created by the German withdrawal after the discrediting and collapse of the Vichy administration. On a local level, the appointed government officials and officers of de Gaulle's GPRF (*Gouvernement Provisoire de la République Française*) sometimes found themselves in competition with communist bodies, certain Resistance movements and even the Americans. However, this power struggle was not very long-lasting and there seems to have been no serious move on the part of the communists to make a bid for power. In a matter of weeks, de Gaulle was able to establish himself as the legitimate power base of the new Republic. His visits around the country from September to November 1944 exerted a calming influence on local populations and he was able to ensure that the government structures he supported were put into place both on a local and on a departmental level.

The war, of course, continued until May 1945, so women whose men were STO workers in Germany, prisoners-of-war, or held in concentration camps, continued to live without them. Their personal war only came to a close with the return of the men, but even this often led to difficult problems of readaptation after what could be up to five years of separation (see Chapter 7). Indeed, it was not until 1948 that daily life returned to some form of normality with more consistent supplies of food and other essentials.

Historiography of the Second World War

The experience of military defeat, foreign occupation and liberation has been a major concern of historical research on twentieth-century France. The Occupation has been much written about and discussed since 1945. The mainstream history of the war has been political in focus and has concentrated on events and the political development both of resistance and of collaboration. It has varied considerably over time. The first accounts were written by resisters, who dominated the field.[6] But it is a period which has also held much fascination for British and American scholars, most notably Robert Paxton, who made the most striking contribution to opening the debate.[7] In the last twenty-five years, French scholars have produced research indicating a need to come to grips with this period in their past.[8] But interest in the period has not been confined to a few specialist academics. The extent to which Vichy and the Occupation has remained present in the consciousness of the French was first ably demonstrated by Henri Rousso in his book on the 'Vichy syndrome', and more recently in *Vichy, un passé qui ne*

6. The *Comité d'Histoire de la Deuxième Guerre Mondiale* was formed in 1951 with Henri Michel as its President. It published many accounts of Resistance in its *Revue d'histoire de la deuxième guerre mondiale*. Other early Resistance accounts include: Jean Cassou, *La Mémoire courte* (Paris, 1953); Henri Michel, *Les Courants de pensée de la Résistance* (Paris, 1962); Charles de Gaulle, *Mémoires de guerre* (Paris, 1950–60).

7. Robert Paxton, *Vichy France. 1940–44* (New York, 1972); Bertram Gordon, *Collaborationism in France during the Second World War* (Ithaca, 1980).

8. Yves Durand, *Vichy 1940–44* (Paris, 1972); Claude Lévy, *Les Nouveaux Temps et l'idéologie de la collaboration* (Paris, 1974); Pascal Ory, *Les Collaborateurs 1940–45* (Paris, 1976).

passe pas.[9] The early 1990s have seen a series of events organized to celebrate the fiftieth anniversary of the war, which culminated in 1995. These celebrations led to a spate of memorials, including the official recognition of 16 July 1942, when thousands of Jewish men, women and children were rounded up in the Vélodrome d'Hiv in Paris and deported. The fiftieth anniversaries of various events as they arrived, the Liberation, the end of the war and so on, were also marked by a number of conferences around the country (Caen, Rennes, Rouen, Bordeaux, Toulouse, Aix-en-Provence) which focused on local experiences of the war and the Occupation, but with the main emphasis on the Resistance. The discussion which surrounded the publication of Pierre Péan's book on Mitterrand's youth and the description of his links with the Vichy government also drew considerable public interest.[10] The focus has also been sustained to a considerable degree by the ongoing war trials which have taken place throughout the 1980s and 1990s. In 1987 Klaus Barbie was tried, and in 1993 Paul Touvier was the first Frenchman to be condemned for crimes against humanity. Bousquet was shot in June 1993 before coming to trial, and most recently Papon has been sentenced to ten years for 'complicity in crimes against humanity'. All these cases have attracted much media attention.

The main emphasis of French scholars has been to concentrate on the chief political actors and events, and most of these historians have had very little to say about women or gender divisions. However, it would be wrong to say that there has been no literature about women. For example, although official accounts of the Resistance made little or no mention of women, a large and (still) growing collection of narrative biographical/autobiographical writing has appeared. In these books, women recount their wartime resistance experiences; many have been re-edited and republished to coincide with the recent interest in the period.[11] The most popular of these has been Lucie Aubrac's *Ils partiront dans l'ivresse* (translated as *Outwitting the Gestapo*), which became the film *Lucie Aubrac* (1997, Claude Berri).[12] A key text on women's participation in the Resistance was put together in 1977 after a conference organized by the Union

---

9. Henri Rousso, *Le Syndrome de Vichy* (Paris, 1984); with Eric Conan, *Vichy, un passé qui ne passe pas* (Paris, 1994).

10. Pierre Péan, *Une Jeunesse française* (Paris, 1995).

11. Marie Chamming, *J'ai choisi la tempête* (Paris, 1965/1997); Brigitte Friang, *Regarde-toi qui meurs* (Paris, 1970/1989).

12. Lucie Aubrac, *Ils partiront dans l'ivresse* (Paris, 1984), translated as *Outwitting the Gestapo* (Nebraska, 1994).

des Femmes Françaises and contains enormously rich material about all aspects of women's involvement.[13] This material contains some valuable social data, but is predominantly anecdotal and lacks an analytical overview. Its focus has been almost exclusively on acts of resistance, which has meant that other aspects of women's experience, their everyday lives, and in particular their involvement with collaboration, have been virtually ignored.

Recently, there has been a notable shift of interest towards a more social history of the Occupation years. Henri Amouroux's extraordinary series of books on everyday life drew a picture of wartime experience that most French people were able to recognize.[14] The *Institut d'Histoire du Temps Présent* (which replaced the *Comité de la Deuxième Guerre Mondiale*) commissioned a number of local studies as the archives become more accessible after 1981 and these appeared in their journal. Most recently they have put together an extensive study from their own correspondents.[15] A book by Dominique Veillon, one of the researchers based there, was the first of its kind to give a full overview of everyday life during the war.[16] However, this research too has so far failed to fully address women's experience by contrast with men's.

On the other hand, a number of publications in women's history have appeared both in French and in English and these concentrate specifically on women and the war. Paula Schwarz has produced some key articles on women's involvement in the Resistance.[17] The sociologist Francine Muel-Dreyfus recently published an extremely thorough study of the origins of Vichy policy towards women.[18] Miranda Pollard, by exploring Vichy policy and discourse towards women, has written about the ways in which Vichy intended to prescribe roles for women.[19] Françoise Thébaud edited a collection of essays from a number of key researchers in the field on Resistance

---

13. *Les Femmes dans la Résistance*, UFF (Paris, 1977).

14. Henri Amouroux, *La Vie des Français sous l'Occupation* (Paris, 1961); *La Grande Histoire des Français sous l'Occupation* (Paris, 1977–97), Vols 1–10.

15. *Les Cahiers de l'IHTP: le temps des restrictions en France (1939–1949)* (CNRS, 1996).

16. Dominique Veillon, *Vivre et survivre en France 1939–47* (Paris, 1995).

17. Paula Schwarz, 'Redefining Resistance: Women's Activism in Wartime France', in M.R. Higonnet, J. Jenson, S. Michel and M.C. Weitz (eds), *Behind the Lines: Gender and the Two World Wars* (New Haven and London, 1987); '*Partisanes* and Gender Politics in Vichy France', *French Historical Studies* (Spring 1989).

18. Francine Muel-Dreyfus, *Vichy et l'éternel féminin* (Paris, 1996).

19. Miranda Pollard, 'Femme, Famille, France: Vichy and the Politics of Gender, 1940–1944', unpublished PhD thesis (University of Dublin, 1990), and *Reign of Virtue: Mobilizing Gender in Vichy France, 1940–44* (Chicago, 1998).

and the Liberation.[20] Research is now also beginning to emerge on the hitherto almost taboo subject of collaboration. Peter Novick and Herbert Lottmann began discussion of the purges and the head-shaving of women which was part of this phenomenon.[21] A number of scholars, including the anthropologist Alain Brossat, have opened up the subject further.[22] More articles on other forms of collaboration concerning women are now beginning to appear as the archives open up, though to date no book has yet appeared which is devoted to the subject.

While providing a synthesis of existing research on the period, this book draws upon the existing literature on women and the Occupation in both French and English. It also uses extensive primary material, both from archives and from oral interviews. It aims to give a fuller picture of women's lives at this time. It analyses the disruption brought to women's lives by the war and explores the political choices made by women. What were the circumstances which influenced them one way or another? What were their choices and their constraints? It does not claim to be a definitive history of French women during the war, but to advance the debates and emphasize existing lacunae in our knowledge on the subject.

Theoretical and methodological approaches

Feminist theory and women's studies have brought historians to explore how gender along with class can be an important element in historical analysis. Early work in this field was directly inspired by the feminist movement, which sought to uncover women's experience of the past, experience which had previously been hidden or invisible. This body of work was motivated by the need to 'restore women to history' and to show that women were also makers of history. This process led to the development of new visions of history.

20. Françoise Thébaud, *Clio: histoire, femmes et sociétés, résistances et libérations* (Toulouse, 1995).

21. Peter Novick, *L'Epuration française, 1944–49* (Paris, 1985); Herbert Lottmann, *L'Epuration 1943–1953* (Paris, 1986).

22. This is further explored in Chapter 6. See Alain Brossat, *Les Tondues: un carnaval moche* (Paris, 1993); Corran Laurens, 'La Femme au turban: les femmes tondues', in H.R. Kedward and N. Wood (eds), *The Liberation of France: Image and Event* (London, 1995), pp. 159–73; Fabrice Virgili, 'Les "Tondues" à la Libération: le corps des femmes, enjeu d'une réappropriation', in Thébaud (ed.), *Clio*, and 'Les Tontes de la Libération en France', in François Rouquet and Danièle Voldman (eds), *Les Cahiers de l'IHTP*, 31 (1995).

It became more than just a question of uncovering new information: the material forced new readings and interpretations of the past.

> The search for women's history has encouraged reflection on what such history could be, what implications it holds for the rest of historiography, and what its relationship to a truly general history should be, a history in which women and men equally have a place.[23]

This realization inspired a great deal of theoretical writing around the concepts of women's history, feminist history and gender history, which are all terms that have been used to label the work produced by historians who see women as their main historical subject.

There are a number of theoretical debates concerning the ways women were affected by the two world wars.[24] Generally speaking, the great wars of the twentieth century have been presented as watersheds for women. They offered women new opportunities to demonstrate their capabilities and thereby enabled them to challenge prejudices which confined them to a separate sphere. The wars also brought women political rights (women acquired formal citizenship in the UK, USA and Germany after the First World War and in Italy and France after the Second), which suggests that their good behaviour and their contribution to the struggle were more important than the organized suffrage movements. Debates also centre around the long- and short-term impact of the war. For some, the structures which were established or improvised during the war brought changes which revolutionized women's lives. For others, like Alain Milward and Angus Calder, war does not bring abour major change but merely accentuates or hastens existing processes. According to this argument, the radical changes for women brought by the war were merely interruptions in 'normal' gender relations for the 'duration' of the war.

This book explores these arguments in the context of women's wartime experience in France. The Liberation has traditionally been taken as a watershed in twentieth-century French history. Thus, most contemporary histories of France have tended to take 1944–45 as their ending or starting point. This book covers the period 1939–48 with the express intention of questioning this periodization. It therefore takes its analysis of women's wartime experience beyond

---

23. Gisela Bock, 'Women's History and Gender History: Aspects of an International Debate', *Gender and History*, 1/1 (Spring 1989).
24. These debates are most clearly summarized in the introductory essays to Higonnet *et al.* (eds), *Behind the Lines*: see Joan W. Scott, 'Rewriting History', pp. 21–31, and Margaret Higonnet and Patrice Higonnet, 'The Double Helix', pp. 31–47.

the end of the war to re-examine the assumption that the Liberation or 1945 represents a particular watershed as far as women's experience is concerned. Furthermore, the second half of the book also asks how far women actually experienced any kind of 'liberation' at this time.

The book arose out of a thesis on women's history and aims to provide new information to balance the male-dominated war history and the very stereotyped representations of women in much of the existing literature. It is concerned with the material forces which shaped women's lives and experiences and the structures which caused them to adopt certain patterns of behaviour. For example, how did women actually 'experience' Vichy government policy and discourse. The material collected here is the basis for showing up the complexities of women's lives, and the focus on women suggests new perceptions of gender relations and identities in the war years.

Sources about women are often difficult to find and this is even more the case for the Second World War where many of the archives have been inaccessible until very recently. The nature of the period and the subject has meant that it has been virtually impossible to provide consistent statistical data to substantiate all the points that are made here. Official statistics were often not maintained during the war; some were destroyed at the end of the Occupation accidentally or because of Allied bombing, and sometimes with deliberate intent in cases where they might have been considered compromising. As only very few documents are officially classified as relating to women, the historian is obliged to trawl through a mass of documents concerning every aspect of daily life, in order to find references that might be of use. This was my experience when conducting research for my local study in Toulouse, the subject of my doctoral thesis which was limited geographically. However, although this book draws heavily on my findings from the local study in Toulouse, it is also extensively supplemented with other primary material. Some of this comes from the Finistère in Brittany, a coastal area which had a very intense German presence from May 1940 onwards. By contrast, the people of Toulouse experienced the administration of the Vichy government until November 1942 when the Germans moved into the occupation of the Southern Zone. Further material is taken from the national and local archives in Paris and concerns the lives of women who remained in the capital during the period. France is such a varied and rich country with so much of its culture locally based that it would be impossible to write a national history that truly accounted for its regional differences.

This book does not claim to understand these contexts completely, but by examining the experiences of women in a number of different parts of the country, it offers some awareness of both general trends and regional differences.

One of the hallmarks of women's history is that it has been enterprising in looking for source material and has gone beyond traditional sources. Thus, in addition to traditional archival sources which are the basis of the primary evidence collected here, I have also used oral sources, and I cannot overestimate the value of these for gaining insights into people's lives (particularly women's) and into aspects which are not covered by the documentary material. For my study of Toulouse, I was able to conduct a complete series of 64 interviews which included women and some men from a range of different socio-economic backgrounds.[25] Although this sample is skewed towards the experiences of one particular generation (those who were young in the 1940s), these interviews offer an extensive picture of women's lives at the time. I was able to add a further 15 interviews which I conducted in the Finistère, as well as information from the oral archives held in the Archives Nationales. Interviews have some obvious shortcomings as source material, and oral testimony can never provide an unmediated account of the past. I appreciate that some historians criticize oral sources as '*archives provoquées*', but even if the information is to some degree 'interpreted' for the benefit of the researcher, it is no less thought-provoking as a representation of the past.[26] A telling example of this is the work of Lucie Aubrac. Her first publication about her resistance experiences was a history of the resistance movement she was involved with expressed in non-gender terms.[27] Her second book, *Outwitting the Gestapo* (mentioned above), is her account of her experience as a woman resistance worker, and in it she offers a very different narrative of her own role in events both as an individual and as a woman.[28] It seems that the reliability of these different accounts is not what is at stake, as each kind is both helpful (recounting information

25. Hanna Diamond, 'Women's Experience during and after World War Two in the Toulouse Area 1939–48: Choices and Constraints', unpublished PhD thesis (University of Sussex, 1992).

26. Hanna Diamond, 'Oral History: An Assessment', in Maire Cross and Sheila Perry (eds), *Voices of France* (London, 1997), pp. 59–77. For other discussions of the use of oral history see The Personal Narratives Group (eds), *Truths: Interpretating Women's Lives* (Bloomington and Indianapolis 1989); Sherna B. Gluck and Daphne Patai (eds), *Women's Words: The Feminist Practice of Oral History* (London, 1991).

27. Lucie Aubrac, *La Résistance: naissance et organization* (Paris, 1945).

28. Aubrac, *Ils partiront dans l'ivresse.*

not available elsewhere) and constructed (putting a particular spin on events in retrospect). We cannot ignore either of them but we have to apply our usual scepticism to both.

In this study, oral history is used to complement official sources found in national and regional archives. It is a valuable addition to the book and makes a revelatory contribution: it reveals responses to policies (and that these responses were sometimes different from the expectations of policy-makers, for example in terms of women choosing to work in order to get benefits that were intended to obviate the need for them to work); it reveals local and personal coping strategies (see particularly Chapters 3 and 7); it reveals local and personal practices and passions (Chapters 4, 5 and 6); and it reveals subjective responses to political 'liberation' (Chapter 8). I have always accounted for information that I acquired from oral sources, and where possible I have allowed the women's voices to be heard directly.[29] Their accounts add a supplementary texture to this history. This also means that readers can accept or reject the evidence as they would that of any other historical source. In practice these oral sources may cross-fertilize with archival sources to build up a more complex picture of women's lives. They provide us with considerably more elements to help us better understand patterns of women's experience at this time. There are, however, some areas of women's experience which are not adequately explored here, most notably that of Jewish and immigrant women. This is material which is extremely difficult to obtain, although other researchers are now beginning to open up the field.[30]

Structure of the book

The book is divided into two main parts. Part One deals with women's wartime experiences and explores a number of themes which are then taken up in the second part of the book and re-examined in the context of the immediate postwar years. Chapter 2 is concerned with how women acquired the financial resources they needed to survive. It shows how the benefit system put into

---

29. To protect the anonymity of witnesses, their names have been changed. All translations from the French are my own.

30. See the work of Karen Adler: 'No Words To Say It? Women and the Expectation of Liberation', in Kedward and Wood (eds), *The Liberation of France*, pp. 77–91; 'Idealizing France, 1942–1948: The Place of Gender and Race', unpublished PhD thesis (University of Sussex, 1998).

place by the wartime and subsequent Vichy government was not a serious attempt to compensate women for their missing bread-winners. Many women took on paid employment during this period, although they were alternately welcomed and pushed out of the labour market as government policy dictated. Having established where women's financial resources came from, Chapter 3 explores how the money was spent and how women were able to ensure both their own physical survival and that of those around them. Men and women experienced this aspect of daily life very differently, and it was women who took on the burden of the extra work brought about by wartime restrictions and rationing. Women were called upon to mobilize other skills, and their attempts to cater for their families might easily have brought them into contact with the author-ities in a number of ways.

Chapters 4 and 5 are concerned with women's political choices and activities during the Occupation; Chapter 4 deals with collab-orations and Chapter 5 with resistances. I position myself within the recent re-evaluation of collaboration and resistance which sees them not as clear cut and static, but full of complex graduations, taking several and various forms and above all changing over time.[31] Histor-ians have already done much to redefine women's resistance, and an investigation of the relations between circumstances and motiva-tion is included in Chapter 5. Questions are now being asked about women and collaboration, as historians examine the collaboration trials and explore women's experience of the purges, but the focus has been particularly on head-shaving which is in fact a spectacular reaction to presumed collaboration of a more personal than polit-ical nature. Much of the existing literature still operates on the level of apportioning praise or blame. This voluntaristic approach does not correspond to much of the evidence and testimony from the time. French people of both sexes might have taken certain courses of action which seemed appropriate at the time for whatever reasons and found themselves inadvertently drawn into a web of Vichy or anti-Vichy culture. Because politics penetrated everyday life, women initially sometimes found themselves in a position vis-à-vis the regime by simply continuing their daily lives. As the war went on, both women and men found themselves increasingly forced to take up an attitude towards collaboration and resistance. A distinction can be

---

31. Pierre Laborie, *Résistants Vichyssois et autres: l'évolution de l'opinion et des com-portements dans le Lot de 1939 à 1944* (Paris, 1980); H.R. Kedward, *Resistance in Vichy France* (Oxford, 1978); John Sweets, *Choices in Vichy France* (Oxford, 1986).

made between the sexes. Women often had to make choices in circumstances which were very different from those of men, and women were not on an equal footing in terms of collaboration or resistance either with each other or with men. Furthermore, a woman's role in the household frequently created constraints which affected her choice between collaboration and resistance. Historical argument about choices during the war tends to assume that the subject is an independent individual with no responsibilities and complete freedom of action. This study, with reference to women (although a parallel history could be written for men), investigates the complex ways in which choices could be determined, or prevented, or helped or hindered by family and everyday circumstances. It helps confirm the fragmented nature of wartime experience for women.

The second part of the book is concerned with the immediate postwar period. Chapter 6 takes a close look at the events and impact of the purges. The last two chapters explore the same themes that were examined earlier in the book in relation to the war, namely everyday life and work (Chapter 7) and political choices (Chapter 8). This second part of the book shows not only that women did not find the end of the war liberating, except in the obvious sense of the Germans departing, but also how the restoration of order, a process which began as soon as the Germans left, touched nearly every aspect of women's lives, serving to push them back into gender roles that had been to some degree extended and redefined by the war. So, while the war had offered women some openings to become more independent, the immediate postwar governments, while granting women the vote, also encouraged women to move back into their old gender roles. How far was this a real liberation for women, and to what extent did gaining the right to vote change women's lives or enable them to participate in the postwar political scene?

PART ONE

Women's Lives during the War and the Occupation, 1939–44

CHAPTER TWO

Financial Resources and Paid Employment

If, because of the hostilities, a woman might be called upon to play a role outside of her normal attributes, she should be aware that this is only as an exceptional measure. . . . Our female contemporaries should consider this role as a sort of public service for the country, and not as a new career open to them from now on. . . . In wartime as in peacetime, women of France should remember that our civilization has reserved them an important role to play, but they will not be able to play this role unless they remain first and foremost women . . . and in order to do so they should abandon this role at the end of the war to devote themselves to the needs of the home, but above all during the hostilities, they will not be able to behave as true French women unless they remember that their most important role is as a mother and a wife.[1]

On 3 September 1939, when the war was declared, many French families were still on holiday. General mobilization of young men aged 18 to 35 was ordered on 1 September. Only those who were engaged in what was considered to be essential war work were exempt. Family members were often scattered because of the French habit of sending children away to summer camps separately from their parents. Oral sources indicate that there was therefore some degree of panic during these first weeks as families located all their members, reconstituted themselves and came to terms with separation. Women only had their experiences of the last war to help them deal with this one and attempt to organize themselves. Zaretsky found that mothers were often very annoyed at the way call-up was organized and questioned the criteria used to decide which workers

1. Louis Linyeur, Sénateur, *Le Devoir des femmes* (Mar./Apr. 1940).

were kept at home as special cases.[2] There was little formal evacuation, and Dombrowski has shown that departure was not feasible for the majority of working people, who needed the income from their jobs.[3] Many parents arranged for children to be sent away, especially from the larger cities which people feared might be targets for bombing, but working-class mothers were dependent on benefits, the receipt of which determined whether or not they could afford to send their children to a safer location.[4] Thus the outbreak of war led most families to experience separation of some kind. Women in particular were often parted from their sons, husbands or brothers; unmarried women lost boyfriends or fiancés. Structure and authority within households changed as they were constituted differently.

In this context, the war brought added strains to household budgets, and, in the absence of the men, it obliged many women to take on paid employment. The process whereby women were brought into the labour market during the First World War in both France and Britain is well documented, as is women's paid employment during the Second World War in Britain. But very little research has been done on paid employment in France during the Second World War, of any kind, concerning men or women. Access to sources is difficult and statistics are lacking. Historians are confined to census material from 1936 and 1946, and, as Siân Reynolds has pointed out, this does not provide enough information for us to be able to account for work in gendered terms.[5] In short, there is very little available source material for the war period, which makes it difficult to draw a coherent picture of women's paid employment. However, despite the lack of systematic evidence, this chapter draws on extensive oral evidence which provides a valuable alternative source, offering us some insight into the situation through the examples of Brest, in the Occupied zone, and Toulouse, in the Unoccupied zone. These samples serve to highlight the ways in which employment was intrinsically linked to local circumstances and economic pressures, and that women's experience and work opportunities were different in the two zones.

2. Robert Zaretsky, *Nîmes at War: Religion, Politics and Public Opinion in the Gard, 1938–44* (University Park, Pennsylvania State University Press, 1995), p. 48.

3. Nicole Ann Dombrowski, 'Beyond the Battlefield: The French Civilian Exodus of May–June 1940 (World War II)', unpublished PhD thesis (New York University, 1995), p. 62.

4. Ibid., p. 73.

5. Siân Reynolds, *France between the Wars: Gender and Politics* (London, 1996). See ch. 4, 'What did people do all day? The sexual division of labour between the wars', pp. 83–108.

During the First World War, many women had been mobilized to take paid employment in the absence of the men, and the postwar period had seen an increasing number of married women move into the labour market. This became more common and socially acceptable, and most single women worked. However, during the period between the wars, men were still most likely to be the sole breadwinners in the family. The traditional model whereby married adult men were in employment and their wives remained at home was the norm. The outbreak of the Second World War and the often prolonged absence of the men brought disruption to this pattern for many families. As most men were obliged to leave home for at least some amount of time during the five years of the war, their families were left to manage without them. The state made some attempt to help by introducing measures designed to alleviate the financial loss engendered by the departure of the main breadwinner, but, as this chapter will show, the benefits alone were not sufficient to ensure survival. Furthermore, since some were linked to the presence of a working adult in paid employment, rather than lose the benefit altogether because of the absence of a husband, wives often found paid employment themselves, thereby qualifying for these benefits in their own right. Thus, at a time when the Vichy discourse was justifying its policy in terms of a rationale that women should remain out of the labour market, state benefits actually acted as an incentive for them to do quite the opposite. This chapter, as well as offering an overview of women's paid employment and highlighting the unforeseen consequences of wartime policy towards female employment, will argue that French wartime and Vichy government policy related to women's work resulted in a series of ad hoc responses to German pressures and to the economic situations which arose. Women were alternately welcomed, even ordered, into the labour market and then pushed out of it as events and the labour market appeared to dictate.

The state fails to provide

In September 1939, the families of men who were too old to be called up, or who were kept back as specially affected workers, were sheltered from change as the money continued to come in from the regular source; it just had to go further. Other men – civil servants, for example – were able to arrange for their wives to receive some or all of their absent husband's salary. Wives of officers in the army could also have part of their husband's wage paid directly to them.

Officers with at least two years' experience earned a monthly salary fixed according to their rank, marital status, number of dependants and years of service. They could arrange for their families to receive a *délégation d'office* whereby half their monthly income was paid directly to their wives or parents. In 1939–40, this represented about 1,400 francs, more or less the equivalent of an average wage, thus negating the need for these women to find employment. However, this had to be arranged in advance, and many families were not aware of this possibility until it was too late.

Other wives, whose absent husbands were not officers, simply found themselves dependent on a series of different state benefits. The government introduced and extended state allowances in an attempt to compensate families who had lost their breadwinners.

The first of these was the military benefit, which was introduced by decree on 1 September 1939 to cater for the non-working wives of regular soldiers. This was described by the authorities as a benefit for needy families whose breadwinners had been mobilized under the French flag. But the money was not awarded automatically as had initially been expected by the population. Only certain families qualified, and then only if they were in what the government considered to be a 'difficult' financial position. This definition was left very vague and each case was examined individually by local commissions. Unsurprisingly, a large number of families applied for this money. In Toulouse, for example, the town hall transmitted over 17,000 requests. Once it was decided that a family qualified, the benefit was calculated on a daily basis and varied according to the number of children in a family. The procedure was slow and the money sometimes took so long to come through that local councils were forced to use their own funds to help these disrupted families in the short term. The inadequacy of military benefits became apparent very soon after the outbreak of the war. In Toulouse, the *Aide Municipale* reported in 1939 that: 'Very often . . . the father is at the Front and . . . because of the . . . sparing nature with which the military benefits are allocated, the mother needs a supplementary income to be able to bring up her children.' Oral sources repeatedly confirmed that the benefits provided by the state for them and their families were too small and that they were obliged to look for paid employment. One woman explained: 'I went into the explosives factory on 10 November 1939 as the military benefit was not enough, it was not possible to live on.'[6] Many found paid employment, as the defence

6. Interview, Madame Daphné (Toulouse).

factories, in particular, needed them to replace the absent men. These military benefits continued to be paid until after the defeat, in the summer of 1940. Then, in cases where demobilized soldiers were able to return home, family households were re-established and their experience of separation was a relatively short one.

However, 1,850,000 French men were taken prisoner and did not return home, sometimes remaining absent for as long as five years, leaving their wives and families to manage without them. The Vichy government therefore continued to pay out military benefits to their families. But despite a pervasive discourse and extensive visual propaganda extolling the virtues of family life and motherhood, the families of prisoners-of-war families were not adequately provided for and the benefits failed to compensate for the lost salary of the absent husband. In October 1941, when a factory worker could expect to earn 1,200–1,800 francs, a wife with one child received just 630 francs a month, 840 francs a month for two children and 1,060 francs for three. The Vichy Ministry of the Family fought to prove that these military benefits were not sufficient for prisoner families to survive.[7] It argued that the government should make sure that they were well looked after, otherwise there would be problems when the prisoners returned.[8] It claimed that financial difficulties were leading to demoralization, and that the criteria used to calculate military benefits were inappropriate, as no distinction was made between those living in towns and in the country.[9] Jacques Chevalier, a high-ranking official in the Ministry of the Family, even resorted to special pleading by using the argument that the wives of prisoners-of-war had been forced to turn to prostitution to supplement their income, citing a 60 per cent increase in prostitution in Paris.[10] Chevalier's estimation was probably an exaggeration of the true situation, but he did succeed in touching on two nerves within the Vichy government, those of prisoners and prostitution. But while we may be sure that most wives of prisoners-of-war did not take to the streets to supplement their income, the concern was not unfounded. Many experienced severe hardship and their resources were strained. The widespread belief in Vichy circles that the war would not last

7. See Sarah Fishman, *We Will Wait! The Wives of French Prisoners of War, 1940–45* (New Haven, 1991), for more detailed discussion of these debates.

8. AN F60 558, Commission du Retour des Prisonniers de Guerre.

9. AN F60 559, Note sur le Relèvement des Allocations Militaires. Aide aux Femmes de Prisonniers de Guerre, 17 Dec. 1941.

10. AN F60 558, Le Secrétaire d'Etat à la Famille, Chevalier à l'Amiral de la Flotte, Vichy, 2 Jan. 1942.

and that prisoners would soon return had made officials reluctant to act. A measure was finally introduced on 20 July 1942, known as the 'aid to women alone' or the *délégation familiale*, but it was more or less the previous military benefit under a different name. The amounts awarded, representing a minimum of 600 francs a month for a wife and child, 900 francs a month for two children, and 1,200 francs for three children, were not very different from the military benefits and these figures remained unchanged until the end of the war, despite major increases in inflation.[11]

It is true that the wives of prisoners-of-war had other advantages which helped them to survive. Many paid only 75 per cent of their rent (which was often waived altogether by sympathetic landlords, according to oral sources) and they had tax immunity.[12] In the Finistère, generous factory owners continued to pay some or all of absent men's salaries to their wives.[13] But unless wives were able to benefit from this sort of unofficial help, many were forced to find jobs, despite the Vichy propaganda which appeared to want to prevent them from seeking paid employment. An added advantage of working was that it qualified them for another type of benefit known as family benefits.

Family benefits had existed since 1932 and were awarded as a kind of salary bonus.[14] Originally designed for the traditional prewar household with children, they were part of state policy to help increase the birthrate. Thus the amounts awarded increased according to the number of children in a family. The law of 12 November 1938, completed in the Family Code (*Code de la Famille*) published on 29 July 1939, had established the payment of these benefits on a monthly basis, calculated from an average monthly departmental wage, revised annually by local commissions (in theory, although in reality the Germans did not allow this). A lump sum was given after the birth of the first child, and then monthly benefits were allocated amounting to 10 per cent of the wage for the second child, and 20 per cent for the third and subsequent children. The larger the family, the higher the benefit. The Vichy regime was also very keen to encourage women to have more children, so in October

11. *L'Espoir français*, Aide aux femmes seules, 10–20 Aug. 1943, p. 20; Fishman, *We Will Wait!*, p. 186; Henri Amouroux, *La Vie des Français sous l'Occupation* (Paris, 1961), p. 220.

12. Fishman, *We Will Wait!*, p. 186.   13. ADF 200W44.

14. Pierre Laroque, *L'Evolution de la politique familiale en France de 1938 à 1981* (Paris, 1985); Antoine Prost, 'L'Evolution de la politique familiale en France de 1938 à 1981', *Le Mouvement social* (Oct.–Dec. 1984), p. 7.

1941 the government reinforced this family benefit by boosting the percentage awarded for three or more children from 20 per cent of the average departmental wage to 30 per cent. At the same time, another measure was introduced, known as the 'single wage benefit' (*allocation de salaire unique*).

The 'single wage benefit' also originated from one of the measures written into the 1939 Family Code (*allocation de la mère au foyer*), and became law on 29 March 1941. It was designed to encourage women in urban areas not to take paid employment but to stay at home, symbolically compensating them for their 'lost' income, but it did not apply in rural communes where it was felt that women's work already took place in the home. It was awarded to families with only one income, irrespective of whether that income was earned by the man or the woman. Significantly more generous than the family benefits (families who qualified for this benefit received 20 per cent of the monthly departmental salary for one child up to the age of 6, 25 per cent for two children, and a further 25 per cent for three or more children), in some cases it was even awarded to families where both parents worked, but only if the mother earned less than a third of the monthly departmental average wage.

While, in theory, this benefit favoured large families where mothers stayed at home supported by a working husband, in practice it served as a further incentive for women at home – especially wives of prisoners-of-war – to find employment. Vichy appears to have been legislating for a situation where husbands were present, at a time when many were not, thus creating the paradoxical situation that, although the allowance was not directed at working women supporting families in the absence of men, they were able to take advantage of it. According to Pierre Laroque, in 1943 the single wage benefit represented 50 per cent of all government benefits awarded; more than four out of five women with two or more children received it.[15]

Clearly, the introduction and extension of these benefits did not always have the desired effects. Furthermore, commentators of the time felt that they were not as effective as they could have been. Contemporary documents indicate that particular concern was expressed for families with young children, who were often the worst hit by wartime conditions. Discussion concentrated on the setting of the benefit rates, with officials complaining that the benefit was too small, or that the average departmental wage did not reflect the

15. Laroque, *L'Evolution de la politique familiale*, p. 192.

true state of salaries.[16] There were many discrepancies between rates set for rural and urban areas, and other factors including possible access to food were not taken into consideration. Factory workers, who worked in towns but lived in nearby rural areas, were thought to have lost out. All these factors lead to the conclusion that in practice the system designed to help and encourage larger families was hardly effective, indeed that it totally failed. The benefits were more appropriate to the peacetime scenario of mothers at home and husbands at work. The families most in need of help, mothers alone at home with children, qualified neither for family benefits nor for the single wage benefit unless they found paid work. Fortunately, in many cases local benefit offices continued to pay out family benefits despite the absence of the wage-earner, a move which seems to have depended on local judgment and discretion.[17]

There was a further group of women whom one might have expected Vichy to treat sympathetically, and these were the wives of men working in Germany. But these wives were in no way thought to be in the same position as the wives of prisoners-of-war. Whether by choice or because they were forced to do so, their husbands were working, earning well and should have been sending money home. Evidence from Toulouse shows that the money often failed to arrive.

> On Sunday 13 of this month, in the morning a meeting was organized by the families of workers in France. 80 to 90 people attended and the discussions were quite animated, the vast majority of those present affirmed that they were not receiving half the salary that was due to the families of the workers in Germany from their bosses.[18]

These wives did not qualify for family benefits because their husbands were not working in France; and they could only qualify for benefits in their own right if they worked themselves.[19] Vichy officials finally conceded that the women had a point, and from June 1943 they too were able to receive the *délégation familiale* which had originally been designed solely for the wives of prisoners-of-war.

There were other institutions for those who were in the severest distress. One was the *Secours National*. Originally founded during the First World War, and re-created by law in October 1940, this was a charitable institution, and espoused many Pétainist ideas. Another

16. AN F22 1516, Compte-rendu et analyses hebdomadaires de la correspondance concernant Famille, Santé, Jeunesse. 6 Sept. 1940 to Mar. 1941.
    17. Ibid.   18. ADHG 1302/15, Renseignements Généraux, 18 Dec. 1942.
    19. AN F22 1256, Femmes de déportés de travail, July 1942.

was the more neutral Red Cross, which also had the role of providing help where the state failed. As early as September 1940, the government formulated a top-up plan to ensure that families had the minimum of resources essential to survive in cases where legislation failed.[20] But in reality its scope was very limited. Rather than handing out cash, the *Secours National* preferred to help the families of prisoners-of-war, for example, by finding women jobs. Home working *(travail à domicile)* was the favoured solution and had the added advantage that it not only kept women in the home but also occupied them with what were considered to be 'naturally feminine' tasks like repairing and making clothes. Once they had some kind of employment, women could qualify for state benefits. The *Secours National* gave priority to women without children, as it was feared that if they had children even working in the home might distract them from their motherly duties.[21]

The overall picture therefore shows that despite quite a labyrinth of benefits, the little state support provided by government was inadequate, and that since family benefits depended on the presence of a working member of the family, often the husband, many families fell through the net. Many women were left high and dry by Vichy, which failed to provide for those in need. Oral sources indicate that women often developed unofficial strategies which improved their survival resources. Some did so by moving into households with relations, where another family member took on the responsibility for supporting them. Women who lived in the cities sometimes found that their economic position could be greatly improved by moving to the country where it was easier to come by food. Women who lived on farms quickly understood that their income could be supplemented by selling food to city dwellers, and many carried out black market activity on a small or large scale. The Vichy government had inherited a system of allocations in 1940 and has rightly been credited with increasing and extending them despite having reduced resources due to German requisitioning. But these measures were not intended to help mothers or families in need so much as to implement their family policy in a peacetime context, to foster the ideal large family with the mother at home producing and rearing children and the father supporting them. Vichy propaganda was also directed to this end. The wives of prisoners-of-war at home alone with children to support had no part in this picture. Furthermore, the historian is obliged to question whether family benefits were a

20. AN F9 311F, Croix Rouge Française.   21. AN F60 389, Secours National.

serious attempt on the part of the Vichy government to obviate the need for married women to work. The wives of prisoners-of-war had little help from the state, most could barely survive on the benefits provided for them and, unless they were able to develop unofficial strategies of their own, they had everything to gain from going to work, which was precisely what Vichy appeared to want to discourage. Women in these households were therefore often forced to find paid employment. But was there work available for them? In which sectors? Was it the same work that was available to them before the war, or were there new opportunities?

Women's paid employment before the war

In the late 1930s, women represented about 30.5 per cent of the overall workforce in France.[22] The existing figures for women's work in France outside agriculture show maximum participation before and during the First World War and thereafter a steady decline until the 1960s. The number of women workers in agriculture remained constant throughout the interwar period, but it has to be borne in mind that women in agriculture were generally registered as self-employed in family enterprises, and therefore a distinction has to be made between employed women and waged women.[23]

Certain commentators see women's waged employment during the First World War as having been at its zenith. Women took over from men in many work sectors. Tramways replaced mobilized men with women. Women also entered the armaments factories and were subsequently taken on at the Post Office, in banks, at newspaper factories and as teachers. Most had to give up their jobs when the men returned after the war, and Jean-Louis Robert has described how, from 1918, women's employment went into steady decline, although women remained an important part of the workforce during the interwar period.[24] However, Sylvie Zerner has claimed that although the overall figures indicate a decline in the number of women in the labour force because of the industrial changes that took place, certain sectors in the 1920s and 1930s saw a redistribution

22. J.J. Carré, P. Dubois, E. Malinvund, *French Economic Growth* (Hatfield, USA, 1975), p. 49.
23. Reynolds, *France between the Wars*, p. 84.
24. Jean-Louis Robert, 'Women and Work in France during the First World War', in Richard Wall and Jay Winter (eds), *The Upheaval of War: Family, Work and Welfare in Europe, 1914–18* (Cambridge, 1988), p. 263.

of female labour rather than a decline.[25] In administration, the presence of women workers in trade, banking and insurance was a lasting legacy of the First World War. As the role of offices became more important due to the management need for centralization of information, large numbers of women were taken on for secretarial work. In 1936, 23.5 per cent of the female workforce was concentrated in the tertiary or service sector.

Women still tended to give up paid employment on marriage. Despite the massive movement of women into the labour market during the First World War, this did little to erode prohibitive attitudes, in certain social classes, towards married women who worked. The assumption was that 'if the husband had an appropriate job, the idea of working would not occur to the wife'.[26] It was therefore uncommon for married women to work unless financially forced to do so. However, labour shortages during the Second World War in France brought even more married women into waged employment. As in 1914–18, women became a reserve army of labour brought in and pushed out of the labour force as economic conditions required.

Women's paid employment 1939–44

Although it is impossible to quantify statistically, this chapter will show how women's employment from 1939 to 1944 fell into three broad periods, as the war affected different areas of the country in different ways. During the initial period 1939–40, France was at war and had a fairly typical war economy, with women being brought into the factories to replace men. After the defeat, Vichy government policy towards female employment constantly shifted in response to the needs of the labour market. Female employment opportunities also varied significantly according to the presence or absence of the Germans. Under Armistice agreements, the economic output of factories in the *zone libre* was wound down. Here women, like men, experienced unemployment in 1940–42, whereas, in Occupied areas, factories were immediately put to work for the German war effort and the presence of German soldiers in itself also created employment opportunities for both men and women. After full Occupation in November 1942, although the Vichy regime stopped short of

25. Silvie Zerner, 'De la couture aux presses: l'emploi féminin entre les deux guerres', *Le Mouvement sociale*, 140 (Paris, July–Sept. 1987), p. 9.

26. Miranda Pollard, 'Femme, Famille, France: Vichy and the Politics of Gender 1940–1944', unpublished PhD thesis (University of Dublin, 1990), p. 206.

actually forcing women to work in Germany, the drain of male skilled labour, caused first by the *Relève* scheme and subsequently by the compulsory labour draft, again created a need for women workers across the country, a need which became more and more severe as the war went on and women were drafted into the factories to replace the absent men.

LAWS AND THEIR IMPACT 1939–40

The state defence industries were the most significant employers of women during the first period. The industries working for national defence missed their workers who were called up and required labour on a scale that was no longer available. As men became scarce, women were encouraged to come into the factories. In December 1939, for example, the metal industry called for an 'acceleration in the employment of women and juveniles in the establishments working for National Defence'.[27] The Minister of Labour, Charles Pomaret, issued a letter on 6 January 1940 explaining that the French economy had become increasingly obliged to rely on women's labour: 'This labour is necessary to fill in the gaps and to increase a work-force that will soon be inadequate.' He went on to single out priorities in the employment of certain categories of women. The first priority was to recruit wives of mobilized soldiers because they no longer had their 'breadwinner . . . the salary with which they survived'. The second category for particular consideration was the unemployed.[28] On 29 February 1940, a decree was passed making women's work compulsory 'for the duration of hostilities in certain professions, administrations and companies'.[29] The quotas for women were fixed by the Ministry of Labour, which explained that 'The released masculine labour will be allocated to establishments and companies working for National Defence or in the interest of the Nation'. Women responded to these calls for their labour and the Archives of the Ministry of Defence in Chatellerault indicate that women were employed in large numbers in armaments factories across the country from 1 September 1939 to 18 June 1940. The defence sector was still recruiting women in June 1940. On 15 August 1939, there were just 80 women working in the Chatellerault

27. Groupe des Industries Métallurgiques et Connexes de la Région Parisienne. Circulaire c.55.243. 19 Dec. 1939.
28. Groupe des Industries Métallurgiques. Circulaire c.55.973. Texte de la lettre de Monsieur le Ministre du Travail, 6 Jan. 1940.
29. Journal Officiel, 30 Mar. 1940.

arms manufacture factory: by 18 June 1940 the figure was 1,248;[30] 1,976 women were taken on in the explosives factory in Pont de Buis (Finistère) and 3,579 in Toulouse.[31] The employment lists indicate that most were brought in as unskilled workers, and that some had already worked in these factories during the 1914–18 war. Priority was given to wives of mobilized soldiers whatever their previous work experience. At the same time as women were being taken on in certain sectors, however, other women were being made redundant as factories had to shut down because of lack of raw materials and transport facilities. Shops reduced the number of their employees and many textile workshops closed.

Industry was not the only sector which needed women: they were also brought into administration in large numbers to replace the absent men. In some cases, jobs were created by the conditions of the war itself. The Food Distribution Centres, for example, took on large numbers of female staff. In Toulouse, 150 permanent staff were recruited, 150 who worked fifteen days a month, and 500 others who worked two days a week for the monthly distribution of ration-cards in the different urban centres.[32] Some women were thus able to gain access to white-collar jobs for the first time, but women were rarely recruited on a permanent basis. The Post Office took on young women under 24 as temporary auxiliaries in huge numbers to replace the 35,000 mobilized male employees.[33] As in industry, wives whose husbands were at the Front were told that it was their patriotic duty to replace them.

AFTER THE DEFEAT

In the summer of 1940, factory production ground to a halt amidst the chaos of defeat, after which came demobilization and the return of many men. In accordance with their family policy, the newly established Vichy government immediately proposed that agricultural workers be sent back to the farms and women to their homes. On

30. Claude Lombard, *La Manufacture nationale d'armes de Chatellerault 1891–1968* (Poitiers, 1987), p. 326.
31. Contrôle nominatif des ouvrières embauchées pour la durée des hostilités, Centre d'Archives de l'Armement, Délégation Générale pour l'Armement, Ministère de la Défense, Chatellerault.
32. M.F. Manalesco, 'La Municipalité de Toulouse 1940–44', unpublished Mémoire de Maîtrise (University of Toulouse, 1987), p. 159.
33. Henri Delvincourt, 'Problèmes relatifs à l'emploi dans les PTT pendant la deuxième guerre mondiale', *Revue d'histoire de la deuxième guerre mondiale* (Jan. 1965), p. 42.

7 July 1940, a circular was sent round to all the main industries, both private and public, explaining that redundancies should correspond to the policy of 'return to the soil' and 'the return of women to the home'. The latter required that most women stop working except for war widows, single women, women supporting their family, wives of non-demobilized soldiers and women occupying jobs which were traditionally put aside as female jobs.[34] The majority of the defence factories were wound down completely, most reducing their staff over three months from June to September. The explosives factory in Bergerac laid off 8,256 people: of 1,136 employees left in September, 60 were women.[35] The explosives factory in Toulouse, the largest in the country, lost a total of 11,891 workers (4,445 women and 7,446 men) between June and September 1940.[36] Women were given several months' pay and, in accordance with government policy, where possible widows were kept on if they were thought to be in need. Women who did not belong to the government's exempted categories were laid off by the end of 1940. Thus, only 237 women, 13 per cent of the workforce, remained at the Toulouse explosives factory in September 1940.

The immediate economic impact of the defeat was therefore an increase in national unemployment.[37] One of the most firmly held ideas within Vichy ideology was that a woman's place was in the home with her husband and children, and that she had no place in the workplace, particularly if it was financially expedient to exclude her. Unemployment was an excuse to back up this ideology with legislation on 11 October 1940 with the *Married Women's Work* act. This law forbade the employment of married women in the public sector when husbands were in a position to provide for the family, and called for women to retire at 50.[38] It did not therefore apply to wives of prisoners-of-war or unemployed men, but it did apply to women 'living in a shared household with a man'. Although this law was directed at the category of women whose husbands were present, the extent to which these women were actually affected by

34. Groupe des Industries Métallurgiques. Circulaire c.65.109, 25 July 1940.

35. Variation des effectifs des établissements des poudres, du 1er juin au 1er septembre 1940, Centre d'Archives de l'Armement, Délégation Générale pour l'Armement, Ministère de la Défense, Chatellerault.

36. Hanna Diamond, 'Women's Experience during and after World War Two in the Toulouse Area 1939–48: Choices and Constraints', unpublished PhD thesis (University of Sussex, 1992), pp. 100–1 for full figures for this factory.

37. Alfred Sauvy, *La Vie économique des Français de 1939 à 1945* (Paris, 1978), pp. 172–3.

38. AN F60 628, Main d'Œuvre Féminine.

it is debatable, and lack of evidence makes it particularly difficult to assess the impact of Vichy policy on the private sector, which was not strictly speaking affected. But in the same month as the publication of the law, the Prefect in Toulouse had the following comments to make about private sector industry locally:

> The dispositions decreed with a view to reabsorbing unemployment notably resulting in forbidding married couples to have two salaries have been received with a certain reserve both by employees and employers. Certain branches of industrial and commercial activity: department stores and the shoe industry, would be placed in a critical situation if these measures were to be applied in too strict a fashion.[39]

The lack of reference to it by the Prefect of the Finistère suggests that this was not such an important issue there, but in the Haute-Garonne the law was not welcomed by those in industry and commerce.

Most commentators acknowledge that the law immediately increased women's unemployment. As overall national figures for unemployment gradually dropped, women's unemployment increased from 26 per cent of the figures in October 1940, to 54 per cent in July 1941 and 60 per cent in October 1942, suggesting that men were able to find work as a result of this ban on married women working.[40] As far as taking early retirement was concerned, unless they were forced to, women were unlikely to volunteer for it. A very slim dossier held in the archives of the Finistère testifies to the lack of interest in this aspect of the law. It contains several chits to the Prefect from employers indicating that none of their female employees wished to take early retirement. Whether or not they were obliged to is difficult to ascertain.[41] It seems possible that the law was not applied as rigorously in industry as in administration, where many women over 50, particularly teachers, were forced to retire. Here, the compulsory retirement provisions of the law caused considerable hardship and the National Archives contain many letters addressed to Pétain, particularly from First World War widows complaining about the law and demanding exemption from it.[42] These women would again seem to be victims of Vichy's double discourse. Some were forced to leave their jobs. The evidence in Brest indicates that the 1944 purge commission there reinstated a number

---

39. AN F1 cIII 1154, Rapport de Préfet, Oct. 1940.
40. Michèle Bordeaux, 'Femmes hors l'état français 1940–44', in Rita Thalmann (ed.), *Femmes et fascismes* (Paris, 1986), p. 143; see also Pollard, 'Femme, Famille, France', pp. 231–2.
41. ADF 200W202, Travail Féminin 1940.
42. AN F60 620, Main d'Œuvre Féminine.

of teachers who had been forced to retire in 1940.[43] The work of
Paul Aries on hospitals in the Lyon area is a further indication that
the letter of the law was followed more closely in administration.
Thorough investigations were conducted into the marital situation
of female employees, and a total of 70 women were dismissed.
(Three-quarters of them were to return to their jobs after Vichy's
policy change in 1942.)[44] Indeed, despite the law, many administrations were forced to employ women. After demobilization, women
auxiliaries who had been employed by the Post Office in September
1939 were laid off. But the Germans would not allow the movement
of staff between zones, therefore to compensate for the drop in
staff productivity due to their lack of qualifications and the difficult
conditions of life, more women were employed in spring 1941.[45]
Between December 1941 and December 1943, the SNCF also recruited 20,000 women auxiliaries.[46] In April 1942, the Prefect of
Toulouse expressed concern that there were more female clerks
in their employment than men, in contradiction to the spirit of the
October law. He concluded that the law on women's work could
not stay in place for much longer in public administration.[47]

In practice, the law of 11 October proved difficult to implement,
particularly in the face of German demands on French industry
and ensuing labour shortages. In April 1941, the Vichy intermin-
isterial committee charged with the economy noticed that the law
'no longer seemed opportune in present conditions. It would be
abnormal to give pensions instead of paying wages when France
needs all its productive force.'[48] The Prefect of Toulouse reported
in October 1941 that the industry of the region was 2,000 workers
short. 'In this context the measures against the cumulation of two
salaries, against women's work, do not help and just aggravate the
situation', he complained.[49]

The government was forced to introduce a new law on 12 September 1942 and announced that, in view of the notably different

43. See Chapter 6.
44. Paul Aries, 'Les Personnels hospitalier lyonnais entre détresse and l'espoir',
in Denis Peschanski and Jean-Louis Robert (eds), *Les Ouvriers en France pendant la
deuxième guerre mondiale* (Paris, 1992), p. 92.
45. Delvincourt, 'Problèmes relatifs à l'emploi dans les PTT', p. 43.
46. Paul Durand, 'La Politique de l'emploi à la SNCF pendant la deuxième
guerre mondiale', *Revue d'histoire de la deuxième guerre mondiale* (Jan. 1965), pp. 22–3.
47. AN F1 cIII 1154, Rapport de Préfet, 8 Apr. 1942.
48. Bernd Zielinski, 'Le Chômage et la politique de la main d'œuvre de Vichy
(1940–42)', in Peschanski and Robert (eds), *Les Ouvriers*, pp. 301–2.
49. AN F1 cIII 1154, Rapport de Préfet, Oct. 1941.

situation, most of the terms of the law of 11 October 1940 were suspended. Married women could now work in any sector, whatever the situation of their husbands. The ideological motivation behind the October law had no relation to the reality of the labour requirements of the country and the government had been forced to make a dramatic policy U-turn. Once constraints were lifted, women continued to move into the labour market as they were needed, replacing men who were increasingly forced to work in Germany. At first men started to leave under the voluntary *Relève* scheme, which had more of an impact in some areas than in others. The different examples of Brest and Toulouse suggest that there was a distinction between the two zones. In Brest, in the occupied north, the *Relève* had rather less impact, perhaps because of the presence of the Germans there who generated so much employment locally,[50] whereas in Toulouse more workers were attracted by the offer of well-paid jobs in Germany. The Prefect complained that the departure of workers to Germany was draining local industry of labour, and it was reported in December 1942 that 'certain factories . . . are suffering from the departures of specialists under the *Relève* scheme'.[51] In an attempt to counteract this, emergency measures were introduced to enable industry to employ more women. By August 1943, labour shortages were so severe that employers complained that they were being forced to employ young people from 14 to 19, or women wherever possible, and in December 1943 the Prefect of Toulouse wrote that the numbers of women taking men's places in workshops, factories and administration were increasing daily.[52] This phenomenon increased with the compulsory labour draft, and, as German demands were never satisfied, nearly 25,000 auxiliaries, most of whom were women, replaced permanent staff in 1944 to ensure the functioning of the Post Office.[53]

Another indication of the extent of the labour shortages was in the police force, where Vichy decided that women should be one of the groups targeted for recruitment.[54] By May 1944, 685 women were employed in the *Corps des Surveillantes Auxiliaires*, a structure created especially for them, and it was planned to increase this

50. ADF 31W313, Rapport Mensuel, July 1945.
51. ADHG 1302/15, RG, 11 Dec. 1942.
52. AN F1 cIII 1204, Rapport de Préfet, Aug. 1943, Dec. 1943.
53. François Rouquet, 'Identités, antagonismes, et esprit de corps chez les agents des PTT', in Peschanski and Robert (eds), *Les Ouvriers*, pp. 499–555.
54. Simon Kitson, 'The Marseille Police in their Context, from Popular Front to Liberation', unpublished PhD thesis (University of Sussex, 1995), pp. 187–8.

figure to 1,572 by the end of that year. Yet again, this call for women to join the police was in apparent contradiction with Vichy policies towards women. Simon Kitson offers the following explanations for this. First, there was a general perception that women were influenced by the Church, which presumably made them good law-abiding citizens, and therefore they were likely to be in agreement with much of Vichy's policies. Furthermore, it was believed that women would not be as tempted by professional contacts with prostitutes as men. Strict rules were put into place concerning their tasks. They were not allowed to engage in office work except in cases where they were obviously pregnant (as this was felt to be inappropriate on the street), their powers of arrest were limited, they were not to perform night shifts, they were excluded from dangerous missions and they were not to be armed. Their duties included the supervision of food distribution, and overseeing old people, animals, children and other women in the streets and public places. There was no question that women should police men.

WORKING FOR THE GERMANS IN FRANCE

No study of women's employment during the war would be complete without examining the case of those who worked for the Germans. It is a sensitive area, particularly since it is difficult to distinguish between those who volunteered to work for them and those who were forced to do so. Despite German wishes to the contrary, women were never obliged to work in Germany in the same way as the men were. The need for labour in Germany was such that the Germans had expressed an interest in drafting women workers, and the call-up of women and girls had been rumoured in early 1943. The French Church immediately dismissed this as inconceivable and its disapproval may well have prevented the Germans and Vichy from carrying this area of policy to fruition. For example, in 1943, having been notified by the JOCF (*Jeunesse Ouvrière Chrétienne Féminine*) that 50 women working in a military hospital in Lille had been warned that they would have to go and work in Germany, Cardinal Liénart wrote to the German commander there in protest.[55] The Commander replied that there had been a misunderstanding and that the women would not be sent to Germany. A law was nonetheless passed on

55. W.D. Halls, *Politics, Society and Christianity in Vichy France* (Oxford, 1995), pp. 330–1; Jeanne Aubert, *La JOCF. Qu'as tu fait de nos vies? La Jeunesse Ouvrière Chrétienne Féminine 1928–45* (Paris, 1990), p. 143.

1 February 1944 extending the September 1942 law on compulsory labour for men, to include single and married women with no children, aged between 18 and 45, specifying that they were to be placed in jobs in France, near to their homes if they were married, so that they could return there in the evenings. The ACA (*Assemblée des Cardinaux et Archevêques*) immediately intervened, and the Archbishop of Toulouse, Cardinal Saliège, expressed his outrage at the treatment of women. He wrote that the attitude of the Vichy government was towards 'women as slaves, women as machines that one moves around, women as merchandize to be shipped hither and thither. . . . History will one day [excecrate] what might be termed "the traffic in girls and women".'[56] He maintained that a woman's place was at home and that it was the state's responsibility to keep them there. But concern was not limited to members of the Church. There was widespread anxiety in the population as it was feared that women would be forced to carry out physical labour for which they were not really prepared; many also saw the measure as a first step towards requiring them to work in Germany.[57] The Prefect of the Finistère sternly reported that if a law obliging women to work in Germany were to be seriously enforced, the government should expect the same number of *réfractaires* among women as there were among men.[58]

Vichy hypocrisy is again apparent as they allowed legislation to be passed which required women to work in certain jobs in France. Further legislation in March 1944 stipulated even more severe control of all categories of women. It was even stipulated that tasks previously carried out by men should be carried out by women where possible.[59] Work in Germany seemed even closer for women and rumours about this possibility spread. In June 1944, in Quimper (Finistère), it was said that in Paris the German authorities were rounding up single and married women without children and sending them to work in Germany.[60] The Liberation arrived before the Germans were able to put such a policy into practice, but it seems likely that they did intend to do so.

Inside France, the German forces created considerable work opportunities for local populations. Women were particularly called upon to help look after their personal needs. Cleaners, housekeepers,

56. Halls, *Politics, Society and Christianity*, p. 331.
57. AN F1 cIII 1204, Rapport de Préfet, 5 Feb. 1944.
58. ADF 200W43, 6–13 May 1944.
59. AN F22, Ministère du Travail, Commissariat aux Affaires Sociales. Carton 6. III A,3.4. Paris, 17 Mar. 1944.
60. ADF 200W44, Rapports Mensuels des RG 1941–44, June 1944.

cooks, laundry workers, for example, were all much in demand by the Occupying forces. Sometimes they were requisitioned, but mostly they did not need to be. The Germans paid women well for their work. The financial gains were obvious. In the Finistère, for example, there was a big difference between salaries paid by different employers. A cleaner could earn 5 francs an hour from the French authorities, 5.50–6 francs an hour from a private individual, and at least 7 francs an hour from the German authorities.[61] Burrin suggests that, from 1940 to 1942, those who worked for the Germans mostly did so voluntarily. Many left other jobs to work for the Germans because of better pay and access to extra food supplies.[62] Fear of unemployment was also a major incentive to work for the Occupier. The same was true of women who provided secretarial skills in the offices of the Occupying forces. Women who worked as typists, telephonists and translators certainly benefited materially from this work and might often be more implicated in terms of collaboration. Cobb claims that in Paris they were paid double what was on offer in the French private sector, and perks included access to German canteens and to goods which had disappeared from the shops.[63] In Occupied areas, the Germans themselves stimulated and commissioned work, providing employment for French men and women in industry. Employees in factories working for the Occupier were also paid as much as double those working for the French economy.[64] This employment of French people also had an impact on local economies, since the high salaries paid by the Germans increased the cost of living in some areas.[65] In the forbidden zone, areas on the coast where there was a particularly intense German presence, local agricultural workers were often requisitioned to work on fortifications. This work was not as well paid as that in the factories, which made it unattractive. The result was that many complained that they were being taken away from their normal work to do badly paid work, leaving their women to manage the farms on their own (see p. 42).

Working for the German occupier seems to have been more common in the northern zone, where the Germans were implanted for longer, although the same phenomenon existed to some degree

61. ADF 200W281.
62. Philippe Burrin, *La France à l'heure allemande 1940–1944* (Paris, 1995), p. 288.
63. Richard Cobb, *French and Germans, Germans and French: A Personal Interpretation of France and Two Occupations, 1914–1918/1940–1944* (Hanover, 1983), p. 105.
64. AN F1 cIII 1153, Rapport de Préfet Finistère.
65. ADF 200W35, Renseignements statistiques sur le département 1942–43.

in the southern zone after November 1942. However, a comparison between Toulouse and Brest suggests that the German presence provoked nothing like the same work opportunities for women in Toulouse as it had in Brest.

Although not strictly requisitioned, another category of women who were involved in working for the Germans were those who worked in the entertainment industry. Many of them were put in an invidious position. Theatre, ballet, opera and concerts continued throughout the war and the Germans were enthusiastic patrons of these events. Radio-Paris became an overtly propagandist pro-German radio station but also served to keep many French singers and musicians in work. Some spent time with Germans and went on tour in Germany. These individuals were eagerly exploited by the collaborationist publication *Signal*, which published photos of these actresses and singers delighting German audiences.[66] Although it is said that Edith Piaf was able to help the wives of prisoners-of-war identify their husbands from the pictures that were taken of her there, all those in the entertainment industry appeared before a commission who judged them at the end of the war (see Chapter 6).

If some actresses and singers agreed to work in Germany for certain periods of time, the French and German governments also attempted to encourage other women to work there too. As women were never actually obliged to go and work in Germany under the laws passed by Vichy, their position was rather different from that of the men. However, thanks to convincing and widespread propaganda, many women left the country on the *Relève* scheme to work in Germany throughout the Occupation. Since this move indicated a more serious acceptance of the Germans, it is further explored as a facet of collaboration in Chapter 4.

Prostitution was another area of labour (sometimes requisitioned) which was linked to the German presence. Vichy introduced legislation which sought to define prostitutes and to control their activity. Levels of prostitution increased significantly during the war. In 1935, there were an estimated 300,000 to 500,000 prostitutes in the country and only 1,235 registered brothels with a few thousand prostitutes working in them. In 1940, in Paris alone, there was an explosion of an estimated 100,000 street prostitutes, while only about 2,000 prostitutes worked in brothels.[67] Burrin quotes a figure of five to six thousand women prostitutes who carried bilingual cards.[68]

66. Cobb, *French and Germans*, p. 104.
67. Halls, *Politics, Society and Christianity*, p. 263.
68. Burrin, *La France à l'heure allemande*, p. 211.

Some of the increase in numbers may have been due to the wives of prisoners-of-war temporarily taking advantage of the situation to supplement their income, but it was also proportional to the increase in the number of clients. In accordance with the French tradition of policing prostitution, the reaction of the Vichy government was to take measures to attempt to control and regulate its levels by attempting to drive all prostitutes into the brothels.[69] Like the fascists in Italy who had also been worried about tolerating prostitution, which they saw as degrading to motherhood, the government hoped to shield illicit sex from public view, drawing a sharp line between 'good' and 'bad' women, to preserve the site and purpose of legitimate sex in marriage.[70] On 24 December 1940, Vichy addressed a circular to all Prefects in the Occupied zone suggesting that brothel keepers should be given a monopoly on prostitution. The police (*brigade des mœurs*) regularly raided bars and night-clubs and questioned people. Women suspected of prostitution were sent for medical checks at the local hospital and fined. These clean-up campaigns were particularly intense in the towns visited by Pétain in 1942, where prostitutes were sent to local camps for the duration of his visit as they were considered to be a danger to security and to offer an undesirable moral image. The effects of this early legislation were limited, but Vichy policy towards prostitution took another turn in June 1942, when a new system of regulation was introduced across the country. Under this system, prostitutes had to carry cards and undergo twice-monthly checks designed to keep venereal disease under control. Once a month they had a more in-depth check entailing blood tests.[71] They were formally banned from soliciting in the street, bars or any public places. Laws concerning pimps, which were passed on 20 July 1940 and 2 March 1943, were more difficult to enforce because proof was too difficult to find and most of those who should have been prosecuted were protected by their relations with the Gestapo – an indication of how difficult it is to assess this form of labour both at the time and in retrospect.

Other female prostitutes were requisitioned by the Occupying authorities, who like Vichy were concerned to control them and were used to the strict controls in place in Hitler's Germany. In the first

69. Alain Corbin, *Les Filles de noce: misère sexuelle et prostitution aux 19e et 20e siècles* (Paris, 1978), pp. 499–500.
70. Victoria de Grazia, *How Fascism Ruled Women, Italy 1922–1945* (Berkeley, 1992), p. 45.
71. This information comes from a report on prostitution by *Commissaire* Georges Zanetti, Marseille, 8 Feb. 1946, Archives Départementales des Bouches-du-Rhône, 23J3.

days of the Occupation the *Kommandatur* visited and requisitioned certain brothels for the use of German troops. In 1941, 29 brothels were put aside for the sole use of German troops in the Paris area, two being for officers. No Jewish or black women were allowed.[72] In these brothels, a group of nurses waited for clients at the door. The client then selected a woman according to the price he was prepared to pay and was given a visiting card with the name of his partner and their room number. If he had health problems subsequently, he only had to pass on his card to the army authorities.

Security was a major concern, and in the brothels requisitioned in Toulouse it was stipulated that:

> These brothels . . . can only be frequented by members of the German army. In fact it is of the utmost importance that these brothels should be reserved for the sole use of the German military and that no French soldier or civilian should enter the brothel at the same time. This is necessary to avoid the possibility of any incident.[73]

In December 1942, a rumour spread that prostitutes were voluntarily contaminating German soldiers and this led to a *Wehrmacht* order that any prostitute responsible for such a crime would be sent to a forced labour camp. Indeed, prostitutes were very tightly watched and had little freedom of action, as one witness described:

> You could see a queue of German soldiers in the road waiting to go to the brothel and that day Frenchmen could not go for security reasons. A woman in a brothel as they were organized during the war was under the total control of her employer. She was not even allowed to go down into the street.[74]

Despite Vichy and German attempts to push prostitutes into the brothels, the war actually brought a decline in the number of women who were based there. More women were working on the streets as clandestine prostitutes at the end of the war than in the brothels. Thus, though Vichy policy may have helped in terms of hygiene and the control of venereal disease, it could not control those prostitutes who probably took up the trade just for the duration of the war. In addition, attempts to control prostitution failed because there was little time or inadequate personnel to deal with it.[75]

72. Burrin, *La France à l'heure allemande*, p. 211.
73. AMT Maisons de Tolérance 1931–46, Note à Monsieur le Maire de Toulouse, 25 Nov. 1942.
74. Interview, Madame Antoinette (Toulouse).
75. This is an argument made by John Sweets, *Choices in Vichy France* (Oxford, 1986), p. 43.

WOMEN IN AGRICULTURE

Agriculture was the sector affected most dramatically by the war. Peasants were the first to be affected by mobilization and, while some workers were kept back in industry, this was rare in the agricultural sector. As in the First World War, the lone wife often had to take on the entire responsibility for the running of the farm and it was certainly the domain where women had the most difficulty managing without the men. Once again, despite extensive propaganda about 'back to earth' and the idealization of the peasant woman, little was done to replace the missing workforce on the land. Hélène Viannay recounts that country folk were suspicious of women and foreigners, though they needed the extra labour: 'I went to several farms thinking the men are prisoners, they need help, but they were never interested in me.'[76] In this context, women found that they had to do alone what they had formally shared with husbands and sons. The extra responsibilities were not always welcomed by women, and many, many women wrote to Pétain and the local German authorities begging for the return of their husbands, attempting to gain sympathy and favour. The following is an example of the kind of letters they wrote:

> I want to tell you about my sad situation. I am alone with my 10-year-old daughter to farm a 10 hectare property. My father is elderly and ill, and my recently widowed mother-in-law is handicapped with a 14-year-old daughter. I have repeatedly asked the French authorities to transmit a request to you for the liberation of my husband, but as this has never been done, I am writing to you directly because you are honest and good . . . so I am totally confident that you will have him released.[77]

In reality, women were rarely left completely alone to cope. Villagers or family rallied round to help at harvest time and older men and refugees were often brought in as extra labour.[78] There was a feeling of solidarity, and in certain areas all the farm workers co-operated to help solve problems. In some extreme cases, women were not prepared to take on this extra burden and went elsewhere for the duration of the war, sometimes leaving their land under the care of someone else.

76. Hélène Viannay, 'Témoignages', in Françoise Thébaud (ed.), *Clio: histoire, femmes et sociétés, résistances et libérations*, pp. 236–7.

77. Antoine Lefébure, *Les Conversations secrètes des français Sous l'Occupation* (Paris, 1993), p. 140.

78. AN F1 cIII 1504, Rapport de Préfet, Dec. 1941.

In some areas of France, particularly coastal regions, there were mixed economies. Here, family members often worked a bit of land, as well as working in local industry which included fishing and the preservation industries. These were important employers of women. In the south of the Finistère for example, most fishermen's wives worked in these factories. Lack of petrol during the war brought problems to this sector, and in October 1940 the canning factories, lacking tins – and indeed fish – were threatened with collapse.[79] By December 1941 the situation had not improved, and without employment these women could not qualify for any benefits. But people were inventive and found ways of surviving. By June 1943, at a time when some of the problems had receded and more jobs were available, it became apparent that the women of the south Finistère had turned to lacemaking, which they preferred because it brought in more money than working in the fish conservation factories.[80] Furthermore, when, in February 1944, the fishermen of Penmarc'h were forced into virtually total unemployment, they and their families launched a new business of their own. They made and sold grass brushes and this brought them substantial profits. The grass, collected by teams of women and children, was attached to a wooden handle. An average artisan could make two or three brushes a day and sell them for 130–140 francs each or exchange them for other goods.[81] This is perhaps one example of the French capacity for finding ways of surviving even in the most difficult of circumstances, otherwise known as the 'System D' (*le système débrouillard* – playing the system).

WOMEN'S EXPERIENCE OF WORK

For some bosses, the arrival of large numbers of women in the workplace led to concerns about 'morality'. In Chatellerault, the unprecedented recruitment of women in the armaments factory prompted the following note from the Director to his employees on 6 April 1940:

> The wartime functioning of the factory has led to a profound modification in recruitment namely the massive use of female workers. . . .
> I would have liked to organize workshops to have been exclusively staffed by men or women. But for technical reasons this has not

79. AN F1 cIII 1153, Rapport de Préfet.
80. ADF 200W44, Rapports Mensuels des RG, June 1943.
81. Ibid., Industrie de la brosse en chiendent dans la region de Penmarc'h, 21 Feb. 1944. This is also confirmed by oral sources. Interviews, Mesdames Lucie, Claudine and Joséphine (Finistère).

been possible. I am therefore obliged to let men and women coexist in the same workshops. I do not anticipate that this coexistence should degenerate into licentiousness. . . . I have decided to apply the following sanctions in cases of disobedience:

1. Men will be punished severely.
2. Women will be sacked without notice, whatever their family situation.[82]

Tensions also existed between employees. Men feared that they might be sent to work in Germany and this led them to feel threatened by the presence of women on the factory floor. One woman explained: 'I sensed that the men were not pleased to see me. When they saw that I could manage quite well, they were afraid. They thought that women would take their places and that they would be sent to the Front or to work in Germany.'[83] Those women who moved into jobs where there was a well-established labour force could experience hostility from workers who thought they worked too fast. One woman explained how they could get a bonus if they worked faster than the recommended times. As her fingers were finer than the men's she was able to work much faster than them. 'I was summoned by the foreman who told me that if I carried on like that, I would cause the starvation of several workers who could not work so fast. So I had to slow down.'[84] Another oral source explained how she was young and dynamic compared to those women workers who had been there since the 1914 war and she was not very well liked because she worked faster than them and did too much.[85] Another study reports how one woman found that the farm labourers resented her authority: 'At mobilization, I stayed alone in a 30 hectare farm with two children, two workers and a 15-year-old girl worker . . . my husband was adamant that I should continue to farm the land . . . but they found it more and more difficult to accept the authority of a woman.[86]

Married women who worked, whether their husband was present or absent, normally also had responsibility for the household: supplying and cooking food, cleaning and so on. Any free time was used to find food. Women who worked in factories had a long day. In October 1943, the Prefect reported that in some factories in the Toulouse area women were working up to 60 hours a week.[87] Women

82. Lombard, *La Manufacture nationale d'armes*, pp. 325–7.
83. Interview, Madame Delphine (Toulouse).   84. Ibid.
85. Interview, Madame Flore (Toulouse).
86. Jacqueline Deroy (ed.), *Celles qui attendaient* (Paris, 1985), p. 15.
87. AN F1 cIII 1204, Rapport de Préfet, 5 Oct. 1943.

also worked night shifts. One woman explained: 'The week that I was on nights I did not go to bed. I did the cleaning in the morning and I took the kids for a walk in the afternoon. It was hard . . .'.[88] On top of this, travel to and from work could add hours to the working day.

Women who worked in defence factories earned about 4.55 francs an hour or 1,000 francs a month in 1940.[89] *Employées* were paid monthly and *ouvrières* were paid weekly. Some were hired on a daily basis, paid by the hour, but women's wages were always less than men's. Evidence of the systematic difference between men's and women's salaries during the war is provided by the Galocherie factory in the Finistère. Although men and women were often employed to do different jobs, where they were employed to do the same task a woman's hourly rate was 3 francs less than a man's.[90] A 1944 report on women's work by the *Union Féminine* also confirmed that nationally women's wages were less than men's.[91]

In conclusion then, what was the impact of the war on the structures of women's employment? In her case study of women workers in Paris, Catherine Omnès maintains that the shortness of the period of women's employment in the munitions factories, just 9 months, prevented it from having the same impact as the 1914–18 war on female labour. It merely served to absorb existing female unemployment, and did little to erode the existing cleavage between male and female employment in the metallurgy sector.[92] She found that in her sample, once the hostilities ended, women who were laid off were unable to find work for the rest of the Occupation period and some left the labour market definitively. Overall, she concludes that the Occupation depressed levels of female employment in the Paris region. However, she found that the textile industry offered a rather surprising picture. Paradoxically, after redundancies had been made at the onset of the war, the employment of women stabilized, whereas it had previously been dropping annually. She argues that the shortages created by the war and the need to make the most of existing clothes sustained small workshops which specialized in mending and repairing clothes. At the other end of the market, the Germans

88. Interview, Madame Sara (Toulouse).

89. Centre d'Archives de l'Armement, Chatellerault.

90. ADF 200W207, Grèves.

91. An 'Enquête sur le travail des femmes en France' was carried out by the *Union Féminine* in Feb.–Mar. 1944.

92. Catherine Omnès, 'Les Trajectoires des ouvrières parisiennes', in Peschanski and Robert (eds), *Les Ouvriers*, pp. 62–3.

stimulated haute couture. The industry was thus able to keep its most qualified staff, in stark contrast to the devastation this traditional female sector experienced during the First World War when most of these women workers were forced into munitions factories.[93] There is, however, some conflicting evidence here. Both Veillon and Moreau found in their research that women in the textile industry had the opposite experience and that women seamstresses and hairdressers were often obliged to move into the munitions factories.[94] More research needs to be conducted in the field in order to clarify this picture. As far as the administrative sector is concerned, Catherine Omnès indicates that this was the only area of the labour market where there was any real mobility for women. Women became office workers, typists, clerks and telephonists and there was some degree of redeployment of women factory workers into the administrative sector, a process which had already begun before the war.[95]

As married women were brought into the labour market during the war, it might be considered that something had to be done about providing them with facilities for the children. But these needs do not seem to have been taken particularly seriously by a government that was calling for women to work. As Siân Reynolds has shown, crèches continued to exist throughout the war, even if in theory they did not meet with government approval.[96] They were even officially recognized in the Statute of 22 December 1942, which included them in its general provisions. It is therefore worthy of note that in Toulouse some extra facilities were built even if they were still piecemeal by comparison with demand. Reynolds' view is that during the war the use of crèches became increasingly legitimized and that workers in better-paid jobs were willing to use them. This trend intensified after the war, when they gained a middle-class clientele (see Chapter 7). In Germany, day nurseries and crèches were widely supported and action was taken to help working wives and mothers combine professional and family duties.[97] In Italy, some changes were also made which ironically made it easier for women to work outside the home. Improvements in maternity leave and breast-feeding

93. Ibid., pp. 64–5.

94. Dominique Veillon, *La Mode sous l'Occupation* (Paris, 1990), p. 35; Anne-Louise Moreau, 'La Traversée de la guerre et ses effets sur les itinéraires professionnels d'une cohorte de retraités et retraitées nés en 1919 et résident en Loire Atlantique', in Peschanski and Robert (eds), *Les Ouvriers*, p. 49.

95. Omnès, 'Les Trajectoires des ouvrières parisiennes', p. 68.

96. Siân Reynolds, 'Who Wanted the Crèches? Working Mothers and the Birth-Rate in France 1900–1950', *Continuity and Change*, 5/2 (1990), pp. 189–90.

97. Ute Frevert, *Women in German History* (London, 1990), p. 225.

rooms were really motivated by the desire to offset the alleged negative impact work could have on women's reproductive capacities.[98] Vichy did not go to such lengths, and in France, most commonly, mothers made personal arrangements to have someone to look after the children. Extended family, grandparents and aunts, very often played this role. Children were also often sent to stay with family in the countryside. Sending children out of town to stay with relatives had the added advantage that they were often better fed and in the minds of their parents safer. The municipality also had a system whereby parents made an application for children to be placed in families, a sort of evacuation. One witness explained that she sent her daughter 'to the peasants who boarded children'.[99]

During the Second World War in France, although perhaps not on quite the same scale or in the same circumstances as during the First World War, women were brought into almost every sector of paid employment which had previously been filled by men, but only on a temporary basis. Women worked in the absence of men, but did not take their jobs. Some women were trained to do new types of work and overwhelmingly responded to calls for their labour, but they had to be flexible and be prepared to change sectors as the job market varied in different regional contexts. In 1939, with the outbreak of the war, the vast majority of women who wanted and needed to find paid employment were able to do so, if not in industry, in administration. Those women who already worked in agriculture tended to stay there for the duration of the war and their responsibilities were often increased. Employment opportunities had as much to do with regional socio-economic factors as with the presence or absence of the Occupied forces. Provision for childcare was limited, and the added difficulties of daily life in wartime made it even harder for women to assume the double burden of the home and the workplace.

Vichy attempted to regulate female employment through direct laws and their system of benefits, and did so with some success by comparison with the regimes in Germany and Italy. Perry Willson concludes that, in Italy, quotas and fascist measures had little or no discernible effect on the number of women in waged employment.[100] In Germany, as in France, Nazi policy was constantly shifting where the issue of female labour was concerned. But, despite promises in

---

98. Perry Willson, *The Clockwork Factory* (Oxford, 1993), pp. 5–6.
99. Interview, Madame Delphine (Toulouse).
100. Willson, *The Clockwork Factory*, p. 10.

the election propaganda to keep women out of the labour market, National Socialism had little success in driving out married women, particularly after the outbreak of the war.[101] If the Vichy government did manage to keep married women out of the labour market for some of the time, to some degree, the circumstances of the war and the Occupation made it impossible for them to sustain such a policy. Ideology could not compete when economic pressures were pulling women into the workforce. Policies introduced by Vichy seemed to have more relevance to a peacetime scenario, conforming to their ideological ideals which had little to do with the actual economic realities. These measures even had some consequences which were quite the opposite of their original intentions, and married women who really wanted to find employment were often able to do so despite the attempts made to discourage them. This chapter has shown in detail that not working for money was, by the end of the war, not an option for many women, whatever their family situation, and that regional factors played a very important role. Whether the war made any longer-term differences to female labour is discussed in Chapter 7.

101. Frevert, *Women in German History*, pp. 217–18.

CHAPTER THREE

Physical Survival

In the days after the Liberation, the French were all more or less convinced that they had spent four years fighting the Occupier, whereas, their daily timetable, if it had been kept up to date, would have shown the time that was taken by looking for rabbits in the farms on Sundays, or shoes, or even shoe laces to replace those of the children who had grown; there were also, in this obscure domain, several acts of heroism, of abnegation, but the life-struggle of a mother of four children inspired no bard, no poet as it is so inglorious to merely try to survive.[1]

To observe that women took the main responsibility in most households for the physical survival of its members during the war would be neither surprising nor particularly new. Few were able, like one female member of the Resistance group Défense de la France, to reject the idea of queuing and rely on others to do it for them.[2] The oral and documentary sources indicate unequivocally that most women, unless they were lucky enough to have someone else who was prepared to do it for them, were involved in these activities at least to some degree – in any case more so than the men, who, if they were present, almost always had women around who did this kind of work for them. This chapter will argue that although personal wealth played an important part, physical survival was intensely gendered and was a key factor in women's experience of the war. Furthermore, women's activities and everyday lives were affected by the following variables: first, by the efficiency or lack of it of the local authorities and the structures that were put into place to ensure the fair distribution of food and household stuffs; secondly,

---

1. Alfred Sauvy, *La Vie économique des Français de 1939 à 1945* (Paris, 1978), p. 10.
2. AN 6AV 637–640.

by women's capacity to mobilize other skills and find other strategies for survival, which often meant that they could find themselves in a situation of illegality or part of a counter-culture simply by attempting to do their best for their families and continuing with their daily lives; and thirdly, by their relationship with their men.

Obtaining food

'Looking for food, this was a major concern.'[3]

During the first eight months after the outbreak of the war, despite the separation experienced by many families, most of the structures of everyday life, in terms of food supply at least, were near normal. But after the defeat, from the summer of 1940, German requisitioning immediately led to food shortages and obtaining enough food became a dominant preoccupation.

OFFICIAL SOURCES OF SUPPLY

Rationing

Until June 1940 the war had little impact on eating habits as most people had stocks which saw them through for a while.[4] But this changed radically three months after the German occupation of the north of France when rationing was introduced on 17 September 1940. From that time, tickets had to be exchanged for almost everything. Everyone, rich and poor alike, had a quota of what they could buy to eat, as well as how much heating fuel they were allowed and the clothes they could acquire. People belonged to one of eight different ration categories according to their age and type of work.[5]

E   children under 3
J1   children from 3 to 6
J2   children from 7 to 13
J3   children from 13 to 21
A   adults between 21 and 70 who were not involved in heavy labour
V   people older than 70

3. Interview, Madame Gwen (Toulouse).
4. Antoine Lefébure, *Les Conversations secrètes des français sous l'Occupation* (Paris, 1993), p. 80.
5. Sauvy, *La Vie économique*, p. 113.

T   workers (*travailleurs*). There were two groups within this
     category who received more generous rations:
     T1   those doing heavy work
     T2   miners and sick men
C   agricultural workers over 21 (*cultivateurs*)

Two distinctive categories were created according to gender: FE was
the card for pregnant women (*femme enceinte*) and FA the card for
breast-feeding mothers (*femme allaitante*). Holders of these two cards
were allowed to go directly to the front of queues and had more
generous milk rations. A breast-feeding bonus (*prime d'allaitement*)
was also awarded by government for four months after the birth
of a baby, 175 francs a month for the first baby and 250 francs a
month for subsequent children.[6] In April 1940, a family card was
introduced for families with five children under 21 all living under
the same head of household. This also gave cardholders the privilege
of jumping the queues. On 11 December 1940, it was decided by
arrêté that the 'T' card would also be given to women not working
outside their homes, if they had at least three children under 12 to
look after. But otherwise women had the same rations as men, with
the notable exception that, from August 1941, they did not receive
ration tokens for tobacco.[7] The Vichy government felt that women
who smoked were not compatible with the moral regeneration
of the country. Effectively, therefore, women lost out for moralistic
reasons on what became a valuable currency of exchange for male
non-smokers, and women who were addicted to nicotine were very
unhappy. Some even attempted to get doctor's prescriptions to allow
them to obtain cigarettes.[8]

Monthly ration cards were distributed from the local town hall,
allocated on a departmental basis; ration allocations for the area
appeared in the local press. Newspapers were passed around as
not everyone had access to one. In Penmarc'h (Finistère) women
described how one male member of the community assembled
everyone after the Sunday mass outside the church and listed the
ration allowances; women recounted how they went to this particular church on foot just to obtain this information despite the
fact that it was a long distance away.[9] Although supplies were distributed according to local availability, goods frequently failed
to appear on the market until some time after they had been

---

6. *L'Espoir français*, Aide aux femmes seules, 10–20 Aug. 1943, p. 9.
7. Sauvy, *La Vie économique*, p. 121.   8. Interview, Doctor Rosier (Toulouse).
9. Interview, Madame Denise (Finistère).

announced in the papers. The tickets had to be honoured, but it was a frustrating process as no one ever knew when; deliveries were very irregular and there could be two- or even three-month delays for some products.

Obtaining bread was a particularly difficult and complicated affair. It was always of poor quality and there was never enough of it. In the countryside it was common practice for some peasant families to make their own flour and then take it to the local baker and exchange it for bread.[10] Commercially, the sale of fresh bread was forbidden; bread on sale had to have been baked the day before, the theory being that people would eat less if the bread was stale and hard. The police spent much of their time monitoring food supplies and one of the most common minor crimes recorded across the country was that of people selling fresh bread illegally. Other crimes included deception in the weight of bread, which carried a 500 fr fine; adding water to milk, with a 200 fr fine; and illicit pricing of goods, which was punishable with three months in prison and a 300 fr fine.[11] In April 1941, bread rations for the civilian population were reduced from 350g to 275g per day.

The rations of fats, particularly important for cooking, were often diminished or suppressed altogether. Rural families were not considered to be short of fats since if they slaughtered their animals they had fat from the beast, so from January 1943 holders of category 'C' ration cards received no fats. Milk rations tended to vary, and when milk disappeared altogether its absence mobilized considerable discontent among women (see Chapter 5). Eggs were distributed from time to time, but were more often sold directly from the farms. There was, in theory, a free market for fruit and vegetables. Farmers could sell their goods in the village and town markets at the going price. Even so, only early shoppers could be sure of getting anything. Stalls normally sold vegetables such as cabbages, swedes, Jerusalem artichokes and carrots, which were the most readily available during the war, perhaps because they were easily cultivated and lasted longer than most other fresh vegetables.

Shopkeepers opened on different days and times, but frequently ran out of supplies, encouraging unsatisfied customers to come back later in the day after a possible new delivery. This was frequently a frustrating experience for the hard-pressed housewife. The following

10. Interview, Madame Pauline (Toulouse).
11. Danielle Costa and Jocelyne Joussemet, 'Femmes des Pyrénées Orientales', unpublished Mémoire de Maîtrise (University of Toulouse, 1981), p. 87.

extract from the diary of a Parisian housewife in October 1942 reflects this experience:[12]

7.30	The bakers'. Bread. There will be biscottes at 11am.
9.00	A meat day. The butcher says it will only be distributed on Saturday.
9.30	The cream shop. He will only have cheese at 5pm.
10.00	The tripe shop. My number 32 will come up at 4pm.
10.30	The grocer's shop, there will be vegetables at 5pm.
11.00	Return to the baker's. There are no more biscottes.

Queuing

The only way of legally collecting rations from the shops was to get to the shop before the goods ran out, and since everyone else had the same idea in mind, this inevitably meant queues. Therefore, those who did not queue received nothing. One woman recounts that she took the decision to refuse to queue as part of her political commitment to the Resistance and she nearly starved.[13] (In reality, other people ended up doing the queuing for her.) Images of women queuing are among the most pervasive at this time. It was a particularly urban phenomenon and has remained a lasting memory of the war. But queuing in itself was no assurance that supplies would last until everyone in the queue had been served. It was a regular occurrence to find that by the time it was your turn there was nothing left. The common practice of joining any queue was discouraged because queues became too long and as a system it was unfair. People were required to register with their local shopkeeper instead.[14] This soon became the common procedure for all shops. As soon as the markets opened at five or six in the morning queues began to form, and women sometimes waited several hours on the way to work. Although queuing sometimes meant long and exhausting waits, little or no allowance was made for gender or age. Pregnant women and mothers of large families were often reluctant to take advantage of their priority cards to go to the front of queues because it was greatly resented by other women who might have been queuing for several hours. But, as a general rule, the more time one invested in queuing, the more likely one was to obtain something.

These structures for acquiring food required considerable adjustment. People took some time to reorganize their daily lives as they

12. Dominique Veillon, 'La Vie quotidienne des femmes', in Jean-Pierre Azéma and François Bedarida (eds), *Le Régime de Vichy et les Français* (Paris, 1992), p. 631.

13. AN 6AV 637–640.

14. AN F1 cIII 1204, Rapport de Préfet, 5 Dec. 1942.

adapted to rationing and the changes created a heavy burden for women. Housekeepers had to be extremely organized both with their time and their energy, for not only did they have to cope with queuing but they had the added strain of trying to juggle the budget to pay for what was needed. To obtain what they could have acquired in an hour of shopping before the war, several hours – sometimes an entire day – had to be put aside, without any guarantee of success. However, women, as it was mostly women who were involved, soon organized themselves and developed strategies to deal with these official ways of obtaining food. In large households different members were called upon to queue according to their availability and children were often brought in to help. Some women even hired themselves out to queue for others. It served to cultivate one's own shopkeepers, who would put aside goods for those they knew, or sometimes miraculously find extra supplies for them. In this way those who were 'foreign' to the area, refugees or who had settled from other parts of the country were disadvantaged. All sorts of bits of information became important: knowing which door to the market was to be used that day could make the all-important difference. This kind of rumour played an important role in helping women to know when to be in the right place at the right time.

Women in paid employment were disadvantaged in that they had less time to queue, but working could have compensations, quite apart from their wages. They sometimes had contact with extra survival mechanisms and could more easily gain access to food and the many exchanges which took place at the workplace. Employers would often try to compensate their employees in kind. For example, a woman in Brest who worked for a wine dealer had a monthly allocation of wine which she used to obtain flour.[15]

The difficulties of obtaining enough to eat, particularly for those in urban areas, meant that many turned to charities for help. Children were a major concern, and a number of initiatives were implemented to arrange for them to spend time in the country and benefit from better diets. The *Secours National* and the *Mouvement Populaire des Familles* thus collaborated in St Etienne with the *Ligue Agriculturelle Chrétienne* and the *Jeunesse Agricole Chrétienne* to have children placed in peasant families for one to two months.[16] Some children had school dinners, to the relief of their mothers, who could

15. Interview, Madame Geneviève (Finistère).
16. Jean Nisey, 'Naissance et développement du MPF à Saint Etienne', in Denis Peschanski and Jean-Louis Robert (eds), *Les Ouvriers en France pendant la deuxième guerre mondiale* (Paris, 1992), p. 381.

at least count on them having had one square meal a day, but in fact the authorities in Toulouse expressed concern that the meals provided by the schools were inadequate.[17] Some municipal charities dealt with women's specific needs. The *Goutte de Lait*, for example, founded in 1919, and the *Maison Municipale des Mères*, founded in 1921, were originally designed to help combat infant mortality. Both charities took on an active role during the war. The *Goutte de Lait* supplied pregnant and breast-feeding women with valuable extra rations of sterilized milk. Unemployed women could also qualify for help from the municipality to the sum of 12 francs a day in 1940 if they fulfilled a number of conditions, the most important of which was to have dependants and no other wage earner, i.e. husband.[18] The *Goûter des Mères* was financed by the *Secours National* and provided tea-time food for pregnant mothers. Other charities including the Red Cross tried to find paid work for women with no resources (p. 27) and attempted to serve meals at reasonable prices (see p. 67). However, there was relatively little on offer to help those in real distress.

FROM OFFICIAL TO UNOFFICIAL SOURCES

How successful, then, were the authorities in creating a fair and equitable food distribution system? It is noticeable that most accounts of the war emphasize that people did not have enough to eat. In fact, it is difficult to establish whether the French people really had enough to eat during the war or not. Did rations suffice to feed local populations? Or were rations inadequate and rarely honoured? There were certainly substantial regional variations and there is no doubt that some regions were better served than others. The food distribution authorities were generally considered to be corrupt and inefficient. For example, the department of the Alpes Maritimes experienced severe food shortages throughout the war. This was largely because it produced little for itself apart from fruit. The fishermen could not go out to sea as the ports were mined and its position at the extreme tip of the country made transport difficult. The belief was widespread in the population that deliveries destined for them were hijacked at Avignon or Marseilles.[19] Yet, in Toulouse,

17. M.F. Manalesco, 'La Municipalité de Toulouse 1940–44', unpublished Mémoire de Maîtrise (University of Toulouse, 1987), p. 154.

18. AMT, Archives du Bureau de Travail, Etats numériques des chômeurs 1938–42.

19. Lefébure, *Les Conversations secrètes*, p. 366.

despite popular mythology to the contrary and the fact that oral sources complained that there had not been enough to eat during the war, it would seem that rations were normally honoured when backed by tickets, except for meat.[20] Furthermore, most rural populations in Brittany were always able to buy their rations and there does not seem to have been much suffering from shortages of food. People in large cities, notably those living in Paris, were undoubtedly the worst hit and had the most trouble buying according to their ration allocations.

In areas where food was short, the problem seems to have been not only one of whether or not the rations were met, but that the number of calories they allowed for was too low, so people were forced to find other ways of feeding themselves.[21] Ration allowances were never more than 1,200 calories, which was too little to lead a normal life. In this context, women attempted to supplement rations by procuring food in other ways. The comfort and survival of the household to which they belonged could depend on the networks and the strategies that women devised to obtain what they needed. These attempts sometimes led them to develop less official, even illegal methods of acquiring food.

There were some strategies that people were encouraged to develop in order to acquire more food. Vegetable gardens, for example, took on a new importance during the war, particularly in the towns, where every bit of available space was used to grow vegetables. Public land was rented out and private gardens were converted. In Toulouse, 210,442 square metres of land was rented by associations and companies for this purpose and given to workers.[22] A law was passed on 18 August 1940 that all unused urban land should be handed over to the heads of large families and associations of factory workers. 'Family gardens' appeared in the suburbs of large towns, and most were allocated to factory workers. Dominique Veillon cites that in Lyon, 600 gardens of 200 square metres were distributed in the autumn of 1940.[23] This made it possible for some of those living in the cities to grow their own green vegetables. Many households also attempted to raise chickens, rabbits or ducks if they had the space.

---

20. Rolande Trempé, 'La Région économique de Toulouse aux lendemains de la Libération', in Gérard Cholvy (ed.), *Histoire du Languedoc de 1900 à nos jours* (Toulouse, 1980), p. 122.

21. Henri Amouroux, *La Vie des Français sous l'Occupation* (Paris, 1961), p. 122.

22. Manalesco, 'La Municipalité', p. 155.

23. Dominique Veillon, *Vivre et survivre en France, 1939–1947* (Paris, 1995), p. 171.

Affluent town-dwellers who had country houses were able to organize their gardens to grow vegetables. As food could legally be transferred from one property to another within one family they could therefore benefit from this. In the same way, families in big cities who originated from the surrounding rural areas or nearby departments took advantage of parents or extended families living nearby who sent them food. Thus, people who lived in towns 'rediscovered' relatives in the countryside who sent them family parcels packed with goods which were impossible for them to find in town. In 1942 alone, 13,500,000 parcels were sent.[24] In agreement with the *Jeunesse Agricole Chrétienne*, the *Jeunesse Ouvrière Chrétienne Féminine* twinned peasant families with the families of industrial workers who were then able to exchange parcels.[25] There was also the phenomenon of paid relations, peasants who sent food for payment. City dwellers put advertisements in the rural press to find peasants who were prepared to do this.[26] For those who had contacts in rural areas or who could afford to pay, such parcels made their lives much more comfortable, and sometimes even prevented starvation.

As food became more difficult to find in town, and rations proved increasingly inadequate, townspeople started to look for other ways of acquiring food from the countryside. The authorities recognized that farmers found it much more convenient to sell from the farm than to bring their goods into the markets because of the transportation difficulties and the loss of valuable time they could be spending on the land when there was such a shortage of labour. A clandestine market resulted from this which benefited those with relatives in the country and those with time to go there. Food was obtained in ways which ranged from the legal to the less legal on foraging expeditions. But these trips were fraught with difficulty, and a special pass (*Ausweis*) was required to move around the country, to cross from one department into another and particularly to cross from one zone into another one. There were few private cars on the roads since both oil and petrol were rationed. Trains continued to run, but services were unreliable and there was no guarantee that a train would arrive at its destination. Sometimes trains would stop in the middle of nowhere, obliging passengers to complete their journey on foot, or by whatever means they could. In some areas local transport was organized to help those who wanted to go on

24. Lefébure, *Les Conversations secrètes*, p. 85.
25. Jeanne Aubert, *La JOCF. Qu'as tu fait de nos vies? La Jeunesse Ouvrière Chrétienne Féminine 1928–45* (Paris, 1990), p. 134.
26. Veillon, *Vivre et survivre*, p. 174.

foraging excursions in the surrounding countryside. Although the authorities officially objected to these trips, they did nothing to stop the extra SNCF train services which were provided on Sunday afternoons to facilitate them. One woman who lived on a farm out-side Toulouse described how 'People came by train to fetch things that we had prepared for them: eggs, rabbits, potatoes, dry beans. It was mostly family, people came to us because they knew us, we did not do it for people we did not know, only for family and some intimate friends who wrote to us.'[27] Many women would either walk or bicycle to the local farms. Possession of a bicycle was often a key factor in being able to acquire food from some distance away. Bicycling became the most convenient form of transport and bicycles increased in number from 8,320,042 in 1939 to 10,711,808 in 1942.[28] Their use was strictly controlled and many were requisitioned by the Germans. Tyres were difficult to find as rubber was rationed and very expensive. Still, people would travel up to 60 kilometres in one day to acquire a chicken or a litre of milk.

Police checks were set up at all the entries to the towns, on the roads and at railway stations. Passengers were searched for 'illegal' food. Women found various means of fooling the police on their return journey; disguising themselves as pregnant was a favourite ploy and an effective way of hiding their goods. The French police seem to have carried out the checks with varying degrees of assiduity: 'At the station exits there were controls for food supplies and when they saw a pregnant woman they said that she really needed to eat. When they saw that it was not for commerce and for personal con-sumption they let you go through.'[29]

Often goods were paid for by exchanging them for something else in a barter process. This was extremely important as currency was of considerably less value. Most people wanted something useful in exchange. These kinds of exchanges were generally tolerated by the authorities, but in cases of outright black market dealing, where large sums of money changed hands, they were less happy and the police had a continuous battle to enforce the accepted price levels. Shopkeepers were not allowed to sell rationed goods without the production of a ticket, and what they did sell had to be at regulated market prices. All transactions were logged by the shopkeeper and records had to be presented to the town hall. Inevitably, many indulged in under-the-counter selling, and what began as an option

27. Interview, Madame Sandrine (Toulouse).
28. Amouroux, *La Vie des Français*, p. 519.
29. Interview, Madame Bathilde (Toulouse).

to boost the rations of the privileged few who could afford it became, as oral testimony confirms, extremely widespread and almost essential to survival. The black market was often the only way to acquire goods which had disappeared from the shops and was seen by much of the population as legitimate. Factory workers in towns who were the most affected by problems of food supply particularly resented the fact that those with extra financial resources could find other ways of getting food on the black market and repeatedly called for the state to ensure that the normal quota of rations suffice for their survival.

The authorities were not able to provide increased rations, but they did make considerable attempts to control black market activity. Warnings were given to shopkeepers who were caught selling and transporting rationed goods without tickets or authorization.[30] In September 1941, a price control committee in Toulouse confirmed that vigorous repression was necessary to make sure that prices were respected.[31] Despite the law of 15 March 1942, which excluded transgressions of the law which were carried out for essential family survival, the black market was extremely widespread.[32] In 1942, *Le Midi socialiste* reported 129 prison sentences for 'black market' crimes, 578 people were fined and 71 shops were closed down.[33] The courts could impose maximum sentences of two years' imprisonment and a 200,000 fr fine, though they rarely went that far. The black market was, in fact, more of a 'grey market' – an acceptable alternative way of procuring food for those who were fortunate enough to be able to afford it. Women, who often controlled the resources for buying or selling, were well placed to take advantage of it. Evelyn Sullerot has pointed out how it was very empowering for peasant women:

> The peasant woman who was at the bottom of the ladder in the thirties, the one who worked without paid holiday, without education, and who was made fun of because she only knew her village and the neighbouring one . . . here she became relatively powerful. She kept her keys in the pocket of her apron and she said yes or no to those who came to see her, she dictated her conditions.[34]

Between 1940 and 1944 official prices increased by over 100 per cent, a rise which represented 292 per cent in real terms, so women

---

30. ADF 200W59, Activités des Services de Police, Nov. 1940.
31. AN F1 cIII 1154, Rapport de Préfet, 1–30 Sept. 1941.
32. Amouroux, *La Vie des Français*, p. 144.
33. *Le Midi socialiste*, 27 Feb. 1943.
34. Evelyn Sullerot, 'La Condition de la femme dans la France de Vichy', Le Journal de la France, les années 40, *Historia*, 129, p. 943.

	tax price (fr)	friendly price (fr)	black market price (fr)
butter (kilo)	42	69	107
12 eggs	20	35	53
chicken (kilo)	24	38	48
pork (kilo)	17	46	74
potatoes (100 kg)	161	393	544

had to shop according to their means, legally or illegally.[35] Michel Cépède has established that there were three price levels in 1942, and these are illustrated in the table.[36] A kilo of potatoes bought for 3 francs in the countryside sold for 15 francs in Paris. At a time when the monthly salary of a factory worker was about 1,500 francs for a man and 1,300 francs for a woman, one can imagine how difficult it was for people to eat their fill if they were entirely dependent on black market food.[37] Some women also found that they could help their situation and that of those dependent upon them by moving to the country, not only because it broke the cycle of continuous queuing but also because they then had access to the 'friendly priced' goods.

It seems to be evident that the French attach a great deal of cultural importance to their food, and certainly as far as their memories are concerned it cannot be denied that this was a time of deprivations which can only have been compounded in areas where the Germans were present and where obvious iniquities existed. The enormous regional variations in food supply make it impossible to give a general picture, but people in towns suffered a great deal more than those in the countryside, particularly in polycultural regions. Those who lived in the monocultural wine regions, for example, and those who lived on the coast also had less access to food. It is difficult to establish the extent to which the French people went hungry since food supply could vary dramatically from region to region. What is certain is that some social classes suffered more than others. The families of factory workers experienced particular hardship since they were completely dependent on rations and had no extra cash to buy on the black market, nor could they supplement their income by selling goods, which often helped rural families. A study carried

35. Amouroux, *La Vie des Français*, p. 151.
36. Michel Cépède, *Agriculture et alimentation en France pendant la deuxième guerre mondiale* (Paris, 1961).
37. Lefébure, *Les Conversations secrètes*, p. 95.

out in Toulouse in May and June 1941 on 'The budgets of the families of workers in Toulouse' concluded that they experienced real difficulty.[38] Life was inevitably much more difficult for larger families, and the adolescent ration category J3 suffered more than other age-groups because they needed more food.[39]

However, in most households, strategies were devised so that, although material conditions deteriorated, once networks had been established and money budgeted so that something could be put aside to buy certain essentials on the black market if necessary, the suffering lessened. Family parcels saved the lives of many families in towns. But, once food had been acquired, it then had to be prepared and served as meals. Everyday life also embraced issues like clothes, health and leisure activities. For each of these aspects of their lives, women developed strategies which enabled them to make the most of their situation. The following section describes how women were able to be even more innovative and to develop further strategies when they were confronted with the laws and regulations passed by the authorities. The problems presented by the shortages might also have brought them to break some rules simply by continuing their everyday lives.

Patterns of everyday life

COOKING AND PREPARING FOOD

The process of cooking and preparing food required more thought and became more time-consuming than it had been before the war. Heating fuels and gas for cooking were rationed and supplies were irregular, varying across the country. Electricity was rationed in the cities and the larger towns, and there were many rural areas, as in Brittany, for example, where there was still no electricity. Traditional ways of cooking had to be abandoned if there was a lack of fuel and fats. Housewives had to make rations of fats go as far as possible and find alternatives to the normal habits of frying food. They were called upon to be inventive, to come up with new recipes for the bland vegetables or the tasteless *ersatz* or artificial foods that were to be found. Magazines and the newspapers offered suggestions and advice about how to cook food, how to make it go further and

---

38. AN F1 cIII 1154, Rapport de Préfet, Oct. 1941.
39. Ibid., 4 Aug. 1942; AN F1 cIII 1204, Familles nombreuses; and J3 on 4 May 1942; AN F1 cIII 1152. See also Raymond Ruffin, *Journal d'un J3* (Paris, 1979).

how to make it taste better. It certainly was a challenge to attempt to make nourishing meals out of the skimpy rations. Those housewives who had come to depend on tinned factory-processed food could no longer find it stocked in the shops. The old habits of processing and preserving food came to the fore, and grandmothers with these skills were called upon to help make the meagre supplies last longer, at a time when both sugar and vinegar, essential ingredients for preserving food, were hard to find.[40] This was particularly important in those families where there was a prisoner-of-war: only imperishable goods could fill the parcels that were sent to them. In this way, some of the skills that were beginning to be lost, especially in the cities, were revived, and grandmothers found that they had an increased value in the household.

The distribution of food was normally a task which fell to women. Sources show that the traditional image of the mother depriving herself for her husband and children contains much truth. Women's oral and written testimonies often bear witness to how they had to cope with seeing their children undernourished and how they often deprived themselves for the sake of their children.

KEEPING WARM

In January 1941, clothing was also brought into the rationing system. Women had to clothe themselves and other family members. Each family was allocated a certain number of points and women would have to use them to provide themselves and their children with a wardrobe suitable for their lifestyle in all seasons; pregnant women were allowed some extra coupons.[41] The procedure for obtaining clothes was lengthy. For example, a woman needing clothes for her 7-year-old daughter had to present herself at a distribution centre and go through a series of procedures in order to procure a textile ration ticket. Once she had acquired this, she had to find the article she was looking for in the shops, and exchange it for the ration ticket which represented the weight of the piece of clothing she wanted. After paying for it, the item was hers.[42] But in Toulouse the problems of getting clothes were at times so great that, in March

40. Sullerot, 'La Condition de la femme', p. 940.
41. Clothes allowances for pregnant women: vouchers for one dress, 2 night-dresses, 2 pairs of trousers, a coat and sheets if giving birth at home; A *carte de layette* of 240 points for the new baby; a new card of 140 when the baby reached 1 year and another at 2. *L'Espoir français*, p. 10.
42. Interview, Madame Sophie (Toulouse).

1942, the Prefect was forced to recognize that because women could not clothe their children they were obliged to keep them at home instead of sending them to school.[43]

Most people therefore simply tried to make things last. Dresses and trousers were lengthened by adding odd scraps of material. Curtains, tablecloths, everything possible was mobilized to be made into some item of clothing. Women indulged in knitting crazes and in winter even used newspaper as an extra layer for warmth. Women's magazines advised them how to manage. Both the *Petit Echo de la mode*, which increased its circulation enormously, and *Marie-Claire* were very popular.[44] Women had to learn to be imaginative and to improvise both for themselves and for their families. For example, in the absence of bras, women had to be inventive with bits of material, which they tried to fit in helpful ways. Stockings started to disappear from spring 1941.[45] Although Elizabeth Arden invented the idea of dyeing legs with a lotion, women adapted it in their own particular way: 'We did not have any stockings so we climbed onto the table and drew a line with a pencil, but when it rained it started to drip and you would have thought it was milky coffee.'[46] One pair of shoes per year was allowed for in the rations. But the leather shortages meant that wooden soles had started to become widespread from 1941. These were noisy and clumsy and it was impossible to run with them. Interviewees complained that they did not really allow for a discreet return home after curfew. In 1942, finding a pair of shoes became even harder as there was no question of going to buy them in shops. People went to small artisans, small shoemakers and passed on addresses to one another.[47]

In this context, Veillon holds that clothing could indicate approval of or resistance to the Vichy government and its ideology.[48] What is certain is that those involved in collaboration normally had more money to spend on clothes or going to the hairdresser and this made them stand out.

HEALTH AND CHILDCARE

Keeping clean is the basis of good health and this was not always easy during the war. Soap was scarce: it was one of the first commodities to be rationed, at 100g a month, and it soon went out of

43. AN F1 cIII 1154, Rapport de Préfet, 5 Mar. 1942.
44. Dominique Veillon, *La Mode sous l'Occupation* (Paris, 1990), p. 106.
45. Ibid., pp. 95–7.   46. Interview, Madame Marion (Toulouse).
47. Interview, Madame Dolorès (Toulouse).   48. Veillon, *La Mode*, p. 106.

circulation altogether. Each household found recipes and ways of improvising. But it was necessary to have at least some fats to mix the soap with.

The health of the population was a high priority of the Vichy government and women benefited from the measures designed to keep a closer control on the well-being of the nation as well as an almost obsessive concern to protect childbirth. 'Marry young!' screamed the propaganda. 'Have children young, they will be more beautiful, stronger and healthier.'[49] The health record book was introduced in 1942 along with the pregnancy record book in line with the belief that motherhood and childcare should be closely supervised by experts. Vichy provided for mothers to make regular free visits to doctors and health visitors. Linked with these concerns was the premarriage certificate, which required women to be free of venereal disease before they could marry. Indeed, Vichy was very preoccupied with the spread of venereal disease, and throughout the war the Prefects kept regular rubrics in their reports devoted to social hygiene, charting the progress of the various diseases in the area. Particular care was also taken to control prostitution and to carry out medical checks on women who were picked up by police patrols.

Women and the family were specifically targeted by Vichy. The 'family' was a crucial part of Vichy's National Revolution. As Pétain explained to the nation in a radio speech, the family was 'the essential cell, the basis even of the social edifice, it is on this that we must build'.[50] Vichy discourse laid part of the blame for the defeat of France on the decline in the birthrate and the diminishing importance attached to the family. The creation of a Ministry of the Family (*Secrétariat à la Famille*) on 12 July 1940, just two days after Pétain came to power, shows the priority given to this area of policy (though its importance soon diminished when it became the *Commissariat Général à la Famille* in 1941, with a much smaller budget than other Ministries, and its Minister was excluded from the inner circle of government).[51] It was the French people, and notably women, who had failed to produce enough male children to replace those who had died in the First World War, who were therefore largely responsible for the defeat. Thus they were offered the ideal of the peasant woman with many children. Once again, legislation and propaganda conformed more to a peacetime scenario at a time

---

49. Brochure edited by the Sécretariat Générale à la Famille, 1942.

50. Philippe Pétain, *Paroles aux Français* (Paris, 1941), p. 128; for a more detailed analysis of Vichy's family policy, see Miranda Pollard's work (n. 19 to Ch. 1).

51. AN 2AG 605, Politique Générale de la Famille, 1941.

when a large number of families found themselves in the opposite situation from that desired by Vichy. Separated couples were widespread and many wives of prisoners-of-war became temporary single mothers. Despite the absence of the men, the Vichy government wanted to encourage all women to have children. Even women who found that they were alone when they were pregnant were helped in an attempt to discourage them from having abortions. Propaganda repeatedly encouraged women to stay at home and have children.[52] The family had to be preserved at all costs. Under the April 1942 law it became impossible to divorce during the first three years of marriage. Adultery was no longer sufficient reason for divorce and abandoning the family was severely punished. Wives of prisoners-of-war were fined if they were caught having adulterous affairs.

This perceived need to improve the birthrate led to a campaign against abortion, which was seen as a major social enemy. Concern about the birthrate had long been present in French political discourse, and worries about population figures as a result of the losses experienced during the First World War heightened government attempts to control women's fertility. The 1920 law against contraception introducing anti-abortion measures was strengthened in the *Code de la Famille* in September 1939, increasing sentences from 5 to 10 years in prison and fines from 5,000 to 20,000 francs. In 1941, Vichy further reinforced this area of policy by making abortion a treasonous crime against the state both for the woman having the abortion and the person carrying it out: a path already taken by Mussolini in 1926.[53] A special state tribunal was established to try these cases, along with those of people accused of Resistance activity. Between October 1942 and August 1943, eleven people appeared before it for abortion-related crimes. The minimum sentence was 15 to 20 years forced labour and fines of 60,000 to 120,000 francs, several were imprisoned for life and two were executed. One of these was a man from Le Mans who had performed abortions on three women in spite of the fact that he had already served two previous prison sentences for this crime. The decision of the tribunal was that these prison sentences had failed to deter him and that the guillotine was therefore the only solution.[54] The other, Marie-Louise Giraud, was executed on 30 July 1943 at La Roquette prison for

---

52. Miranda Pollard, 'Femme, Famille, France: Vichy and the Politics of Gender, 1940–1944', unpublished PhD thesis (University of Dublin, 1990).

53. Victoria de Grazia, *How Fascism Ruled Women, Italy 1922–45* (Berkeley, 1992), p. 55.

54. AN 4W15 dossier 5.

performing 27 abortions (22 pre-dated the law). It is quite apparent from the accounts of the trial that she was condemned as much for her lifestyle and personality as for the crime. The report justifying the decision of the tribunal mentioned that Giraud 'acted with a disconcerting cynicism, conducting the abortions in her own home where both her young children were aware of what was going on'.[55] The fact that she also rented out rooms to prostitutes and made considerable financial gains (she earned over 13,000 francs from the abortions) helped to create a picture of moral degeneration which the Vichy regime had to make an example of. Her story is re-created in Francis Spinzer's novel *Une Affaire de femmes, Paris 1943, exécution d'une avorteuse*, which was made into a film by Claude Chabrol.[56] Across the country, the number of convictions for performing abortions increased from 1,225 in 1940 to 3,701 in 1944.[57]

Work has already been done which shows Vichy's intentions embodied in these laws.[58] But is there any evidence that these laws had any effects, that more babies were born, that more illegitimate babies were kept and that aborting was reduced? This sort of evidence is difficult to find. Sauvy has remarked upon the surprising national increase in natality during the war, from 13.1 per thousand in 1941 to 15.7 per thousand in 1943, which he sees as a result of the family policies implemented from 1939.[59] Sauvy also records that there was an increase of over 20 per cent in the number of illegitimate children. But statistics can give no more than a minimal base for hypothesis. Indeed, it would be interesting to discover the extent to which Vichy propaganda encouraging women to have more children impinged upon the everyday life of women. Although awareness of family propaganda appears to have been fairly widespread, the evidence remains inconclusive.

KEEPING CHEERFUL

Leisure time was as an important part of everyday life during the war, as at any other time – perhaps more so, as having fun and trying to

---

55. AN 4W13 dossier 5.

56. Francis Spinzer, *Une Affaire de femmes, Paris 1943, exécution d'une avorteuse* (Paris, 1986).

57. Roger Henri Guerrand, *La Libre Maternité, 1896–1969* (Paris, 1971), p. 110.

58. Pollard, 'Femme, Famille, France'; see also Cheryl Koos, ' "On les aura!": The Gendered Politics of Abortion and the Alliance Nationale Contre la Dépopulation, 1938–1944', in Hanna Diamond and Claire Gorrara (eds), *Modern and Contemporary France, Special Issue: Gendering the Occupation of France* (Feb. 1999), pp. 21–33.

59. Sauvy, *La Vie économique*, p. 194.

forget the war for a while helped to maintain morale. It was not always easy, but, as one women explained, 'anything was a pretext for us to get together'.[60] Cafés remained a particularly male domain during the war years, and, as was the case for restaurants, there were alcohol and non-alcohol days. Laws on 24 August and 7 October 1940 prohibited the unlicensed distillation of spirits and sale of alcohol on certain days. The strength of pastis was limited to 16 degrees. Opening hours were strictly controlled according to electricity supplies and curfew regulations. Restaurants required ration tickets and served a 'normal meal' at a very high price – in fact people could easily spend a month's wages on one meal. Other restaurants catered for the less affluent by offering mainly vegetables, although clients had to bring their bread ration tickets. Black market restaurants also existed that everyone knew about, but few could afford. Popular restaurants or canteens were common, particularly in the towns and cities where people worked away from home during the day and therefore could not prepare their own food or return home for lunch. The *Secours National* organized such canteens with considerable success, providing a total of 60,000 meals in the southern zone.[61] One centre in Toulouse served 600 meals a day, costing between 3 and 5 francs.[62] This was still quite expensive except for those with a reasonably generous wage. Large companies and administrations organized restaurant-canteens where people could eat for 'normal' prices.

Several collaborationist groups also saw this as an area where they could mobilize female members and members' wives. In 1943, for example, the local *Légion Française des Combattants* in Toulouse opened three *restaurants légionnaires* for those in need, whether members of the *Légion* or not. In the department of the Haute-Garonne, centres in Toulouse and Saint Gaudens served 470,247 meals between January and April. The *Ligue des Familles Nombreuses* in collaboration with the *Légion* also organized for cooked dishes to be sold cheaply in certain areas of Toulouse.[63] Mass canteen style restaurants were also established, offering rather more expensive (10 fr) meals. One in Brest attended by local factory workers was created under the auspices of head of the *Croix de Feu*, Colonel de la Roque, but its prices excluded all but those who were relatively well-paid.[64]

60. Interview, Madame Bathilde (Toulouse).
61. AN F60 389, Soupes Populaires, Secours National.
62. Manalesco, 'La Municipalité', p. 153.
63. Henri Mauriès, 'Manifestations publiques de la Légion Française des Combattants en Haute-Garonne, 1940–44', unpublished Mémoire de Maîtrise (University of Toulouse, 1987), pp. 36–7.
64. ADF 200W43, 3 Feb. 1944.

The theatre was limited to the wealthy minority of the population who lived in towns. In Paris most of the big theatres remained open, as did the Opéra. The cinema was a major distraction and many people were dependent on the propagandist newsreels for information about the war. American and British films were banned but the cinemas were regularly packed, though less so for films known to be outright propaganda. Married women with families to support were less likely to have any extra spending money, so the local authorities often organized special cinema viewings for families of prisoners and those working in Germany, at reduced prices.[65] Single women were more likely to have something over from their budget to spend on entertainment, but like married women who found themselves alone, there were severe social constraints which prevented them from going out without a chaperone. Dutiful wives of prisoners-of-war therefore had to settle for spending evenings together knitting and writing letters, exchanging news about their men. As the war went on some plucked up the courage to go out to the cinema together, but often only after getting permission from husbands. Women who lived in the countryside rarely came to town because transport was so difficult and most working women had to use precious spare time to look for food.

However, there were also ways in which enjoying their free time could cause women to come up against the authorities. Listening to the British radio, for example, was an activity which could be dangerous as people were encouraged to denounce those who listened to it. Going out during curfew was a direct infringement of the rules. Clandestine dances were often held, although they were frowned upon by the Pétainist authorities (and forbidden in the Occupied zone). It was seen as scandalous to dance when so many Frenchmen were in prison camps. Yet these 'illegal' evenings could be big events, particularly in rural areas. Prefects' reports both in the Haute-Garonne and in the Finistère suggest that they took place regularly. In Brittany, in June 1943, the local population believed that invasion by the Allies was imminent and therefore a number of balls were held. They charged participants an entrance fee which would allow them to pay off the fine if they were caught. Should they escape detection, the money was paid back at the end of the evening.[66] Most of these festive evenings managed to escape notice as they were often held in farms well away from the German strongholds. However, on the occasions when German troops did make an appearance

65. ADHG M2277, 22 Sept. 1943.   66. ADF 200W44.

and demand that the party should finish, there could be serious clashes between them and the local population. On one occasion shots were fired and one of the organizers was injured.[67]

Strategies for survival

These were some of the ways women found to overcome the shortages imposed by the conditions of the war and the Occupation. Many found ingenious strategies which improved the quality of their lives. However, they were also sometimes obliged to transgress some of the rules and regulations that were put into place by the authorities, simply to ensure their own well-being and that of those dependent upon them. A major factor which could have an important bearing on women's experience of the war was the presence or absence of their men. Women whose husbands were present often experienced very little change in their lifestyle except in adapting to changed conditions. In some cases the presence of the husband served to insulate women from the more difficult problems brought by the war. Rather than extending their role, they were expected to perform their wifely and maternal duties even better than before, making a little food go further and being inventive with what provisions they did have. It is possible, therefore, to see the Occupation as having had a restrictive effect on some married women. By contrast, women whose circumstances were radically altered by the war because of absent husbands, and who had extra responsibilities, children or ageing parents, had much more to cope with. They were often forced to take on roles traditionally considered to be male. Absent husbands could not always provide a steady income and their wives were often forced on to the labour market, temporarily becoming the head of the family. Life was easier for them if they lived in the country. An important strategic move for young wives or mothers could be to move back home or in with relatives in the absence of their husbands. Some older women moved in with their daughters and helped them to run the business or the farm that the wife was maintaining in her husband's absence.

Most historians think of housekeeping and homemaking as tasks that were done solely by women and extend this to saying that 'all women' were preoccupied with this throughout the war.[68] It is true that women remained the guardians of the home and had main

67. ADF 200W43.   68. Amouroux, *La Vie des Français*, p. 192.

responsibility for the preparation of food and clothing the family. Consequently it was women who had to invest more time on survival techniques than men. Their traditional role as homemaker was therefore extended during the war. Those in small households, especially those living alone, single working women or men, or students, found it particularly hard to get enough to eat as they had no time to establish networks or to join queues. Elderly or middle-aged men and women who lived alone might simply die of neglect if they could not get about or were not looked after. The *Secours National* reported in February 1943 that much of their financial assistance went to the elderly or women alone.[69] But if she was part of a household a grandmother was able to participate in all areas of everyday life.

But the most important aspect highlighted in the chapter is that even if much of the evidence confirms the traditional picture of women's lives dominated by struggle for survival, the key issues which ruled women's everyday lives at this time were their relationship with their men, and their capacity to circumvent the rules established by the authorities. As women began to notice that food seemed to be disappearing before their very eyes, the Germans were increasingly blamed for rationing and food shortages. This contributed to a general feeling of antipathy towards the Germans. Thus lack of food and the need to find ways round the laws could push them to question existing laws. The main argument of the chapter is therefore that physical survival brought women into contact with structures which often forced them to confront the authorities and to stretch definitions of legality. This in turn might bring them to be critical of the regime, a point which is further explored in Chapter 5.

69. AN 2AG 154, Secours National.

CHAPTER FOUR

Collaborations

There were women who collaborated firstly for financial reasons, who collaborated because they were good-looking chaps, the Germans, then others collaborated because one of their family had been arrested and they collaborated to get them released. Then there were women who had been arrested and clubbed who collaborated to save themselves.[1]

The difficulty of access to the material and the fact that collaboration remains a highly sensitive issue in France is one of the reasons why historians have been more reluctant to deal with this aspect of the history of *les années noires* than that of Resistance. Feminist and women's historians working on the period have been more concerned to stress resistance and volition, and have not wanted to appear to be apologizing for women involved in making the 'wrong' choice. The phenomenon of women whose heads were shaved during the Liberation has acted as a symbolic representation within which all aspects of women's collaboration have been collapsed. Thus, most existing studies of collaboration have assumed that apart from what is referred to as 'horizontal' or sexual collaboration, collaboration was a predominantly male activity. However, increased access to the transcripts of the trials that took place in the postwar years, and detailed local studies of the Occupation, indicate that women participated in a spectrum of patterns of behaviour which ranged from acceptance of Vichy to outright collaboration with the Occupying forces. This chapter will argue that women were involved with collaboration on a number of levels. It will also demonstrate that there were certain forms of collaboration activity that were gender-specific or which, because of the circumstances of the war, concerned women more directly.

1. Interview, Madame Dolorès (Toulouse).

Collaborationist behaviour is normally seen as behaviour demonstrating or displaying support for Nazi Germany.[2] But this perception has been formed, to a large extent, by what was defined as collaboration in the postwar trials. Certainly, the word 'collaboration' implies a degree of voluntary action which carries a heavy ideological load and can be indefinitely extended to include all those who were directly or indirectly involved with the Germans, even all those who did not react against them. In this context collaboration also covers a *mentalité* of collaboration in which women as well as men certainly participated.

Steps towards collaboration

After the signing of the Armistice and in the highly confused situation following the invasion, most French people did not challenge the legitimacy of the Vichy regime. Once the initial shock at defeat abated it was succeeded by a general sense of relief that the war was over. Most people, men and women, had little awareness of the political implications of the Armistice. In the Occupied zones, the arrival of the Germans was nothing like as frightening as the rumours that preceded them had suggested. Oral sources suggest that they were seen to be polite and made a serious effort to make themselves as agreeable as possible. In the Non-Occupied zone, where people were spared the presence of the Germans, Pétain appeared to be a familiar and reassuring figure. Even if there were some individuals who were shocked by the events of the defeat and the Armistice, few knew what action to take. Most people were unaware that there was any alternative. Very few heard de Gaulle on 18 June 1940 and the majority did not openly question the existence of a legally established government headed by the *victor de Verdun.* The priority for everyone was to return to a 'normal' lifestyle, to get on with the business of surviving. As was seen in Chapter 3, these immediate everyday problems inevitably became very time-consuming and acted as a force of inertia which encouraged a certain political numbness and worked in favour of the Vichy regime. Other concerns seemed more important, particularly for those women who had to take on the burden of the extra work created by the conditions of the war and who were not explicitly concerned with political affairs. In this context, women could be brought to support Vichy through their

2. Pascal Ory, *Les Collaborateurs. 1940–45* (Paris, 1976).

everyday lives, a position which once achieved could undeniably lead to acceptance of or even more pronounced collaboration with Germans in later years. There is, of course, an important distinction to be made between acceptance of Vichy from 1940–42 and active support of Vichy authorities and Germans after 1942 and this must be borne in mind. However, in 1940, Vichy set out to win women's support and, through specific structures like the Associations for Prisoner-of-War Wives, sought to prevent them from withdrawing their support from the regime.

After the defeat, the overriding concern of women with soldiers in their family was for their absent husbands, brothers and sons. Some returned home, but others waited in vain. Those women whose soldier husbands did return in 1940, unless one or the other was of a political turn of mind, were most likely simply to acquiesce to conditions which they had no power to change, especially if they were sheltered from the problems of food supply. Women in these families had no reason to think badly of the Vichy regime unless they were Jews or communists, who were singled out by the regime for persecution.

Other women were less fortunate and many waited and waited for the promised return of husbands. This separation could act on women in two opposing ways. Some refused to accept a regime which allowed their husbands and sons to remain prisoners in a foreign country (see Chapter 5), but most were particularly receptive to Pétain's reassuring discourse which promised their imminent return. In the months that followed the Armistice, a number learnt from the Red Cross that their husbands had been taken prisoner and were in camps in Germany. The authorities were aware that they had to work to keep the support of the wives of prisoners-of-war and to try to counter the natural feelings of resentment that these women might have towards a regime allowing their husbands to remain prisoners in a foreign and conquering country. Pétain therefore made careful use of the prisoners to gain support, promising that his policies would bring the end of the war and their return. As Sarah Fishman explained, 'the majority of the leaders at Vichy shared and encouraged the sentiment that the prisoners would soon be liberated'.[3] Informants sometimes reflected the disappointment with the regime which was the result of dashed hopes. Wives of prisoners-of-war described how they waited for husbands to return

3. Sarah Fishman, *We Will Wait! The Wives of French Prisoners of War 1940–45* (New Haven, 1991), p. 155.

for weeks and weeks before they finally had to accept that they were not likely to return in the near future.

From the first, the Red Cross acted as a great socializing force. It informed women of their husbands' whereabouts and in each village parcel-sending groups were organized. Thus it did much to make an abnormal situation appear normal. Women would come together and make up their parcels for their absent husbands. What could be more reassuring than meeting up with other women in the same position? What could seem more legitimate than the Red Cross? These women, who would apparently have strong reasons to be hostile, were arguably being socialized into supporting the Vichy regime. What is more, the idea was taken up by the wives of prisoners-of-war themselves. Groups of these wives started to appear at the end of 1940 in certain large towns in France.[4] They subsequently formed themselves into associations which enabled women to locate each other and organize themselves within each commune. In 1941 they gave themselves the general name of the Federation of Prisoner-of-War Wives' Associations (*Fédération des Associations de Femmes de Prisonniers de Guerre*) to cover the various different groups. They had 12,000 members in March 1942 and 40,000 members by May 1943.[5] The existence of these Associations shows that these women recognized themselves as a category with special needs and shared experience. Christophe Lewin sees this organization as operating rather like a trade union which represented the interests of wives of prisoners-of-war.[6] Their activities included holding meetings, setting up parcel-making centres, organizing holiday camps for children and sending out a bulletin which was published in Lyon and which printed up to 130,000 copies in 1943. Members saw their role as contacting other women who were in the same situation and passing the publications on to them. 'We tried to talk about our problems and keep our morale up. When we were together, we talked about the prisoners. We felt that we shared some of the same problems.'[7]

The Federation declared itself to be apolitical by explaining that members should 'carefully avoid all deviation onto political or partisan territory' and tried to distance itself from the official government agencies which represented the interests of prisoners-of-war

4. Christophe Lewin, *Le Retour des prisonniers de guerre français* (Paris, 1986), p. 25; Fishman, *We Will Wait!* (in Ch. 8 she details the formation and activities of the 'Associations des Femmes de Prisonniers de Guerre' but does not surmise as to whether they had any political significance).

5. Fishman, *We Will Wait!*, p. 155.

6. Lewin, *Le Retour des prisonniers de guerre*, p. 25.

7. Interview, Madame Margaux (Toulouse).

and their families. Sarah Fishman has shown that it 'intellectually reinforced traditional family values', and its magazine was full of paternalistic propaganda about how to be a good wife and mother.[8] Independent action was discouraged and women were advised to behave as if their husband was still present, to write to him and to consult him on all family issues. In a 1944 issue of *Femme de prisonnier*, wives were described as having a 'current mission as guardian of the home, as wife and mother', emphasizing that this 'mission' was therefore only temporary. A recurrent image was that of the waiting mother as 'suffering but triumphant'.[9] This sort of discourse had a remarkable similarity to other Vichy publications about motherhood and housewives, urging them to concentrate all their energies on the home – propaganda to which the wives of prisoners-of-war, feeling isolated, could be particularly susceptible.

While these Associations acted as a channel for women to create valuable support networks, they were networks which encouraged them to suffer and accept rather than to fight and reject. In no way did they foster resistance. These Associations which were created, financed and organized by the wives of prisoners-of-war themselves therefore helped to bring them into a position of acceptance, notably in the early stages of the Vichy regime. Although it is impossible to prove, there seems to be a strong case for the argument that the support provided by the Associations and the Red Cross helped to ensure the continued support of the wives of at least some prisoners-of-war, as it became increasingly clear that Pétain's promises were not to be fulfilled and that the prisoners were not going to return.

Wives of prisoners-of-war were to experience more disappointments throughout the course of the war. Many believed that the *Relève* would bring back their missing men and most experienced it as a particularly frustrating episode. Those wives who had still not broken with Vichy after this experience might be drawn into more and more active co-operation with the regime. Wives who realized that their husbands were not going to return may have endeavoured to show themselves to be good Pétainists to ingratiate themselves with authorities in the belief that this could help to obtain the release of their prisoner husbands. Lefébure describes how in Perpignan, and other towns nearby, word spread that you could get a prisoner liberated by helping a soldier of the *Wehrmacht*. Mme P. was thus inspired to write the following letter on 20 November 1941 to the German commission at Vichy.

> Sir,
> I am for collaboration and I am going to prove it by proposing a practical application of it.
> My husband is a prisoner in a Stalag in Westphalia. Free him, send him back to us and with him an injured German. I promise to look after both of them with the same care. Your compatriot will be in a family. We will care for him, even spoil him as best we can . . .
> Send them both for Christmas please.[10]

Other wives were taken in by a radio broadcast urging them to sign up for membership of the collaborationist group the RNP (*Rassemblement National Populaire*) to hasten the return of their husbands, whereas in reality it was merely a device for the group to boost their membership.[11] These wives are therefore an interesting example of a group that could be drawn into a position of going along with Vichy because of its own vulnerability, a vulnerability created by the conditions of war.

If the population was generally sympathetic to the wives of prisoners-of-war throughout the war, women whose husbands left to work in Germany voluntarily under the *Relève* scheme found themselves in a rather different position, and they were often badly thought of by the local population who assumed that they were benefiting from generous salaries that husbands were sending home, although this was not always the case (see Chapter 2). In some areas they were threatened: as one police report quoted, certain members of the population did not tire of telling these wives that when they returned their husbands would be shot.[12] Although not seen as collaborators, these families were thought to have sympathies towards the Vichy government. For example, Zaretsky found that in Nîmes, families whose members had volunteered to work in Germany were treated with scorn and derision. In Montaren, one official refused to furnish a local woman whose son had left for Germany with her monthly allotment of gas and bread.[13]

10. Antoine Lefébure, *Les Conversations secrètes des Français sous l'Occupation* (Paris, 1993), p. 147.

11. Yves Durand, *La Vie quotidienne des prisonniers de guerre dans les Stalags, les Oflags et les Kommandos, 1939–1945* (Paris, 1987), p. 221; Fishman, *We Will Wait!*, p. 35.

12. AN F14610.

13. Robert Zaretsky, *Nîmes at War: Religion, Politics and Public Opinion in the Gard, 1938–44* (University Park, Pennsylvania State University Press, 1995), p. 215.

Working for the Germans in Germany

Choice of workplace, in so far as there was an element of choice, could also demonstrate an attitude of conforming to the regime. As was seen in Chapter 1, many factories were set to work towards the German war effort after the Armistice in Occupied areas and many more after the occupation of the southern zone. Since the Germans were present in the northern zone from 1940, there were more opportunities for employment there than in the south, where the Germans only took control of industry after October 1942.

Most people knew when a factory came under German control because soldiers would be present in the premises.[14] Women who worked in these factories were therefore aware that they were directly contributing to the German war effort, but for them it was a means to make a living, sometimes the only means open to them. Some were therefore grateful for the German presence, particularly since salaries were advantageous. In this context, the Prefect of the Finistère reported in September 1943 that the workers in the region were beginning to wonder if the high salaries that they were getting from the Germans would be maintained after their departure, as some were already anxious about a possible change in their circumstances in the near future.[15] The decision to leave a well-paid job when the factory was taken over by the Germans was clearly a difficult one, but there were individuals who refused to stay in a factory under German control. Annette Leiris, who was responsible for establishing the social services in the Arsenal in Brest, left in 1940, as soon as the Germans took over the factory, without even asking for what was still due to her.[16] Those who continued to work in such factories, however, cannot reasonably be accused of collaboration, and once forced labour legislation was introduced in 1943–44 there were many young unmarried women who were drafted into jobs against their will (see Chapter 2). At the same time, these French workers were objectively helping the German war effort, and the recorded actions of some individuals who refused to stay in these factories suggests that there was an element of choice open to them. Furthermore, the numerous women who worked for the Germans, although they did not necessarily support them, were often labelled as collaborators at the Liberation. Indeed, this was one of the ways they might come into contact with the Germans and subsequently

14. Interview, Madame Irène (Finistère).   15. ADF 200W43, 11 Sept. 1943.
16. AN 2AV 544, Annette Leiris.

find sexual partners amongst them or be drawn into more organized political collaboration.

Women who were prepared to go as far as travelling to Germany to find paid employment were surely indicating a more pronounced tolerance and acceptance of the Nazi regime. It is difficult to unravel the extent to which women were coerced, and, despite German denials, it seems plausible that there were women who were forcibly sent to work in Germany. Rayna Kline gives the example of ten young women from the Finistère who were forced to sign contracts in early 1943, and despite appeals from a Douarnenez priest they were sent to Essen.[17] As was shown in Chapter 1, legislation stopped short of explicitly forcing women to work in Germany, but German propaganda was widespread and the desire to encourage women to work in Germany was real enough. The collaborationist press advocated the departure of couples, and women who wanted to join their husbands were particularly targeted. On 9 October 1942 Radio-Paris announced the opening of a home near Rouen for the children of workers leaving for Germany.[18]

Lefébure documents a recorded telephone conversation between a German placements officer in Grenoble and a young woman enquiring about work in Germany. The former tried to be friendly and persuasive, explaining that foreign women could work in factories, as nannies, or as chambermaids and cooks. He assured her that she would be able to choose where she worked as she wanted to be near her prisoner husband in Leipzig. He then offered her a one-year contract with two holidays, one paid and one unpaid.[19] These conditions must have seemed attractive. Another propaganda technique was to devote press coverage to the women who were already working in Germany. On 25 August 1943, a series of articles about the experiences of a local girl appeared in *La Dépêche de Toulouse*, presenting her experiences in the most positive of ways. Such reports conveniently glossed over the reactions these women received if they came home for a holiday or when they had finished their terms of service. The effectiveness of such tactics varied according to the economic conditions of each region and most importantly the availability of work. In the Finistère, for example, propaganda had little influence on male or female factory workers in the region as there was enough work on offer at home. The only women who

17. Rayna Kline, 'Partisans, Godmothers, Bicyclists and other Terrorists: Women in the French Resistance and under Vichy', *Proceedings of the Western Society for French History* (1977), p. 377.
18. Ibid.   19. Lefébure, *Les Conversations secrètes*, p. 188.

were tempted to go to Germany, according to the Prefect, were those of little virtue.[20] There was, however, a steady trickle of women who left to work in Germany from across the country, particularly from the south where job shortages were most severe. Jankowski recounts that in early July 1942, 1,541 volunteers left Marseilles for Germany, including 26 women.[21] According to Burrin the number of women leaving to work in Germany increased considerably from spring 1941, and by July 1942, of 77,000 French workers in the Reich, 23,000 were women. In September 1944, between forty and fifty thousand French women were working on German territory. Most worked as factory workers, others as cleaners or shop assistants.[22] Corbin claims that a further five to six hundred prostitutes signed contracts to work in the Occupied territories. Some opened bank accounts in Paris into which payments were made by the Germans.[23]

Why would a woman go to Germany? Probably because she knew she would find employment and needed the money. Others went because they wanted to try to be close to prisoner husbands, as was emphasized in the propaganda. Laval's speech on 21 October 1942 encouraged wives to join their prisoner husbands and work with them for a year under a 'spouse's contract'. One interviewee was understandably attracted by this proposition:

> I heard on the radio that prisoner-of-war wives could go and work with their husbands. I said to myself, I am going to go there. Whether I live here or there, I would rather be with my husband (we did not have any children). I wrote him a letter hidden in the bread. My husband wrote to me that I should not go, that it was a mistake, that he did not want to see me behind barbed wire and that I would end up like lots of women who served for amusement purposes.[24]

Fortunately, this woman heeded her husband's advice and was not taken in by such promises, unlike other women who were often bitterly disappointed and rarely saw much of their husbands in nearby camps. Helga Bories-Sawala in a case study of 1,000 French workers in Bremen during the war found that only 37 were women. For the most part, these rare women had come to join their husbands. She

20. ADF 31W313, July 1945.

21. Paul Jankowski, *Communism and Collaboration: Simon Sabani and Politics in Marseille. 1919–44* (London, 1984), p. 89.

22. Philippe Burrin, *La France à l'heure allemande 1940–1944* (Paris, 1995), pp. 288–9.

23. Alain Corbin, *Les Fille de noce: misère sexuelle et prostitution aux 19e et 20e siècles* (Paris, 1978), p. 504.

24. Interview, Madame Camille (Toulouse).

found that although these women were represented by the men she interviewed as women of little virtue, most had respectable professions and she suspects that these accusations were unjustified.[25] Burrin depicts the women who worked in Germany as poorly qualified and in bad health. Of those who offered themselves to work in Germany 10–15 per cent were refused after medical checks because they were suffering from tuberculosis or venereal disease. A third were prevented from leaving until they had completed a course of treatment or undergone further tests.[26]

Once they arrived in Germany, some had a more satisfactory time than others. The reality of their experiences could be very different from the propaganda. Lefébure again provides valuable source material, citing the cases of two women. One went to Germany because she had been out of work for two months. She found that the food was good and the pay reasonable, in spite of high taxes. His other example, Annie Botto, left Nice for Germany in September 1942, and was cruelly disillusioned by her experience. She wrote home in a letter:

> We live in a large wooden house, it's really disgusting. In Dijon we had a speech about how we would be the Ambassadors of France here. In fact Ambassadors are no more than prostitutes. My room mates wander around at night, then they come in at all hours to tell us all about it, how much they earned etc. . . .
> There is worse, and what I worry about all day, they steal everything from our bedrooms.[27]

Other accounts suggest that this was a common experience. Work conditions were very difficult, women were often lodged on site in camps and factories, hygiene was poor, there was a great deal of promiscuity and many women turned to prostitution.[28] Furthermore, German reports indicate that these voluntary workers were ostracized both at their departure and at their return. Burrin cites the case of a young girl from the department of the Gard. She lived with her parents, who were on good terms with the Germans. In August 1943, probably because she already felt isolated from the local community, she decided to go and work in Germany. The day before her

25. Helga Bories-Sawala, 'Les Travailleurs français à Brême', in Denis Peschanski and Jean-Louis Robert (eds), *Les Ouvriers en France pendant la deuxième guerre mondiale* (Paris, 1992), p. 22.

26. Burrin, *La France à l'heure allemande*, p. 290.

27. Lefébure, *Les Conversations secrètes*, p. 193.

28. Jeanne Aubert, *La JOCF, Qu'as tu fait de nos vies? La Jeunesse Ouvrière Chrétienne Féminine 1928–45* (Paris, 1990), p. 144.

departure her head was shaved by her male cousin and his friends.[29] When these women returned to France, many had their heads shaved, a phenomenon that is further explored in Chapter 6.

These were the structures through which women, in particular, could come into contact with the Germans, but they represent degrees of behaviour building up towards collaboration but stopping very far short of it. There were also other women who became involved with types of activity which could more accurately be called outright collaboration, behaviour which entailed more than just going along with events, but which manifested a conscious and real support for the Germans, the consequence of which was invariably beneficial to the German cause and certainly detrimental to French men and women who may or may not have been involved in Resistance activities.

Choice translated into action

Although there is certainly no doubt about its existence, the character of women's collaboration makes it particularly difficult to quantify. Some facets of female collaboration can be identified by arrests during the immediate post-Liberation period when a significant number of women were tried and often sentenced for collaboration-related crimes. These crimes varied in gravity from black market and economic collaboration to serious treason and involvement with the murderous activities of the Nazis. Some women were sentenced to death in these courts, though most were later pardoned by General de Gaulle. This trial process and the ways in which there was a gendered element to the way the purges were conducted is explored in Chapter 5; here it is worthy of note that the testimonies and the records of the trials give valuable insight into the kinds of collaboration activities which specifically involved women.

To what extent was 'active' collaboration gendered? The existing evidence remains so limited that it is difficult to offer a convincing sociological analysis of women's participation, but some general trends do emerge from my material and the existing secondary sources. Sexual collaboration is the form of collaboration that is normally associated with women. Other activities included denunciation or *délation*, the writing of anonymous letters to the authorities

---

29. Burrin, *La France à l'heure allemande*, p. 213.

denouncing others for breaking the law. Such acts could have extremely dangerous consequences for those transgressing Vichy or German rules. Those denounced might have been escaped prisoners-of-war, political refugees, Jews or individuals who were involved in the Resistance. On the basis of this information the Vichy or German authorities might then have made arrests and, depending on their 'crime', detainees could have been shot or deported. Denunciation has often been seen as a form of behaviour which involved women in particular, though men were certainly also guilty of it. As far as the most serious collaboration activities were concerned, namely participating in collaborationist groups, men were more likely than women to become members, although the collaboration trials show that women also became involved in this kind of active collaboration. The most serious collaborationist crime, as defined by the courts, was to have joined the *milice* and to have been involved in fighting alongside the Germans against the Resistance. Although there were women members of the *milice*, on the whole they were involved in less serious activities than the men.

SEXUAL COLLABORATION

Sexual collaboration has dominated all accounts of women's collaboration. The film documentary *Le Chagrin et la pitié* is a good example of this. Here men's collaboration is political and women's collaboration is sexual.[30] Many commentators share the opinion expressed by one male resister that 'for many people, to have seen a women with a German was enough to condemn them'.[31] Contemporary French police were aware of this and often reported that French women were seen with Germans.[32] Indeed, at the Liberation women who had been seen with Germans were in danger of being punished by the local population (see Chapter 6). However, there was clearly a difference between the women who spent time with Germans to get a decent square meal or simply to have a good time, and those who sought out the Germans and ended up in complete agreement with their activities and political ends. That both motives for this type of behaviour existed there is no doubt. For obvious reasons the sources, both oral and written, do not necessarily tell the

30. Marcel Orphuls, 'Le Chagrin et la pitié', published in *L'Avant Scène du cinéma* (July–Sept. 1972), p. 63. See also Siân Reynolds, 'The Sorrow and the Pity Revisited, or Be Careful, One Train Can Hide Another', *French Cultural Studies* (1990), p. 156.
31. Interview, Monsieur David (Toulouse).
32. ADHG M2277, RG, 26 Sept. 1943.

whole story. What were the influences at work here? What motivated the women to behave in the way they did? Are there distinctions to be drawn between having a few drinks or dances with German soldiers and establishing regular intimacy with them? Sexual collaboration is a complicated and guilt-ridden issue, but to assume that all women who spent time with Germans were necessarily displaying an in-depth commitment to collaboration would be to oversimplify women's motivations.

Why did women become involved with Germans? In some regions it might have been linked to the absence of available young men, but in most cases women came into contact with Germans in the workplace, and spending time with them was a natural progression from there.[33] Cobb attributes the following motives to such women:

> for the girl concerned only with short-term benefits, a German boyfriend could offer immediate and solid advantages, not just to the working-class girl, but to the *lycéenne* from the XVIème and the VIIIème: *le prestige de l'étranger*, the hint of perversity and adventure, the wonderfully persuasive white dress uniform of the young *Luftwaffe* pilot, dinner in sumptuous surroundings . . .[34]

Even women who were committed to resistance recognized the sexual appeal of the German soldiers. 'They were nice looking boys' was a common attitude. For young women in 1943, who just followed the tide and who wanted to have a good time, having fun could mean spending time with the Germans, but you had to be in contact with them in order to become involved. Many women doubtless latched on to the Germans for what they could get out of them. Some may have been seeking marriage, but German soldiers were not allowed to marry French women or those from any of the other occupied countries. Children were an inevitable consequence of these relationships, and by mid-1943, 80,000 French women in the Occupied zone had claimed children's benefits from the German military authorities and had requested German nationality for their offspring.[35] Burrin gives a figure of three to four thousand children of liaisons with German soldiers for the town of Rouen alone. He estimates a figure of 50,000–75,000 for the whole of France.[36]

---

33. Luc Capdevila, 'La "Collaboration sentimentale": antipatriotisme ou sexualité hors-normes?', in François Rouquet and Danièle Voldman (eds), *Les Cahiers de l'IHTP*, 31 (1995), p. 77.

34. Richard Cobb, *French and Germans, Germans and French: A Personal Interpretation of France and Two Occupations, 1914–1918/1940–1944* (Hanover, 1983), p. 67.

35. Ibid., p. 66.   36. Burrin, *La France à l'heure allemande*, p. 213.

Was involvement with the Germans a political choice? Motivation was the crucial factor which preoccupied the courts when trying to apportion blame, but how far could sexual collaboration be linked with political conviction? (See p. 145.) Spending time with German officers was not proof of political collaboration. One Resistance woman talked about a woman collaborator thus:

> She was not politically convinced, it was a question of money because the Germans, they gave away lots of money and jewels, they paid for tickets to the theatre and shows and things; a woman who just wanted to be a woman, well she was attracted by that.
>
> I lived in the German milieu myself in Paris, with these kinds of women, but they were all coquettes, women who just wanted the good life, to go to the theatre, eat in good restaurants, but I don't think that politically speaking they played a very important role.[37]

Another woman explained how sleeping with a German did not make a woman anti-French: she was only after the good-looking young man who could get her what she wanted.[38] Yet, argues one women who was involved in the Resistance, sexual collaboration was never an innocent choice:

> A woman who was the mistress of a German in 1942 was not innocent. She knew that at any moment this German could arrest her brother and her father. As far as I was concerned, I never looked at a German straight in the face throughout the war, that was the position many women took if they were participating in the Resistance; we did not see the Germans.[39]

Celia Bertin argues along the same lines: 'When I felt the eyes of a German soldier on me, I turned my head to refuse his look.'[40] But take the case of the following Resistance woman who was herself only 17 in 1942:

> We had lived through a dismal period; women wanted to enjoy them-selves, to push away all this dreariness, all the problems, especially in the towns. Who had the money to have a good time at the time? The Occupying forces, the black market racketeers, those who were making the big money. They held secret balls, they ate in good restaurants. These women were rather loose; they wanted to enjoy themselves, to make the most of their lives, because they saw that the years were pass-ing by and that things would not change. There is a moment when you

37. Interview, Madame Flore (Toulouse).
38. Interview, Madame Louise (Toulouse).
39. Interview, Madame Antoinette (Toulouse).
40. Celia Bertin, *Femmes sous l'Occupation* (Paris, 1993), p. 95.

reach the limit. . . . They turned towards one side because it was the only side on which there was frivolousness, whereas on the side of the Resistance, there was only austerity. There were shortages: of money, of food, of supplies, and then there were worries. It was dismal.[41]

This woman explains quite clearly how the choice presented itself to her. Admittedly, this represents the opinion of just one witness – other women described the choice of going into the Resistance as exciting and daring – but spending time with Germans clearly had distinct material advantages.

Who were these women who spent time with Germans? The trials give us some clues. In Toulouse, 94 per cent of the women accused of collaboration in autumn 1945 were in the 18–30 age-group, and most were single or the wives of prisoners-of-war.[42] Luc Capdevila's analysis of the 189 women who were accused in the Lorient of 'sentimental collaboration' shows that 60 per cent of them were under 26, 69 per cent were single, 18 per cent were widows, divorced or separated and 13 per cent were married but had no news of their prisoner husbands. The high percentage of single women in these figures was an excuse for them to be represented as prostitutes, whereas in fact, as Capdevila has shown, most of these women were independent and went to the Lorient to find paid employment and thereby became involved in relationships with the Germans because they chose to do so.[43] Many women who were suspected of sexual collaboration were accused of being prostitutes and, indeed, prostitutes generally were singled out as women who had collaborated with the Germans. At the Liberation many were herded into prison and into internment camps, and most of these also suffered the indignity of head-shaving. Popular support for this belief that prostitutes could not be trusted because of their involvement with

---

41. 'On avait passé des années sombres; les femmes avaient envie de s'amuser, de donner un coup de pied à toute cette tristesse, à tous ces problèmes, surtout dans les villes. Qui avaient les moyens de s'amuser à cette époque? L'occupant et ceux du marché-noir, ceux qui brassaient beaucoup d'argent. Ils faisaient des bals clandestines, ils mangeaient dans des bons restaurants. Ces femmes qui étaient un peu légères, qui voulaient s'amuser, qui voulaient profiter un peu de leur vie, parce qu'elles voyaient que les années passaient et qu'elles allaient rester comme ça, on arrive à un moment où la mesure est pleine. Elles se sont tournées comme ça . . . parce que c'était l'unique côté où il y avait un peu de frivolité, alors que le côté résistant, ça a été plutôt austère. On manquait, et puis il y avait des soucis. C'était sombre.' Interview, Madame Sandrine (Toulouse).

42. Hanna Diamond, 'Women's Experience during and after World War Two in the Toulouse Area 1939–48: Choices and Constraints', unpublished PhD thesis (University of Sussex, 1992).

43. Capdevila, 'La "Collaboration sentimentale"', pp. 73, 77.

the Germans was one of the key arguments which enabled Marthe Richard to pass a law closing the brothels in 1946 (see p. 166). But there is no evidence to suggest that prostitutes collaborated politically any more than anyone else. Moreover there were official reasons why they were dealing with the Germans, as was shown in Chapter 1. What else could these women have done? Can we really consider that granting sexual favours for money equals collaboration? These women were often under instructions to carry out their own particular form of 'work'.

At the Liberation, when the crimes of collaboration came out into the open and the punishments were defined, sexual collaboration was perceived as having been particularly reprehensible. Women were humiliatingly punished and put on public display (see Chapter 6). Was this because it was an especially visible form of collaboration and the guilty parties could easily be singled out? Or was there some more aggressive misogynist force at work? The evidence suggests that sexual collaboration was rarely motivated by thought-out political conviction, but was more often an improvised means of having fun or a mechanism of survival, as in the case of the wives of prisoners-of-war who might have turned to prostitution to supplement their income. Prostitutes who were caught in the structures established by Vichy in the form of brothels were simply earning a living. Historians have been so concerned with this more visible and in some way titillating form of collaboration that, until recently, they have almost ignored the other political dimensions of women's collaboration described below.

DENUNCIATION

Délation, or sending letters of denunciation which were sometimes signed but more often anonymous, was a common phenomenon during the war, and indeed continued afterwards during the purges when letters were written denouncing those who had collaborated. The summaries of incoming mail to Pétain in October 1940 mention 'numerous denunciations of the teaching staff who discussed political questions in front of their pupils'.[44] *Délation* also became particularly common in relation to black market issues. In December 1943, the mayors of the Haute-Garonne, for example, observed the marked lack of community solidarity in the villages as everyone

44. AN 2AG 205. La Famille. CM19E, Compte rendu et analyses hebdomadaires de la correspondance concernant Famille, Santé, Jeunesse, 18 Oct. 1940.

was too busy denouncing everyone else, particularly around issues to do with the food supply.[45] At about this time, posters appeared which offered rewards of up to 5,000 francs for the denunciation of Jews, black marketeers, anarchists, socialists, communists, so-called terrorists and *réfractaires* (those who tried to escape the compulsory labour draft).[46] Designation of these enemies was presented in the propaganda as a civic act. Collaborationist groups expected their members to observe the activities of friends and neighbours and to denounce those around them. Members of the SOL (*Service d'Ordre Légionnaire*), an organization which later became the *milice*, were told to report people who listened to the 'Gaullist radio'.[47] Jankowski explains that the PPF (*Parti Populaire Français*) made a particular point of encouraging denunciation and constantly pressed people to turn on their neighbours or compatriots. He relates the case of an Algerian woman, a former prostitute, who joined the PPF and exploited her position by threatening to denounce anyone in her neighbourhood who annoyed her.[48] Denunciation, and more especially the threat of denunciation, was common in relations at work. Certain individuals took advantage of it to frighten and intimidate people; sometimes these threats were carried out.[49]

Commentators have referred to the presence of large numbers of such letters in the German archives from 1942 onwards.[50] Even the Germans were surprised at the number of letters they received. But John Sweets has shown that the 'police often found these to provide false leads or to have been based on personal vendettas, so they discouraged them'.[51] Furthermore, letters did not always reach their destination as Vichy's postal control intercepted them, and recipients did not always act on them.[52] Yet, in interview, several Resisters ascribed their arrest to a denunciation and claimed that they were often more worried about denunciation by other French people than about detection by the Germans themselves.[53] Indeed, Burrin claims that letters of denunciation were behind the condemnation of most of those who appeared at the German tribunals.[54]

45. ADHG M1551, Association des Maires de la Haute-Garonne, 14 Dec. 1943.
46. John Sweets, *Choices in Vichy France* (Oxford, 1986), p. 23.
47. Fred Kupferman, *Les Premiers Beaux Jours 1944–46* (Paris, 1985), p. 28.
48. Jankowski, *Communism and Collaboration*, p. 133.
49. Burrin, *La France à l'heure allemande*, pp. 214–15.
50. Cobb, *French and Germans*, p. 105.
51. Sweets, *Choices in Vichy France*, p. 100.
52. Jankowski, *Communism and Collaboration*, p. 133.
53. Interviews, Mesdames Adrienne, Juliette and Sandrine (Toulouse).
54. Burrin, *La France à l'heure allemande*, p. 214.

Many Jews, Gaullists and 'terrorists' were tracked down and arrested as a result of such letters. The police who were tracking down Jews were regularly informed by a network of concierges spread around the cities, though there were also those who informed the Resistance.[55] The Germans were certainly helped by the atmosphere of distrust among French people.

The way in which *délation* became so widespread suggests that its germs pre-existed the war. Indeed, Françoise Thébaud has described how women wrote letters of denunciation during the First World War if they felt that people were not being suitably patriotic.[56] That French police were familiar with it and found it useful for law enforcement is illustrated by the fact that the *Commissaire de Montauban* was able to conduct nearly all his investigations in relation to abortion on the basis of anonymous letters, often sent several years after the crime.[57] Where there was already some degree of lack of tolerance, lack of sense of community and lack of civic feeling in France, it was exacerbated by the conditions of the Occupation when letter-writers could gain financial rewards.[58] Certain members of the community easily slipped into the habit, encouraged by the Germans, of making it their business to know other people's business. The Vichy authorities and Occupying forces therefore successfully tapped into this existing predisposition. Thus *délation* could be the result of a local atmosphere, and the Occupation served to catalyse long-standing conflicts between individuals of different political tendencies. Revenge or jealousy might also have played a part. Halimi gives an example of a woman whose husband left her for another woman whom the wife then denounced to the Germans as a Jew.[59] After the war, where it could be proved, women and men were severely punished in cases where their denunciations had led to the arrest, deportation and sometimes death of Resisters and Jews.

Popular mythology maintains that denunciation was an activity which particularly concerned women. There is a memorable example in Jean Dutourd's satirical *Au bon beurre* where the female character writes to a German officer denouncing an escaped prisoner-of-war. The style is a parody of such letters.[60] But, unfortunately, there is little secondary literature available on this form of 'action'

55. Cobb, *French and Germans*, p. 106.
56. Françoise Thébaud, *La Femme au temps de la guerre de 14* (Paris, 1986), p. 242.
57. ADHG 2060/343.
58. I am grateful to Dominique Veillon for helping me to clarify this point.
59. André Halimi, *La Délation sous l'Occupation* (Paris, 1983), p. 25.
60. Jean Dutourd, *Au bon beurre* (Paris, 1952), p. 34.

and existing studies give no analysis of the gender of letter-writers.[61] Letters written by women were only signed if they hoped for some financial recompense,[62] though Antoine Lefébure claims in his analysis of the archives that there were more letters written by women.[63] Cobb suggests that *délation* was the greatest service rendered by women to the German and French repressive authorities.[64] Burrin notes that though relatively few women were judged by the courts, they were over-represented in cases of denunciation. For example, in the Finistère, of 77 denunciation cases, 54 concerned women, and in the Eure, out of 225 cases, three-quarters were women.[65] Françoise Leclerc and Michèle Wending found in a study of the *Cours de Justice de la Seine* that of 901 women who appeared, 687, or 70 per cent were tried for denunciation.[66]

Was this then a particularly female kind of collaboration? It is certainly true that women had more access to information about the affairs of others, and were able to pick up information more discreetly. Because the circumstances of the war were such that the private and the public merged, private lives became indicative of political choice, and so people took more interest in the private lives of others. Women were present, in the households and in the streets, when the men were not, and they were sometimes privy to certain knowledge through privileged relations such as doing someone's washing or cleaning. They were therefore more likely to notice and ask about the presence of strangers in a household, a sudden absence, or the fact that household members kept irregular hours. This became valuable knowledge since informers received remuneration from the Germans, and women may have chosen to use this knowledge, for whatever motives. However, Leclerc and Wending found that the sample of women they studied were much more likely to have made denunciations in the public sphere than in the private sphere. Only 78 women out of 687 were sentenced for denouncing in the private sphere, 58 for denouncing a husband, the others for a lover and, in some exceptional cases, other members of the family. Of the 609 who denounced in the public sphere, 502 were

---

61. Halimi, *La Délation*.
62. There were probably more signed letters than anonymous ones for this reason. Cobb, *French and Germans*, p. 126.
63. Lefébure, *Les Conversations secrètes*.
64. Cobb, *French and Germans*, p. 105.
65. Burrin, *La France à l'heure allemande*, p. 215.
66. Françoise Leclerc and Michèle Wending, 'La Répression de femmes coupables d'avoir collaboré pendant l'Occupation', in Françoise Thébaud (ed.), *Clio: histoire, femmes et sociétés, résistances et libérations* (Toulouse, 1995), p. 139.

sentenced, of whom 94 were members of the German intelligence services.[67] Leclerc and Wending argue that women who found work in German administrations were affected by their daily contact with the Germans and that this was a permanent motivation to collaborate through denunciation. They cite the example of LL, a 48-year-old widow who started work in 1942 as a cleaner in the German administration. In July 1944, she denounced a British parachutist to the German authorities and provoked the arrest of the five men who had been sheltering him. Three were shot, one died in deportation and one escaped. The guilty woman explained that she worked for the Germans because she could not do otherwise to survive. She was condemned to death on 3 November 1949.[68]

Rousso and Cobb suggest we should be wary of condemning these people.[69] In his article on the purges, Rousso wonders whether letters of denunciation were really more numerous during the Occupation than those that proliferate in peacetime, even if the consequences were more tragic. Cobb suggests that the compulsive women *denunciatrices* should not really qualify as collaborators as many of them were just doing what they always did, and would continue to do so equally in the different circumstances of the purges.[70] Burrin concludes that *délation* was the weapon of the weak, and women denunciators were doubly weak: as women they were often in unfavourable social categories, few were in professional positions, and their secondary weakness came from the fact that they could not resist the opportunity to use this exceptional power.[71] There may be some truth to this, but it seems a rather sexist assumption, particularly since men were also guilty of denunciation.

JOINING A COLLABORATIONIST GROUP

Those individuals who chose to join collaborationist groups and associations after the Occupation were the most politically committed to the collaborationist cause, and represent the extreme end of the collaboration spectrum. These were people who became very closely associated with the Germans. The obvious sensitivity of this subject area, and difficulty of access to archive material, means that it is hard to discover how many French people were involved and to

---

67. Ibid., pp. 139–40.   68. Ibid., p. 145.
69. Henri Rousso, 'L'Epuration en France: une histoire inachevée', *Vingtième Siècle* (Jan.–Mar. 1992).
70. Cobb, *French and Germans*, p. 106.
71. Burrin, *La France à l'heure allemande*, p. 215.

what degrees. The existing material suggests that only a very small percentage of the population, probably less than 1 per cent, actually joined 'collaborationist' groups, most of which were concentrated in Paris and the large cities. It seems probable that there was a core of activists who were involved in several different groups. Historians have also emphasized the male nature of collaboration of this extreme kind. Cobb asserts that the ranks of the PPF, RNP, and the *milice* were confined to men with no women's sections.[72] Burrin also claims that partisan involvement in collaborationist groups was a masculine phenomenon. However, recent research and my own findings suggest that this was not entirely the case. Although this research is still in its infancy, it is apparent that women were present in most of these groups, in some cases in substantial numbers, both as fully fledged members who joined of their own volition, and as family members enrolled by their husbands and fathers. It is difficult to give figures for women's involvement. Burrin puts women's participation at 15 per cent, which he concedes was a high figure at a time when they had no political rights.[73] Rough estimates for Toulouse are rather lower, at between 7 and 9 per cent of those on the lists, including those who were family members.[74] Some groups attracted more women members than others. Members lists of the RNP held in the local archives in Paris indicate a very high female membership.[75] Admittedly, not all groups had women's sections but some did form them to cater for the women. The *Jeunesse Française Féminine*, for example, broke away from the PPF in 1942, and were described as 'uniformed girls cavorting with Germans officers, often bored adolescents'. Jankowski found that where women could have freer access to membership their presence was stronger; this he found to be the case with the *Groupe Collaboration*.[76] In Nîmes, the opening of the ranks of the *milice* to women claimed some recruits, particularly amongst women who feared being drafted to work in Germany, in the same way as it had for the men.[77] Women could become German intelligence agents, belong to the *Gestapo* or the *Abwehr* and be involved in military espionage and counter-espionage. For those women employed as radio agents, the financial gains could be

72. Cobb, *French and Germans*, p. 104.
73. Burrin, *La France à l'heure allemande*, p. 433.
74. Diamond, 'Women's Experience during and after World War Two', p. 143.
75. ALP 212/76/1, Carton 12/13 membres RNP, La Seine, Chambre Civique, Arrêts de suspension de droit civique.
76. Jankowski, *Communism and Collaboration*, p. 133.
77. Zaretsky, *Nîmes at War*, p. 207.

considerable – one was paid as much as 6,000 francs a month.[78] Another worked as a typist for the youth section of the RNP and admitted to wearing a uniform and carrying out the Nazi salute in the street with her colleagues. Here the salary was also an incentive.[79] One of the most extreme examples I came across was that of a woman whose lover was head of the German police: she herself joined the police, and her job was to wander around the streets of Paris, listening to conversations French people were having, and denounce them to her lover.[80]

Within these groups women were rarely in positions of authority, but some had important roles to play. In Chateaudun, a woman was named by the PPF to run the local section and the police reported that she seemed very capable of putting the organization of the party in shape.[81] Another woman, in Paris, became head of a section – a librarian at the Sorbonne, she frequently came to work in her PPF uniform.[82] A number of women are recorded as having been seen in the various uniforms, and this may have been important to some, as it was for Anne: 'Anne, 18 years old, joined the *milice* in May 1944 without saying anything to her father, to have some company and to be well dressed thanks to the uniform with its cape, dress, beret and shoes. . .'.[83]

Women more often had roles as secretaries or as head of the women's or young girls' sections.[84] They were also given responsibility for various social services, especially if they were family members. Women in the *Légion Française des Combattants*, one of the earliest groups, organized many 'social' events including artistic galas, fêtes, tombolas, film showings as well as soup kitchens.[85] Women known as *dames SMS (Service Médico-Social)*, a kind of *légionnaire*'s social worker, appeared towards the end of 1942. Their role was to look after the restaurants run by the *Légion*, to organize tea-parties for the children of prisoners-of-war and generally 'fight against all physiological and material discontent'.[86] A group of these women in Toulouse were responsible for evacuating 537 children in the summer of 1943 to

78. Leclerc and Wending, 'La Répression de femmes coupables', p. 140.
79. AN Z5120, no. 5615.   80. AN Z625, dossier 426.
81. AN F14610, 12 Mar. 1942.   82. AN Z5 6028.
83. Danielle Costa and Jocelyne Joussemet, 'Femmes des Pyrénées Orientales', unpublished Mémoire de Maîtrise (University of Toulouse, 1981), p. 153.
84. ADHG M2277, Réunion des membres du PPF de Toulouse, 3 Aug. 1943.
85. Henri Mauriès, 'Manifestations publiques de la Légion Française des Combattants en Haute-Garonne, 1940–44', unpublished Mémoire de Maîtrise (University of Toulouse, 1987), p. 35.
86. Ibid., p. 37.

protect them from possible bombing and to improve their health. Women who were members of the *milice* or who were active in other collaborationist groups often continued doing the same 'good works' as they had as *Pétainistes* or *Amis de la Légion*. Similarly, *miliciennes* organized a social work section to cater for women members, and for the wives and daughters of male members of the *milice*. These works involved sending parcels to prisoners, providing help and medical care for needy families, distributing clothes and offering holiday camps.[87] The national organizers took these activities so seriously that they planned links between the social service activities of the *milice* and the *Secours National*. They were keen that the *milice* should no longer be just a military elite but should have this other side to its activities.[88]

This 'social' role that women adopted within collaborationist groups is particularly interesting because it shows how women's political involvement was expressed through traditional caring roles which were integrated into their everyday lives. The structures which emerged for women were very similar to the kinds of caring, nurturing and supplying-of-food activities which were a large part of women's contribution to resistance described in the next chapter. The evidence is not sufficient to establish whether collaborative women created this role for themselves; it seems more probable that it was a role assigned to them by the men as a way of gaining and sustaining their support. But, in any case, it is clear that this sort of philanthropic activity was a way for women to be politically active and it gave many women who were associated with the collaborationist movement a certain status and a chance to feel that they were fully active partners.

Membership of the groups varied. Burrin found that in his sample, most women members tended to be young and uneducated; early members were not in employment and came from comfortable backgrounds, while women manual workers and employees joined in larger numbers in 1943.[89] Although it is not always possible to establish their motivations, there were a number of structures that operated to bring women into contact with collaboration. The issue of sexual collaboration has already been evoked where initial contact with the Germans was most often made in the workplace. Even if this was flippant and non-political at the outset, such contact

87. AMT 4/1988 422–428, Berthe A., Unpublished diary, 'Mes Barbélès', p. 40.
88. AN 2AG 154, Activité du Secours National, Feb. 1943.
89. Burrin, *La France à l'heure allemande*, p. 435.

could bring women a step nearer to further involvement. A certain Berthe A., a university researcher in Toulouse, explains in her journal that she joined the group *Collaboration* in response to a ministerial directive which was sent out to all civil servants.[90] It was founded in autumn 1940 as a 'French group for continental unity'.[91] Berthe A. claimed that she paid her registration fees but never attended any of the meetings. Her understanding was that the aim of the group was to help French prisoners in Germany and to call for less strenuous measures by the Occupiers; these were the elements that interested her.[92] Those who went to work for the Germans may also have found that they were expected, even obliged, to join one of these groups. Other women may have believed that joining one of the groups would improve their chances of getting paid employment with the Occupier. In one of the trials, a woman claimed that she joined the PPF before the invasion because she worked in a restaurant at the Gare du Nord where most of the clientele were members.[93]

Family and social milieu probably accounted for the vast majority of women, mothers, daughters and sisters who were brought into the groups by their men, husbands, fathers and brothers. Women who appear on lists as members of the *milice* were not all necessarily activists and, as Cobb has commented, it is hard to position these wives and daughters who may or may not have shared the commitment of husbands or fathers.[94] The influence of the family drew women into a certain entourage. Many women joined *Les Amis de la Légion* to support husbands and fathers. Some such *Femmes Pétainistes* took their role very seriously and may have been attracted by Pétain's family policies. One witness recalled seeing eager women in central Toulouse with Pétainist banners attached to their bicycles, and singing *Maréchal nous voilà*, or old war songs against the English. 'When you heard these songs you could be sure that here was someone who was not necessarily for the Germans, but certainly for the Marshal.'[95] Once a family became established in this milieu and if the men progressed into the SOL and eventually the *milice*,

90. The group *Collaboration* appears quite frequently in source material as a group which was patronized by women.

91. Pascal Ory, *Les Collaborateurs 1940–1945* (Paris, 1976), p. 62.

92. AMT, Berthe A., Unpublished diary, 'Ma Prison', p. 127. For more information about Berthe A. see Hanna Diamond, 'Berthe's Diary: the fate of Women Collaborators in Post-Liberation Toulouse', *History Today*, September 1999.

93. AN Z597, no. 4567.   94. Cobb, *French and Germans*, p. 104.

95. Interview, Monsieur Alexandre (Toulouse).

the women often continued to follow. As far as the rest of the population was concerned, once any member of the family joined the *milice*, 'their women and children were also considered to be collaborators', as one witness explained.[96] This was particularly the case for wives.

> They were fascists, those who husbands were. They worked with their husbands and they gave them information.[97]

> The wives of the men who collaborated, they followed the flow. Women at that time, they were not as free as they are now. They were still submissive, they had to follow the directives of their husband, or at least pretend to, they had to stay in line.[98]

However, even in cases where a couple had joined a group, it cannot just be assumed that wives always followed their husbands. Some wives took the initiative and became the more active of a husband-and-wife team. One trial report described how 'the husband followed her directives, his ideas were secondary'.[99]

Political commitment cannot be ignored, and there were women who joined groups because they were attracted to Nazism. One woman declared at her trial that:

> My husband was a police watch during the war. He was not interested in politics and we often had disagreements because personally I talked about politics. I approved of Marshal Pétain's politics and I was convinced that it was in the interests of France to collaborate with Germany and that this policy of collaboration would have good results. I knew about the mass deportations of the Jews, but I thought these things happened under all governments in all regimes.[100]

Such candidness was rare, and this woman must have known that she was likely to be in trouble after the war because she left France with the Germans at the Liberation. One woman who published her memoirs in 1953, after spending a year in prison, presented anti-communism as a reason for her membership of the *milice*. She argues that she saw in the *milice* a way of combating communism and that she was anti-communist because she was a Christian. 'Like many of the *miliciens* I've mentioned, I believed that through my action I was obeying my obligations as a Christian; since the Pope

96. Ibid.   97. Interview, Madame Juliette (Toulouse).
98. Interview, Madame Sandrine (Toulouse).
99. ADHG 3808/6, Cours de Justice de Toulouse, 1945, no. 2540/58.
100. AN Z5 118.

had condemned communism as atheist, the *milice* seemed to me to be one of the best instruments to combat it.'[101]

The aim of this chapter has been neither to excuse nor to condemn collaboration, although collaboration is now seen to have been the 'wrong choice'. My concern has been to look more closely at collaboration as regards women's participation and to move beyond sex-ridden stereotypes. Politically, despite their lack of involvement in prewar politics, some women did join collaboration groups out of conviction. More seem to have joined through family links, which does not rule out conviction but gives an 'excuse'. Few women members had positions of responsibility, but they had an active role in the social services side of collaboration as they did in resistance. *Délation* and denunciation can be classed as part of the most thought-out, virulent forms of collaboration, which were often motivated by a desire to exercise power and to make some easy money. In terms of women's 'private life', I have stressed the gender-specific constraints that might make women less inclined to resist and by the same token more likely at least to pay lip service to Vichy. The need to keep the family together was a particular concern for women in separated families who displayed a tendency to accept the situation without question in order to keep on the right side of the authorities. The need to survive financially was paramount for some women, even if it meant working in factories towards the German war effort or going to work in Germany. There were more opportunities for sexual collaboration in places where German soldiers were in occupation and where local economic circumstances pushed women towards finding jobs with them, and this in turn could bring women into situations of more serious collaboration.

This chapter has shown that if women could be in all sorts of situations which appear collaborative in retrospect, they did not participate on the same scale nor in the same ways as men. Although there were some gender-specific forms of collaboration, relatively few women joined groups and became involved in explicitly political forms of collaboration. Men, on the other hand, appear to have been more involved with collaboration on an organized level. Furthermore, most ultra-collaborationists, if not actively anti-feminist, despised women, seeing them as incompatible recruits to the politics of virility. The language of collaboration was aggressively masculine

---

101. Fabienne Freyssinnet, *Quatre saisons sous les geôles de la Quatrième République* (Monte Carlo, 1953), p. 20.

and Joan Tumblety's research on this is illuminating.[102] There is more evidence of women being involved with collaboration in its more individualistic, opportunistic and unorganized forms, such as denunciation and sexual collaboration. Young women who collaborated 'sexually' probably saw spending time with the Germans in strictly non-political terms at least at the outset. Some may later have been corrupted by the sense of power that it brought them. Adult women who had little or no political education were less likely to join collaboration groups spontaneously. They had no experience of attending political meetings and, in any case, few were at liberty to do so. It therefore seems probable that men, who could draw upon the political experience that women lacked, tended to be more ideologically motivated. All these factors serve to show up the extent to which collaboration was gendered and that women's collaboration was, in the main, rather different from men's.

102. Joan Tumblety, 'Fascist Cultural Politics in France: The Rhetoric of History and Gender in *Je suis partout* 1940–44', unpublished PhD thesis (University of Cambridge, 1998).

CHAPTER FIVE

Resistances

In my parents' house, my father was an official Communist Resistance worker, so he used to have many men and women visiting him.
But it cannot be said that my mother was not involved in Resistance
activities. Who used to get up in the morning to take care of the
Resistance worker who was to leave before sunrise? Who used to
darn socks and do the washing for the Resistance worker who was
sleeping? Who used to prepare the food that he would take away
with him? And who would be at home when the police called during
an alert? I think that in my family my mother was as involved in
Resistance activities as my father.[1]

The last chapter showed the ways in which women might be brought
to take a position of collaboration towards the Vichy regime or the
Germans. The choice to resist was, on the whole, a more difficult
one as it was dangerous and life-threatening not only for the individuals concerned but also for those around them. Resistance to
Vichy and the Occupation, like collaboration, operated on several
levels and, in the same way as for collaboration, women could be
pushed towards resistance through structures in their everyday lives.
Through its analysis of motivation, this chapter will argue that there
were specifically gendered issues which mobilized women to take
an attitude towards Vichy and the Occupation authorities. Women
reacted to issues which concerned them directly, and these were
often (but not always) different from the issues which affected men.

1. Chez mes parents, mon père était résistant, communiste officiel, alors il recevait
un tas d'hommes et de femmes qui venaient. On peut dire que ma mère n'a pas
résisté, mais, qui se levait le matin pour s'occuper du résistant qui devait partir avant
le lever du jour? Qui raccommodait les chaussettes et lavait le linge du résistant qui
dormait? Qui préparait la nourriture qu'il allait emporter? Qui recevait la police
quand il y avait une alerte? Je pense que dans ma famille ma mère a autant résisté
que mon père.' Interview, Madame Constance (Toulouse).

Defining women's resistance

The participation of the French people in the Resistance movement is an area about which much has now been written. The postwar assumption that the major part of the population engaged in anti-Occupation acts has now been more or less shaken off, although certainly many French people had opted for an anti-German position by the latter months of the war. Attempts to quantify the numbers of people involved have mostly been based on those who appeared in the dossiers of the CVR (*Combattants Volontaires de la Résistance*) which were established in the immediate postwar years. In order to appear in these dossiers, individuals had to be nominated by a recognised Resistance organization and have a minimum active involvement of ninety days. According to these figures, women generally made up between 7 and 12 per cent of the Resistance population. The figures recorded in Ille and Vilaine were relatively high: here women represented 12.75 per cent of those involved;[2] in the Hérault, 10 per cent;[3] in the Haute-Garonne estimates vary from 9 to 11.5 per cent;[4] in the Alpes Maritimes, 9 per cent;[5] in the Aveyron, 8 per cent and in Corsica, just 7 per cent.[6] These figures seem low, particularly when we consider that women represented more than 51 per cent of the population at the time. The same story is true where we have figures of women within the different movements. Few were involved in *Combat*, less than 10 per cent in *Franc-Tireur*, 12.5 per cent in *Libération-Sud*, 14 per cent in the network *Jade Fitzroy*[7] and 16.89 per cent in *Défense de la France*.[8] The figure of just under 25 per cent participation in *Témoignage Chrétien* is quite exceptional.

However, recent studies of women's resistance, and most especially work by Paula Schwarz, has shown that the very character of

2. Jacqueline Sainclivier, *La Résistance en Ille et Vilaine 1940–1944* (Rennes, 1993), p. 89.

3. Hélène Chaubin, 'Femmes dans la Résistance Méditerranéenne', in Françoise Thébaud (ed.), *Clio: histoire, femmes et sociétés, résistances et libérations* (Toulouse, 1995), p. 39.

4. Silvie Soula, 'Ceux qui vivent . . . Les Résistants en Haute-Garonne: histoire, organization et sociologie', unpublished Mémoire de Maîtrise (University of Toulouse, 1987).

5. Chaubin, 'Femmes dans la Résistance Méditerranéenne', p. 39.

6. Ibid.

7. Figures collected by Laurent Douzou, 'La Résistance, une affaire d'hommes?', in Françoise Rouquet and Danièle Voldman (eds), *Les Cahiers de l'IHTP*, 31 (Oct. 1995), p. 17.

8. Olivier Wieviorka, *Une certaine idée de la Résistance: Défense de la France 1940–49* (Paris, 1995), p. 16.

women's resistance meant that only a fraction of those involved are represented in these figures.[9] Women who have talked and written about their own involvement in the Resistance have complained that there has been a tendency to concentrate on the more spectacular side of the Resistance in the textbooks, which has not only served to give a distorted picture of what the Resistance was about on a day-to-day basis but has also given priority to the kind of 'military' resistance which involved men. Some women did become involved with activities on the same basis as men, but although some women were involved in transporting and sometimes even taking up arms, as Paula Schwarz has shown, most of the evidence indicates that women who were involved in 'active' resistance tended to have a more secretarial, caring and nurturing role. This was not because this role was considered to be less important, but because it was felt that everyone had to be mobilized and a woman might have easier access to a typewriter and the skill to use it. Women often engaged in activities which would allow them to continue to fulfil their roles as wives and mothers, incorporating their resistance into this process. They centred their resistance activities on the home, and their resistance work became an extension of what they were doing anyway to keep the home running, procuring food and providing shelter. The home might also be used as a post-box, for holding meetings or stocking arms. The nature of this kind of activity meant that it remained unknown both at the time and subsequently. The home camouflaged these activities, and the assumption that the home was essentially private was an advantage to these women since public activity (i.e. Resistance activity) was not expected if there was plenty of evidence of domesticity (small children, washing etc.). As Lucie Aubrac has confirmed, keeping an appearance of normality was one of their main worries.[10] But once the home was discovered to be a cover for public activity, the punishment could be very violent and dangerous.

> Everything was centred on the home. One day the *milice* arrived. Inside there were several Resistance workers who had come to collect some of their belongings. There were scuffles, shots were fired. The Resistance workers escaped through the rear windows. But all

9. Paula Schwarz, 'Redefining Resistance: Women's Activism in Wartime France', in M.R. Higonnet, J. Jenson, S. Michel and M.C. Weitz (eds), *Behind the Lines: Gender and the Two World Wars* (New Haven and London, 1987); '*Partisanes* and Gender Politics in Vichy France', *French Historical Studies*. 16/1 (Spring 1989); UFF, *Les Femmes dans la Résistance* (Paris, 1977).

10. Lucie Aubrac, *Ils partiront dans l'ivresse* (Paris, 1985), p. 8.

three of us, my mother, my cousin and myself, were arrested and deported.[11]

It could be argued that in some ways women implicated in this home-based resistance, who could not defend themselves if they were taken, were more exposed than those who were in more organized military resistance. Indeed, many were sent off to camps if their activities were discovered, while others were arrested just for being present in their own homes when there was suspicion that Resistance activities had taken place, even though they might not have been involved. Many wives and mothers were deported in the place of husbands and children.

> Mum was deported, but they did not take her because she had been involved in the Resistance, because the poor woman, she had never done anything except to try and see us, but they took Mum because she was part of the family, she lived in my house.[12]

But, if they survived the war and were not stopped by the authorities, women who were active in this way do not appear in the figures. Furthermore, if asked, they often retort that they did nothing. Laurent Douzou has expressed frustration with women who are prepared to allow their husbands to take all the credit for this kind of joint Resistance involvement.[13] Several commentators have attempted to explain why this is so. For Ania Francos, women have interiorized and socialized their role to such an extent that they have the impression of 'having done nothing' if they simply 'felt very anxious when they [the men] did not come home at the planned time'.[14] In fact, 'doing nothing' except wait was sometimes the hardest part of their role.

> This role we had of waiting was in my opinion as exhausting as participating in the operation because they were taken up in the ambience of it all. As if he was worried about me! Not because he did not think about it, he was taken up in the movement, whereas for us, well for us it was terrible.[15]

11. Interview, Madame Sandrine (Toulouse).
12. Interview, Madame Flore (Toulouse). The same was true of Madame Verdier, who had not been involved with the Resistance activities of her husband but was deported nonetheless. There are other examples of this in *Les Françaises à Ravensbrück*, L'Amicale de Ravensbrück et l'Association des Déportées et Internées de la Résistance (Paris, 1965).
13. Douzou, 'La Résistance, une affaire d'hommes?', p. 14.
14. Ania Francos, *Il était des femmes dans la Résistance* (Paris, 1978), p. 86.
15. Interview, Madame Flore (Toulouse).

Marie-France Brive has interpreted women's apparent reluctance to value their involvement as part of the conventions of modesty and discretion expected of a woman. For these women, by resisting they had transgressed not just official laws but also the tacit laws of what women should be, so they do not want to be associated with the 'abnormal' character of their involvement. She suggests that we should hear in 'I did nothing', 'I am a complete human being and every human being worthy of the name should have resisted'.[16] Indeed, in a sense, despite the dangers, many of these women were often simply carrying out their normal role in extraordinary circumstances, as the quote introducing this chapter also indicates. Some might therefore argue that since no choice was necessarily involved for these women, their 'resistance' was very different from that of the men who joined the Resistance, or from that of other women who became involved in resistance activities as a result of a conscious and active decision to do so.

However, there were also women who had to actively choose to be involved. The Resistance also needed people who, if necessary, could leave the household, adopt a new identity and go underground. This was more difficult for women who were married with children or who had other responsibilities apart from their clandestine life in the Resistance. As Lucie Aubrac explains: 'There was the everyday existence that had to be dealt with, a house to look after, a husband, a child to feed and the laundry to do.'[17] Let us not forget that it could take a day to do the laundry without a washing machine and with soap that only lathered with great difficulty. Single women had more flexibility to move around; they had more freedom to become involved in the activities required of a liaison or intelligence agent and were able to combine Resistance activities with their normal 'legal' life. One woman explained how her life operated on several levels:

> I had three lives: I was studying for my degree and for me this was very important; I had my illegal life, responsibilities, contacts, rendezvous with fear, tasks to carry out; and my third life was to participate in getting food for my family.[18]

But, if discovered, such women had to be able to disappear. Brigitte Friang wrote that in November 1943:

16. Marie-France Brive, 'Les Résistantes et la Résistance', in Thébaud (ed.), *Clio*, p. 59.
17. Aubrac, *Ils partiront dans l'ivresse*, p. 28.
18. Interview, Madame Antoinette (Toulouse).

It seemed wise to leave the house. There was no point in compromising my parents even more. . . . It was not necessary to add to the exhaustion, the lack of sleep and the nervous tension the added worry that I would drag my parents into a catastrophe . . .[19]

Women often felt that they needed to be completely independent of any home ties before they could become fully involved, as one women Resister explained:

I think that one of the things that I shall never forgive this war period for is the night that my mother died. I spent the night with her; I said to myself, my God, it's as well that she's dead. I was afraid of only one thing, that they would come to arrest me whilst she was still alive and that she would see me leave; that I would disappear, and that I would not be able to stay with her to the end. Immediately after the death of my mother I entered into the Resistance completely.[20]

This kind of situation was almost impossible for married women to envisage, for they were unlikely to risk leaving children with no one to care for them.

Women who did take up the challenge were especially effective as liaison agents. At a time when there were no men available, they were less likely to draw attention to themselves whereas young men were more likely to be noticed, particularly after the compulsory labour draft. Brigitte Friang recounts the attitude of the man who recruited her to his Resistance group:

He preferred the idea of a young woman to a young man for the strong intimacy of the underground existence. In the 1940s, we still had the weakness of paying less attention to a woman and a man meeting, in the road, in a restaurant, in trains, than two men meeting.[21]

The activities of a liaison agent were by definition secret. The nature of their work might even have obliged them to keep their parents in the dark about these activities. Women used code names, which would therefore have been very difficult to trace after the war. Indeed, these women liaison agents, except in exceptional cases, never appeared on any list because the ideal liaison agent continued her normal life, and was often not formally involved in any group. Most were therefore easily forgotten when the war ended.

19. Brigitte Friang, *Regarde-toi qui meurs* (Paris, 1989), p. 33.
20. Interview, Madame Charlotte (Toulouse).
21. Friang, *Regarde-toi qui meurs*, p. 22.

Other Resistance activities which involved women similarly tended to depend on maintaining an appearance of normality, thus rendering their activity essentially 'invisible'. Distribution of the clandestine press was one such task:

> I recruited a group of young women to fold the papers and then put them into envelopes, which were then dropped into different letter boxes throughout Paris. Most of the young women might not be perceived as having been 'actively' involved in our movement, yet they certainly contributed to the cause, risking deportation if caught with the papers.[22]

Women with children could more easily pass unnoticed. The baby's pram might serve as an ideal hiding place for documents.

> When they came to the package with counterfeit papers hidden beneath the baby clothes, I started to cry and talk about my baby and my prisoner husband (neither true) and how my baby needed these clothes and I was going to use the food to make packages to send him. The police stopped searching my bags and put my things back. They asked where in town they could drop off my things.[23]

Women also acted as intelligence agents whose job it was to collect information. Again, they were best able to act if they maintained their daytime jobs. Those who worked at the *Préfecture*, for example, helped the Resistance by acquiring blank identity cards, driving licences, travel permits and so on.[24] Playing the double game, as they called it, was dangerous, but it enabled the Resistance to forge many vital documents. One woman took carbon copies of everything she typed, particularly official documents concerning the Jews. Her position also meant that she was able to give the Resistance advance warning if there was to be a police round-up.[25] Women in the Post Office intercepted letters of denunciation and listened in on telephone calls.[26] Women agents in the SNCF organized clandestine train departures and warned agents of the presence of German officers on the platforms.

22. Geneviève de Gaulle, quoted in Margaret Collins Weitz, *Sisters in the Resistance* (New York, 1995), p. 91.

23. Gisèle Joannès, quoted ibid., p. 81.

24. Interviews, Mesdames Louise, Hélèna, Dolorès, Marie, Marianne, Sandrine, Ghislaine (Toulouse).

25. Interview, Madame Madeleine (Toulouse).

26. Christine Scalisi, 'La Résistance PTT dans la région de Toulouse', *L'Œil et l'oreille de la Résistance: action et rôle des agents des PTT dans la clandestinité au cours de la seconde guerre mondiale*, Actes du Colloque, 21–23 Nov. 1984 (Paris, 1985).

Women also had other important roles they could play. Many took in and helped to save the lives of Jewish children as well as other refugees, for which some paid with their own lives.[27] There were also those who became involved in a form of 'resistance' social service. Bertie Albrecht, in the network *Combat*, organized women to help families whose members were in prison. These women provided them with food and moral support, and arranged for the prisoners to be visited regularly, posing as friends or fiancées. In June 1943, this social service was extended across the Resistance generally. These clandestine social workers were all women and the organization was formalized at the Liberation as the COSOR (*Comité des Œuvres Sociales de la Résistance*). As the Liberation approached and the number of sabotages and violent incidents between the Germans and the *milice* on the one hand, and members of the Resistance on the other, increased, women looked after injured Resistance workers in secret safe houses and worked with trustworthy doctors. On some very rare occasions women also acted as a kind of stool pigeon, playing a double game, infiltrating the Gestapo or trying to lure German officers into places where they could more easily be shot. The *passeurs*, who took groups of Jews and political refugees of various kinds across the Pyrénées to relative safety in Spain, might also have been women.[28] Another role included acting as radio operators and as decoders for messages between members of the internal Resistance groups based on the French mainland and those who were operating out of England.[29]

However, it would be a mistake to assume that being involved with the Resistance was an ongoing, all-encompassing process. Once an initial commitment had been made, involvement could be sporadic and periodic. It was often a question of being available at certain times to carry out certain tasks. There were certainly lulls when women had to return to their normal lives, and it was therefore often preferable for them to have a job or a home to return to, enabling them to continue with a semblance of normality which acted as a good cover for their activities.

27. Rita Thalmann, 'L'Oubli des femmes dans l'historiographie de la Résistance', in Thébaud (ed.), *Clio*, p. 30.
28. Emilienne Eychenne, *Montagnes de la peur et de l'espérance: le franchissement de la frontière espagnole pendant la seconde guerre mondiale dans le département des Hautes-Pyrénées* (Toulouse, 1980).
29. Claire Chevrillon, *Code Name Christiane Clouet: A Woman in the French Resistance* (Texas, 1995).

The following picture therefore emerges. Married women who centred their activity on the home were able to maintain an appearance of normality while men were more likely to be noticed and therefore went underground and operated in *maquis* groups hidden from the authorities. This fully clandestine lifestyle was sustained by women who ensured the delivery of food supplies and themselves often remained visible. *Maquisards* acknowledged the essential role played by women as carers and providers.[30] H.R. Kedward has also referred to the fact that it was always women who opened the door to possible danger and engaged with the Occupation authorities, leaving the men time to escape through the back door. Single women continued to work until such time as they were suspected and were then able to go underground, free from the household constraints which made this difficult for married women with children. Generally speaking, women were able to pass unnoticed as their activities tended to include their traditional roles, although this also meant that much of their contribution was overlooked. A small minority did become involved in acts of sabotage and carrying arms. Perry Willson has shown that the case was the same for women in the Italian resistance.[31] Although some took up arms, as in France, they generally had a more auxiliary role and were engaged in similar sorts of activities; most did not go beyond rigidly defined norms of good female behaviour but participated primarily in a nurturing role.

After the war, few women made anything of these activities. According to Dominique Veillon, 'When the Liberation came, they took refuge in silence and anonymity whereas their male companions in the battle undertook to explain their activities.'[32] There may also have been political reasons for this, as De Grazia maintains there were in Italy. She describes how the enormous participation of women in the Italian Resistance was largely occulted and when the time came to celebrate the victories of the Resistance the contribution of women was by and large kept quiet. In the wake of the liberation of Italy, the left-wing male image of the liberation quickly canonized itself in order to present itself as a legitimate force

---

30. H.R. Kedward, *In Search of the Maquis: Rural Resistance in Southern France 1942–44* (Oxford, 1993), pp. 89–90.

31. Perry Willson, *The Clockwork Factory* (Oxford, 1993), p. 23.

32. Dominique Veillon, 'Résister au féminin', *Pénélope, pour l'histoire des femmes*, 12 (Spring 1985), p. 87.

capable of ruling Italian society.[33] Rita Thalmann has shown that the high number of foreign and Jewish women in the Resistance was a further element contributing to the fact that their participation was easily forgotten, as they were part of minority cultures.[34] Paula Schwarz has indicated that women's names are more difficult to trace as they change when they marry, so they do not appear to the same extent.[35] These are all convincing arguments, but the activities and nature of women's resistance exposed here also serve to show why it has been underestimated.

Who, then, were the women concerned? The existing research suggests that the female Resistance population tended to be young. My sample in Toulouse was necessarily young.[36] Jacqueline Sainclivier also came to this conclusion in her work on Ille et Vilaine where she found that generally the Resistance age was young, but that women were on the whole older than men.[37] In Wieviorka's study, 51.81 per cent of the women were single and only 34.4 per cent married (the marital status of the remaining 13.79 per cent is not recorded).[38] However, he does not see marriage as a hindrance to involvement and suggests that the higher numbers of single women were more to do with demographic factors related to the First World War, or because the kind of women who were likely to resist were independent and might refuse to marry because of this.[39] In any case, as has been seen, it was logical that the women who could devote themselves entirely to resistance were most likely to be those who had fewer family commitments and responsibilities. Middle-aged women who may have been married with children would often follow the lead of their husbands and may have become involved in home-based resistance. Older women between 50 and 60 appear to have been less present in the Resistance, but oral testimony is not available since no one thought it worth collecting before they died. The elderly often had physical limitations which made them more vulnerable, but existing accounts suggest that they certainly had a role in hiding people.

33. Victoria de Grazia, *How Fascism Ruled Women, Italy 1922–1945* (Berkeley, 1992), pp. 278–87.
34. Thalmann, 'L'Oubli des femmes', p. 32.
35. Paula Schwarz, 'Différence des sexes et résistance: bilan et perspectives', in Thébaud (ed.), *Clio*, p. 78.
36. Hanna Diamond, 'Women's Experience during and after World War Two in the Toulouse Area 1939–48: Choices and Constraints', unpublished PhD thesis (University of Sussex, 1992).
37. Sainclivier, *La Résistance en Ille et Vilaine*, p. 91.
38. Wieviorka, *Une certaine idée de la Résistance*, p. 178.   39. Ibid., p. 179.

Pre-Resistance

Various factors served to bring women into the Resistance. A first step was for them to situate themselves in relation to the government and the authorities. Chapter 2 showed how, during the war years, some women found themselves inadvertently transgressing the rules established by the authorities without necessarily changing any aspect of their everyday existence. They arrived at this position by simply carrying on with their lives and endeavouring to survive in a way that seemed appropriate in the context of wartime. Often their daily lives quite simply clashed with the rules imposed by the Vichy or German authorities. This position might serve to predispose them to be less sympathetic to them, whereas, as far as the authorities were concerned, the rules represented a necessary infringement on people's lives to be sure that the population was under control. There may have been no real political stance taken in refusing to obey them, but some were so anxious to fall into line that they refused to dissent from Vichy even on such minor issues. As Vichy continued to introduce legislation related to the National Revolution (see pp. 64–6), a rebellious counter-culture grew among a minority who found themselves 'outside' Vichy without necessarily having taken a decision to be so. Laws were passed which specifically concerned women, relating to paid employment, abortion and prostitution, for example, which made women who transgressed them become part of this counter-culture.

Acquiring food and supplies was a major preoccupation for women, and this was an avenue through which women might come to reflect upon and even reject the authorities in place, to the extent that when they were lacking on a number of occasions women across the country took to the streets demanding more food and better rations. Ivan Avakoumovitch has put together a detailed account of these demonstrations, showing that they were concentrated in the first half of 1941 and 1942, during the most severe and difficult winters of the Occupation.[40] Women could therefore be moved to take a particularly critical attitude to Vichy as a result of its failure to ensure that rations were honoured. The Food Supply Services were known to be corrupt, and Antoine Lefébure's collection of letters and telephone calls suggests that this was often commented on.[41] From the winter

40. Ivan Avakoumovitch, 'Les Manifestations des femmes', *Cahiers de l'histoire de l'institut de recherches marxistes*, 45 (1991), pp. 46–9.

41. Antoine Lefébure, *Les Conversations secrètes des Français sous l'Occupation* (Paris, 1993).

of 1941–42, women across the country made representations to Prefects demanding better quality of bread, more milk for their children and so on. Police reports contain evidence of these demonstrations, which sometimes mobilized large numbers of women. Dominique Veillon found that women in working-class areas were first to demonstrate against the material difficulties which hit them and their families.[42] Guillon has cited a number of movements in the Var.[43] Zaretsky dates demonstrations in all the major towns of the Gard from January to March 1942, though here the women involved were not thought by the police to be 'lower class, but were women of breeding'.[44] Sometimes food protests took on a more explicitly political nature. In Alès, in February 1942, 500 women presented themselves at the sub-prefecture, and their chant 'Bread Pétain!' (*Pétain, du pain*) became 'Down with Pétain' (*A bas Pétain*).[45] The extent to which these demonstrations were politically motivated is difficult to evaluate. Most Prefects took the initial protests as spontaneous, but the role of the communist party in the organization of many quickly became apparent.[46] The party gave them more cohesion and printed tracts for publicity. Most were triggered by the absence of a certain product in the market-place. However, there were some recorded demonstrations in the south which took place long before the arrival of the German troops, and some in areas like St Tropez where the communist party had no stronghold and there were few miners or factory workers.[47] The frequency and effectiveness of these demonstrations increased throughout the Occupation and the range of the areas of their dissatisfaction increased. In October 1942, for example, women in Annecy were recorded demonstrating against the compulsory labour draft. They carried placards with the words 'We do not want our husbands to work in Germany.'[48] Women also set about blocking trains of departing workers. On 6 January 1943, at Montluçon, five thousand people, including entire families, demonstrated. Women lay across the track and eventually the train was uncoupled and all but thirty of the three hundred set

42. Dominique Veillon, *Vivre et survivre en France 1939–1947* (Paris, 1995), p. 223.
43. Jean-Pierre Guillon, 'Y-a-t-il un comportement ouvrier spécifique? Les ouvriers valois', in Denis Peschanski and Jean-Louis Robert (eds), *Les Ouvriers en France pendant la seconde guerre mondiale* (Paris, 1992), pp. 469–76.
44. Robert Zaretsky, *Nîmes at War: Religion, Politics and Public Opinion in the Gard, 1938–44* (University Park, Pennsylvania State University Press, 1995), p. 179.
45. Roger Borderon, *Libération du Languedoc Méditerranéenne* (Paris, 1974), p. 35.
46. Danielle Tartakowsky, 'Ouvriers et manifestations de rue 1940–44: des manifestations ouvrières?' in Peschanski and Robert (eds), *Les Ouvriers*, pp. 420–1.
47. Avakoumovitch, 'Les Manifestations des femmes', p. 28.
48. Tartakowsky, 'Ouvriers et manifestations de rue', p. 425.

for Germany escaped.[49] These hungry women refused to accept a regime which was incapable of resolving their daily subsistence problems, and, as H.R. Kedward has pointed out, their demonstrations did much to sap popular consensus in favour of Vichy and politicized an increasing proportion of the population.[50]

Strikes were rare during the Occupation, but despite the dangers, women also mobilized and supported the men in strike activity. Police reports describe how during the miners' strikes which took place in the north of France from 27 May to 10 June 1941, 'the wives of miners have joined the battle next to their husbands and sons. . . . 3,000 women took an active part in the strikers' pickets, thereby protecting their children from starvation.'[51] Women were, however, arrested, and one woman, Emilienne Mopty, wife of a miner from Pas de Calais, was executed in the courtyard of a Cologne prison on 18 June 1943. Tartakowsky shows how, in some cases, women were able to use strikes to enable them to obtain more food supplies, though she suspects that the communist party may well have been involved here too. In Lodève, on 23 June 1943, when the town hall refused to receive a delegation of women who had come to complain about the inadequate food supplies, the women went straight to the entrance of the mine demanding that their husbands, brothers and sons strike. This alliance of housewives and workers forced concessions, and food was released.[52] Similarly, in Martinet, the food supply improved when a demonstration of women was followed by a three-day strike.[53]

Thus women could be drawn into a counter-culture which might influence them to move towards resistance or, at the very least, question the validity of laws passed by Vichy or imposed by the authorities. The counter-cultures described here operated on various levels. Women became part of a counter-culture when they found themselves disapproved of by the authorities, a disapproval which operated with differing levels of severity. These women, although their position may have been politically ambiguous, were essentially in a position of 'proto-resistance' and, as the war went

49. Rayna Kline, 'Partisans, Godmothers, Bicyclists and other Terrorists: Women in the French Resistance and under Vichy', *Proceedings of the Western Society for French History* (1977), p. 377.

50. H.R. Kedward, *Resistance in Vichy France* (Oxford, 1978), p. 220; see also Paula Schwarz, 'The Politics of Food and Gender in Occupied France', in Hanna Diamond and Claire Gorrara (eds), *Modern and Contemporary France, Special Issue: Gendering the Occupation of France* (Feb. 1999), pp. 35–45.

51. AN F60 1521, Rapports de Gendarmerie.

52. Avakoumovitch, 'Les Manifestations des femmes', p. 12.

53. Tartakowsky, 'Ouvriers et manifestations de rue', p. 426.

on, more and more women joined their ranks. Although this did not necessarily mean that they became involved in Resistance proper, some then established contacts which marked a move from an individual to a collective counter-culture, and gradually various underground survival networks emerged which pre-dated more established Resistance.

There were also pre-Resistance survival networks which operated for the most part through the family. Women tended to be drawn in as mothers and wives and placed in a situation as individuals or through solidarity with others which created a feeling of illegality. A group of women who might have been affected in this way were the wives of prisoners-of-war, who had rejected the overtures, however subtle, made by the Vichy authorities described in the last chapter, and refused to accept separation from their husbands without protest. Many came to reject the Vichy regime that maintained their presence in Germany. They might initially have become involved with illegal activities in their attempts to communicate with absent husbands as they found ways of overcoming the censorship of the permitted monthly letters. Some sent coded letters, or hid letters in their husband's food parcels, often with great ingenuity. For these women, the situation of continued absence of husbands, in spite of promises that they would return, led to a growth of hostility towards Vichy, and, after the Occupation, towards the Germans. In some cases it became a reason for becoming involved with the Resistance.

From November 1942, escaped prisoners-of-war were automatically in a position of illegality both for Vichy and the Germans, and therefore had to remain in hiding.[54] This almost inevitably drew the entire family into clandestine activities. Wives, whether they had been involved in their escape or not, were also implicated. As one wife whose prisoner husband escaped in June 1942 explained, 'I was scared because the Germans said that they would revenge themselves on the families of escaped prisoners'.[55] Yet, as was noted in the previous chapter, wives of prisoners-of-war were more likely to be predisposed to collaborate, so it is not surprising that relatively few became involved in the Resistance, as the evidence suggests. They had much more to overcome in the form of family constraints, particularly if they were solely responsible for young children. In interview, those wives who did become involved in Resistance activities explained that they did so reluctantly; those who found themselves alone with the children felt that they had so much more to risk.

54. AN F60 1484, 'Note pour l'Ambassade', Cabinet de l'Ambassade, 1 Mar. 1943.
55. Interview, Madame Laurence (Toulouse).

From 1943, when the reality of the German Occupation had become more apparent, many women found themselves confronted with more clear-cut choices. After the introduction of the compulsory labour draft, there were certainly women who encouraged their husbands and sons to go and earn good money, but there were also those who actively discouraged them. H.R. Kedward records that women's vociferous presence at demonstrations against the labour draft was a discomforting force for the authorities.[56] One woman described how her mother told her and her brother to stay in the train when they arrived at the station and carry on to the next station as the Germans were rounding up all the young men off the trains and loading them into lorries bound for Germany.[57] A male Resistance worker recalled how pleased mothers were if their sons did not go to Germany on the labour draft. He explained how some mothers would bring their sons to him so they could join the clandestine *maquis* groups and remain in France.[58] The Germans were aware of this kind of family complicity and threatened the families of those men who avoided the compulsory labour draft, particularly when they came to realize that many of these men had taken refuge in the *maquis*. In this way, whether or not wives and mothers were involved in the decision of a husband or a son to avoid going to Germany, they were affected by it and drawn into a certain position because of it. Women with husbands or sons in the *maquis* were therefore much more likely to be sympathetic to the Resistance.

Resistance: choice and motivation

Women with previous political experience were the most likely to make a choice of their own volition to become involved in some form of Resistance activity, or to seek out some kind of action. It was they who were most likely to have some interest in, and understanding of, world events. This was particularly true of communist women or women who were involved in trade unions. Women who had already gained some political consciousness of the events of the Popular Front were also more likely to engage with Resistance and have some notion of what a reaction to the Vichy regime could be. Thus, communist women had a political education and some kind

---

56. H.R. Kedward, *In Search of the Maquis* (Oxford, 1993), p. 90.
57. Interview, Madame Françoise (Toulouse).
58. Interview, Monsieur Frédérique (Toulouse).

of precedent which enabled them to question and even reject the status quo represented by Vichy. Paula Schwarz has done interesting work which shows that women with previous political experience often became involved with Resistance as a natural continuation of their prewar activities.[59] This was also the case for my more modest sample in Toulouse, where 8 out of 25 women interviewed claimed that they became involved in Resistance because of a previous political commitment.[60] It was predictably the communist women who were most able to relate their Resistance activities in political and often also in class terms, whereas the explanations of the Gaullist and Christian women were much more 'politically neutral' by comparison. The famous heroines of the Resistance, women like Danielle Casanova, Marie-Claude Vaillant-Couturier and Claudine Chamat, were all involved with the communist youth organization UJFF (*Union des Jeunes Filles de France*) before the war.

Women who had experienced some socialization in youth groups might also have been drawn to Resistance. Youth groups related to the Church, Scouts and so on were also important because, although not overtly political, they provided women with networks through which they might contact others or be contacted themselves. A number of left-wing political groups also influenced women in a less direct way and could have an important socializing influence, as in the case of members of the JAC (*Jeunesse Agricole Chrétienne*) and the JOC (*Jeunesse Ouvrière Chrétienne*). The JOCF (*Jeunesse Ouvrière Chrétienne Féminine*) was quickly implicated in anti-Vichy and anti-German activities. As was seen in previous chapters, they organized canteens, helped families escaping from the Germans and discouraged women from taking paid employment in Germany.[61] One oral witness described how she became involved in Resistance activities as a direct result of her prewar involvement in the Church.

> I was a departmental organizer of *Combat* and *Témoignage Chrétien Clandestin*. In principle you were not supposed to do all that, but once you were asked, someone had to do it and so you could not refuse. I was known as I had attended the 'Semaines sociales de France' since 1934 and it so happened that we had all opted for the same side, we all went in the same direction.[62]

---

59. Paula Schwarz, 'Precedents for Politics': Prewar Activism of Women in the French Resistance', unpublished MA thesis (Princeton University, 1981); also mentioned in *Les Françaises à Ravensbrück*, p. 26, and UFF, *Les Femmes dans la Résistance.*
60. Diamond, 'Women's Experience during and after World War Two', p. 174.
61. Jeanne Aubert, *La JOCF. Qu'as tu fait de nos vies? La Jeunesse Ouvrière Chrétienne Féminine 1928–45* (Paris, 1990), p. 130.
62. Interview, Madame Ghislaine (Toulouse).

The fact that *Témoignage Chrétien* was able to mobilize high numbers of women was doubtless due to its links with the Church.

It would be a tempting hypothesis to suggest that women in paid employment would have been more likely to evaluate their situation in political terms and would also be more likely to have contacts which might lead them to Resistance networks. They may also have had a better understanding of what was happening in the war and first-hand experience of the German presence in the workplace. By contrast, women at home would have had less chance of coming into contact with organized resistance. However, recent sociological studies of the Resistance seem to indicate that women in paid employment were not the majority of women members. Sainclivier concludes that, in Ille et Vilaine, the fact that women worked was not a determining factor.[63] Hélène Chaubin also found that in l'Hérault and Corsica, many women in the Resistance were not in employment.[64] Only Wieviorka's study of the network *Défense de la France* indicates that most of the women involved were in paid employment, in what he calls 'emancipatory' jobs, which he suggests indicates that these women were attached to some degree of independence.[65] However, this may say more about the particular character of this network than about women's participation in the Resistance in general.

Other than previous political experience, women were most likely to come into contact with the Resistance through their families and because of their social milieu. Resistance did not happen in isolation. Men and women who opposed the Armistice could make little impact by opposing it on their own, though some women did try. Two female members of DF both individually wrote and distributed their own tracts whenever they could before becoming involved in a Resistance network.[66] The dynamics of involvement in the Resistance depended on meeting like-minded people, and in this women were disadvantaged in relation to men. Women's friendship circles and contacts were less likely to bring them into contact with the kind of people who would be active in this way. Furthermore, even if women were motivated, in most circles they would not be expected to have views about the political situation, and would rarely, if ever, be invited to comment, except about problems of food supply. Indeed, unless they were of a particular social class, or owned a radio,

63. Sainclivier, *Résistance en Ille et Vilaine*, p. 95.
64. Chaubin, 'Femmes dans la Résistance Méditerranéenne', p. 44.
65. Wieviorka, *Une certaine idée de la Résistance*, pp. 166–7.
66. AN 6Av 591.

women may not have been all that well informed about what was happening in the war. The milieu to which a woman belonged could also act as an important factor to draw her towards Resistance. Often younger people, who were less afraid, talked amongst themselves more openly about what was happening. Students, for example, were a particularly important group of young people who could be more easily drawn into Resistance. Class and education therefore also played an important role here.

Most of the accounts, whether from oral or written sources, indicate that married women were almost inevitably drawn into the activities of a husband.[67] Many women worked with their husbands from the beginning of their activities and saw themselves as 'following' their husband's lead. This was the case whether husbands were present in the family home or elsewhere in hiding.[68] Some acted because they necessarily did the same as their husband without taking the initiative; some contributed as more equal partners. It was obviously almost impossible for husbands to disguise their activity from their wives. A husband could bring a stranger home once or twice and pass him or her off as a friend, but would have to explain their presence eventually. One woman who worked with her husband realized when her husband was deported in October 1943 that she had to continue with the work where he had left off.[69] Political commitment appears to have been secondary for these women, and any political involvement was often defined by the political preferences of the husband.

Another important familial link which could draw women into Resistance was that between mothers and their children. It has already been seen that mothers sometimes discouraged sons from going to Germany on the labour draft, or defended their children against Germans enquiring after their activities. However, mothers with children involved in clandestine activities were less likely to become involved themselves than wives, who could hardly fail to become involved with their husband's affairs. Families sometimes had a group commitment to Resistance, and someone like Marie Chamming's came into contact with Resistance because of her father.[70] But Wieviorka's study of *Défense de la France* refutes the idea of family recruitment. He claims that most fathers were hostile to the Resistance

67. Schwarz, 'Différence des sexes', p. 82.
68. Interview, Mesdames Flore, Marie, Laurence (Toulouse).
69. Interview, Madame Joséphine (Toulouse). See also *Les Françaises à Ravensbruck*, p. 28.
70. Marie Chamming's, *J'ai choisi la tempête* (Paris, 1997).

and unsupportive. Furthermore, the guerrilla character of Resistance incited activists to keep their sisters away from action they judged to be dangerous, although this was less true in Paris where *Défense de la France* had a strong female element.[71]

Daughters might also have been influenced by the First World War experiences of their fathers. Those who had suffered because of the participation of fathers in the Great War were less tolerant about accepting a second German invasion. Many remembered that the German armies had destroyed their homes and those of their families during the First World War, and since their childhood they had heard stories of German cruelty.[72] Several women related to the experiences of fathers who had been killed in the First World War, believing that through their Resistance involvement they were somehow carrying on the battle for them. One wife of a prisoner-of-war described how she reacted when she was approached by a friend in the Resistance. When asked if she wanted to join the fight against the Germans she explained that they had taken her father during the 1914–18 war. 'Now they have taken my husband and brother prisoner, there were no two ways about it, I'm against the Germans.'[73]

In some cases, the events of the war themselves could have a major impact on women, which could then trigger a further reaction. The 1940 exodus could have a politicizing influence in this way. Those closely involved with refugees, like Gritou and Annie Valloton, could not fail to be moved by their plight and almost inevitably became critical of the Vichy government and the Germans.[74] Those who were persecuted by the regime were necessarily pushed into a situation of resistance. Rita Thalmann describes the case of Yvette Bernard-Fernoux, who replaced Bertie Albrecht after her arrest at the head of the social services of *Combat*. Bernard-Fernoux explained that she had nothing to lose as a Jew as she was already condemned to death. East European women came from a milieu which made them more prepared to adapt to difficult moral and material conditions: they were often more aware of political realities and more used to facing unexpected situations.[75] This was particularly true of Jewish women, communists and Spanish republicans. French communists

71. Wieviorka, *Une certaine idée de la Résistance*, p. 74.

72. Margaret Rossiter, *Women in the Resistance* (New York, 1985), p. 17.

73. Wieviorka, *Une certaine idée de la Résistance*, p. 74.

74. Gritou and Annie Valloton, *C'était au jour le jour: carnets (1939–1944)* (Paris, 1995).

75. Thalmann, 'L'Oubli des femmes', pp. 23–5.

and Spanish republicans already had some experience of resisting established authority. For example, after the French communist party was disbanded in September 1940, both male and female members were forced to carry on their activities underground. Renée Rousseau has argued that women came to play an important role as they were unknown to the police and could move around freely between activists in hiding.[76] They were forced to organize themselves after being pushed into illegality and subsequently fought for their own survival. Spanish communists brought their experience of fighting fascism to the Resistance and their presence was particularly high in the Languedoc and border departments. Chaubin records that 5 per cent of women who resisted in the Hérault were Spanish, of whom half were deported.[77]

Finally, women might also have been brought in by a chance contact or encounter. Women may have been motivated to act, but if they did not have a milieu or familial links which were likely to draw them into contact with Resistance, they were unable to do very much. Admittedly, this may appear to be a rather 'convenient' argument, but many French people complained at the Liberation that they had not known that the Resistance existed, and that if they had known, they would have wanted to be involved. On the other hand, people could also become involved quite by chance. This woman's story is an example:

> My father went out for an hour and during that hour a women came and knocked on the window. 'There are two Intelligence Service agents at the port. The Germans are looking for them. Can you take them?' I looked at Mum. I was alone with her and I said, 'What should we do?' She said, 'I don't know.' So, I said that they had better come. My resistance started on the 5 January 1941. We put them in the attic and that evening they ate with us. They stayed in the house for 7 days.[78]

She later sheltered as many as twelve Allied airmen in her home and they all returned safely to England.

Can we assume that a woman's choice to resist was more difficult than a man's? It would seem so. It is not just the element of fear that was present for both sexes, but that women, by choosing to join the Resistance, were inevitably committing more than themselves to

---

76. Renée Rousseau, *Les Femmes rouges: chronique des années Vermeersch* (Paris, 1983), p. 20.
77. Chaubin, 'Femmes dans la Résistance Méditerranéenne', p. 47.
78. Interview, Madame Cécile (Finistère).

the battle, often implicating children and elderly parents – a major factor in their testimonies, and one which, even if it was a consideration for the men, is rarely evoked by them, suggesting that it was almost certainly a less important part of their decision. Perhaps this was because men were not so worried about the repercussions the choices they made might have on members of the family. It seems fair to assume that men were more used to making decisions which affected themselves alone, whereas women had no experience of this, and were more socialized into seeing any decisions they made about their own lives in tandem with those of their children. As Wieviorka has pointed out, women were still seen as minors and this was a severe social constraint. At a time when commitment to the Resistance implied a negation of the current norms, women had more to overcome than men, thus making it more complicated and difficult for them to become involved.[79]

In the context of retrospective memoirs and interviews, most women resist the idea that their experience was gendered or different from that of the men and therefore were not aware of any discrimination that took place. As H.R. Kedward has put it, 'generally there was a "felt" equality'.[80] They are even reluctant to admit that there might have been specific roles for women in the Resistance. Most were so delighted to be involved, or so scared, that they rarely questioned what they had been asked to do in any case. They claim that it was certainly not the atmosphere of the time to question the decisions of those in control, and even less so for women to express preferences. For example, it is only recently that some women who were involved in the clandestine journal *Défense de la France* have come to realize that they could have written articles as well as printing and distributing copies of the paper. They put this down to their own lack of confidence and inability to consider themselves competent to do it:

> I wrote five tracts hoping that they would have a snowball effect. I couldn't imagine any other way at the time. And then I met Philippe and all those young intelligent people and I never wrote another line. . . . I regretted it afterwards.[81]

Celia Bertin records that women who were involved in the Resistance did not feel that they were underestimated by the men with whom they worked, yet few held positions of responsibility, and, if someone

79. Wieviorka, *Une certaine idée de la Résistance*, p. 180.
80. Kedward, *In Search of the Maquis*, p. 94.
81. AN 6Av 637–640.

had to be sent to London, it was not likely to be a woman.[82] Apart from some rare exceptions, notably Marie-Madeleine Fourcade, who was a founder member and later became head of the network Alliance,[83] and, in Toulouse, Marie-Louise Dissart, who became a recognized chief of the *Françoise* escape network,[84] women rarely held an important organizational position. Yet, if men were arrested or had to escape into hiding, it was often assumed that wives would carry on in their absence.[85] Perry Willson suggests that Italian resistance organizations were more prejudiced against women than those in France, where Resistance organizations were prepared to use women, certainly in the earlier part of the Occupation, when they were less likely to be suspected.[86] Initially, it did not seem to occur to the Vichy or the Occupying authorities that a woman could have a role within the Resistance and, as has been seen, they were often used in cases where a cover was needed or where there had to be an appearance of normality. Men were more likely to be used for visible armed attacks. Even if the authorities might have considered the possibility that women could be involved, the punishments were not as severe, at least at first, as this poster from the Finistère which appeared in October 1941 indicates: 'Men who help, directly or indirectly, teams of enemy aviators . . . by aiding their escape or helping them in any way, will be shot. Women found responsible for the same crime will be sent to concentration camps in Germany.'[87]

How do women see their involvement in Resistance? Did this involvement cause them to become any more politically aware?[88] Unless women were explicitly aware of politics, they tended to see themselves as apolitical. A common view in oral testimony was 'I was in the Resistance, but I was not political'.[89] 'We were not politicised. We were really against the Occupier that's all.'[90] This reluctance to define their activity in political terms was widespread. 'Women in the Resistance didn't talk about politics. We had the principle in the

82. Celia Bertin, *Femmes sous l'Occupation* (Paris, 1993), p. 216.
83. Marie-Madeleine Fourcade, *L'Arche de Noé: réseau "Alliance" 1940–45* (Paris, 1968).
84. Christian Monly, 'Une héroïne toulousaine, Marie-Louise Dissart, alias Françoise', *Revue R4*, 7 (Mar. 1970).
85. Sainclivier, *Résistance en Ille et Vilaine*, p. 89; Thalmann, 'L'Oubli des femmes', p. 29.
86. Willson, *The Clockwork Factory*, p. 238.   87. ADF 200W27.
88. This question is also asked by Hélène Eck, 'Les Françaises sous Vichy: femmes du désastre – citoyennes par le désastre?', in Françoise Thébaud (ed.), *Histoire des femmes, le XXe siècle* (Paris, 1992), pp. 185–213.
89. Interview, Madame Saskia (Toulouse).
90. Interview, Madame Madeleine (Toulouse).

Resistance that it was not about politics, we all had to be in agreement to save France.'[91] Thus, although women were acting 'politically', many of them did not conceptualize their actions in those terms. And, as Celia Bertin put it, 'The political side of Resistance escaped most of us.'[92] This kind of discourse needs to be contextualized within French political culture, which associates everything political with party politics and government at a time when women were not citizens. Despite the findings of Paul Smith, who suggests that politics were much more a part of women's culture throughout the 1920s and 1930s than was previously assumed,[93] most of the testimonies indicate that politics *per se* were not the main concern of these women. Christine Bard acknowledges that few feminist activists became involved in the Resistance.[94]

On the whole, women were much more comfortable articulating their Resistance involvement in terms of anti-German feelings or patriotism. There was a sense in which the family and the nation was being directly threatened and something had to be done about it. 'Things were going very badly for us,' one woman explained. 'We might have become German.'[95] Women's levels of political consciousness probably varied from movement to movement. For the women in *Défense de la France*, politicization came long after the war. One of the women members recognized that '*Défense France* was a very good movement for me because I was extraordinarily apolitical. I was so politically ignorant that it still shocks me.'[96] Another explained that 'My activities were more related to patriotism, they were absolutely not political',[97] and Hélène Viannay, 'We were hopeless [about politics], we had no political consciousness and I think that (. . .) I was the one who knew most about it. We didn't follow what Vichy did, we didn't care about it.'[98] But the most telling explanation comes from another witness, who hints at the feeling also expressed by other women in the movement, that they felt quite reproachful of the men for being too political with their dreams about post-liberation France which distracted them from the pressing concerns of Occupied France.

91. Interview, Madame Sandrine (Toulouse).
92. Bertin, *Femmes sous l'Occupation*, p. 217.
93. Paul Smith, *Feminism and the Third Republic* (Oxford, 1996).
94. Christine Bard, *Les Filles de Marianne: histoire des feminismes 1914–40* (Paris, 1995), p. 444.
95. Interview, Madame Madeleine (Toulouse).
96. AN 6Av 612–613.
97. AN 6Av 513–514.
98. Hélène Viannay, in Thébaud (ed.), *Clio*, p. 259.

When they started to get into really political discussions, I would go and make the sandwiches or the supper, I let them argue amongst themselves. I thought there were more important and more urgent things for us to get on with than to quibble over details like that . . . there was one thing I thought was important: we had to fight against them [the Germans] and help the people who were victims.[99]

However, as has been shown, the fact that women did not see themselves as behaving politically either at the time or later does not mean their contribution to the resistance was any less 'political' than that of the men.

The communist party very quickly realized the political role that women could play and had a clear agenda as far as women were concerned. They wanted to mobilize women and created specific structures which were designed to do so. The UFF (*Union des Femmes Françaises*) saw its role as being to try to politicize women and to encourage a particularly female form of resistance; it worked very closely with the communist party and was effectively a wing of it. The UFF had its origins in the *Union des Jeunes Filles de France* and the *Comité Mondial des Femmes contre la Guerre et le Fascisme*.[100] Both groups were dissolved in 1939 at the same time as the communist party, but during the Occupation women from these groups formed small clandestine networks known as *Comités féminins de la Résistance* which later became the *Union des Femmes Françaises*. Their participation in food demonstrations and strikes has already been described. The communists saw women as important potential agents for mobilization against Vichy and they were certainly responsible for politicizing and mobilizing large numbers of women. They took advantage of women's feelings of discontent about lack of supplies to orchestrate a number of large demonstrations. Lise London's account of the organization of the women's committees describes how the party hierarchy placed her, Claudine Chomat and Danielle Casanova in important positions in order to oversee these activities.[101] They used intense propaganda and committees of women in threes to harangue frustrated women waiting in queues, exploiting outbursts of anger or frustration when housewives realized that rations were not going to be honoured:

little by little, using daily concerns as a point of departure, we carried women along not to passively endure the consequences of the defeat

99. AN 6Av 525–528.
100. See Rousseau, *Les Femmes rouges*, pp. 14–20.
101. Lise London, *La Mégère de la rue Daguerre* (Paris, 1995), p. 141.

and of the Occupation, not to put up with their misery. We marked out the way towards active resistance.[102]

Sometimes the communists used false distribution promises as a pretext to get women to congregate, and the women were left angry and militant when these promises were left unsatisfied.[103] This action culminated in the rue de Buci demonstration when Madeleine Marzin incited a group of housewives to help themselves to jam and sugar from a warehouse of goods destined for Germany. She and her three young male armed protectors were arrested. Lise London was involved in a further demonstration in the rue Daguerre and was also eventually arrested. The communists also realized that the presence of women in demonstrations was valuable because it changed the character of the demonstration. In view of the fact that very real problems existed, officials were often sympathetic to their demands for more food and better rations. Accordingly, the sanctions imposed were much more severe if communist involvement was uncovered, and if men were arrested in this context, they risked worse treatment than that of the women.[104] Furthermore, the UFF can be credited with providing women with structures to express their discontent; however, the most active women were more often communists themselves, or the wives of arrested communists. Women who joined the demonstrations were often simply angry:

> There were masses of women who joined in with us at the time, but politically speaking, well, I am not sure. They were against the Occupier, they were all mothers with several children to feed. There were however, an important number with a political consciousness, a consciousness that our country was occupied, that the food produced in France, the vegetables, the fruit, the meat etc. . . . was sent outside by the Germans.[105]

Nonetheless, the UFF appears to have been efficiently organized and was the only real example of a Resistance group which made an effort to target women and recognize them as a political constituency. Its survivors are well informed about wartime politics from a communist angle and their activities are better documented than those of women's resistance generally. This is no accident, and can perhaps be explained by the influence of the male political party, which no one denies had close links with the UFF. The women's organizations were seen as a particularly successful facet

102. Ibid., p. 107.
103. Avakoumovitch, 'Les Manifestations des femmes', p. 18.
104. Ibid., p. 31.   105. Ibid.

of communist resistance and were, for them, a good investment of time and money. Indeed, the communists mobilized this success as much as they could in the postwar period and recalled their wartime activity as a way of legitimizing themselves. Danielle Casanova, who was arrested and died in deportation, became a martyr. Her role was manipulated by the propagandists throughout the Cold War, as Hilary Footitt has shown.[106]

Resistance therefore emerges as intensely gendered. It has not been my intention to argue either that women's resistance was essentially and inherently different from men's or that it happened in some kind of vacuum. But it can in no way be regarded as identical. In terms of the chronological development, women's resistance developed in parallel with and as part of the Resistance movement in general. In terms of activism, women were in a minority however their activity is assessed. This was partly because the character of women's resistance often took less organized and unofficial forms and was by its very nature less visible. Women's recorded resistance is therefore small in relation to the men's. There were structural reasons why women were less likely to be in the Resistance. They had fewer political antecedents than men, were less likely to belong to networks, and were less politically educated than men. Women also had other commitments and constraints in the form of children or other household concerns which affected the choices they made. It would perhaps be interesting to examine the extent to which the men felt that they were free or constrained by family circumstances – in any case, their position was different. Married men, for example, although they also had certain domestic responsibilities, could leave the home if necessary and go into hiding, confident that the household would continue to function in their absence because they could rely on their wives. In general they were less concerned that their choices might have repercussions on the family as a whole.

Women's contribution to Resistance cannot be denied, but women's inhibition about conceptualizing these activities in political terms is worthy of some consideration as men were certainly not so reluctant to do so. For example, many men were able to carry their Resistance involvement into the postwar period, enabling them to present themselves as politically aware and involved. It is hardly surprising that the women who operated in quasi-isolation as part of a network and who came into contact with few other activists had

---

106. Hilary Footitt, 'Women and (Cold) War: The Cold War Creation of the Myth of "La Française résistante"', *French Cultural Studies*, 8 (1997), pp. 41–51.

little sense of a common political aim other than ridding France of the Occupier. Chapter 8 explores how these women reacted when the dominant political discourse defined their resistance activity in unmistakably political terms. However, it is to the credit of the communist party that they succeeded in developing structures to mobilize women, and that, through them, women were able to participate in what Patricia Gurin and Louise Tilly have called 'protopolitical' activities: making direct appeals to the authorities, enabling them to acquire organizational skills and networks of relationships, and, perhaps most importantly, to gain a consciousness of their collective situation.[107] The extent to which the UFF was able to keep a following is also taken up in Chapter 8.

107. Louise A. Tilly and Patricia Gurin, *Women, Politics, and Change* (New York, 1990), p. 7.

Conclusion to Part One

The evidence collected here demonstrates that indeed women in France, as in other parts of Europe, found that the war offered them a complex combination of both opportunities and constraints, and brought numerous changes, negative as well as positive, to their lives. It is possible when discussing this kind of research to appear to be presenting a descriptive catalogue of women's activity. This is largely because the sources do not allow us to be more precise and because the material collected here is drawn from a number of different sources. However, the existing evidence has served to highlight the immense variety of women's situations. It has shown up the various different patterns of behaviour and the complexity of their lives in wartime conditions. It serves to caution us, as historians, against making sweeping judgments about how people experienced the war. These chapters have shown how women were subject to numerous, often conflicting, complex pressures and constraints which influenced the choices they faced and the decisions they made.

Involvement with the local community was sometimes a further factor which could determine the way women behaved. The kind of collective conformity that existed in villages and rural communities might influence the behaviour of men and women alike, although there was a greater percentage of women present at this time. Thus, some villages would swing one way or the other, and it became more likely that all villagers would comply since it was the 'right' thing to be seen to be doing, saying and thinking. Within villages women were normally sensitive to how their behaviour was perceived by their neighbours. This could often have a restraining influence and might mean, for example, that women were less likely to want to be seen with Germans. The example of the Ile de Sein is very interesting in this context. The men on the island left *en masse* to join de Gaulle in London and their women were all more or less obliged to fall into line with the anti-German position.[1]

Vichy ideology towards women, both in terms of their employment policies and their prescribed role for women, indicates that the state took on an extremely paternalistic relationship to women, but their policies were unable to survive in the face of German demands and wartime economic forces. This ideology had much more to do with a reactionary government attempting to pass off right-wing measures than any practical application to the situation in France. Women may have been influenced by these policies to some degree, and this remains difficult to evaluate, but their lives were more likely to be governed by their personal socio-economic situation, their age, the presence or absence of their husbands and whether they had children or other dependants, as well as by regional factors.

Everyday survival became more difficult and time-consuming for everyone during the war and this was an extra burden that was often taken on by women, who were forced to develop strategies to deal with it. This might often bring them into contact with the authorities and at times lead them to question the situation in which they found themselves and even possibly influence them to take action. Indeed, politically, women were involved in activities which have been defined as collaborative or resistant and in ways which often differed from those of men. Women might have been brought into these positions because of their family and social positions, but women also made choices of their own volition about where their allegiances lay and what benefits they stood to gain from their situation. A number of pre-Resistance and pre-collaboration structures also emerged, serving to push or pull women in certain directions. Because of their relative independence in the absence of husbands, women found themselves in the unusual situation of having responsibility for deciding what to do, although many were affected by numerous constraints.

As far as activism is concerned, the evidence shows that for both collaboration and resistance gendered traits can be recognized. Women were likely to become involved in the more spontaneous, unorganized activities which could more easily be combined with the concerns of their everyday lives. Women might be present as members of collaborationist groups and involved in Resistance networks, but they were present in smaller numbers than men.

1. Interview, Madame Katherine (Finistère).

In fact, paradoxically, the evidence suggests that during the Occupation, the unprecedented merging of public and private which took place brought politics explicitly into women's lives and provided them with an almost unique opportunity to act politically, whether it was by entertaining a German officer or hiding a Jewish family. One woman described her experience of the Occupation thus:

> Women during the Occupation started to find their freedom. Whether they moved towards the Occupier or towards the Resistance, they started to say, I am doing that, I like it. Whereas before, they had been made to be much more submissive by society, the Occupation created a world where women could choose for themselves how they wanted to live their lives.[2]

The experience of all women can certainly not be based on the interpretation of this one witness, but the evidence collected here seems to support the hypothesis that the Occupation forced some women to make choices, organize their lives and gain access to the workplace. They behaved in ways that can retrospectively be seen as political, although the political nature of what they did was not always apparent to women at the time. The events of the purges and the re-establishment of the peace also suggest that men recognized that women had experienced a measure of newfound independence, be it political or otherwise, which was somewhat threatening to them and which in any case could not be allowed to continue. The second part of the book deals with the immediate postwar years and explores how women experienced the purges and analyses whether the Liberation and the end of the war brought any real change to their lives. It also shows the extent to which women's experience of making 'political' choices during the Occupation was carried into the postwar period when they were newly equipped with the right to vote.

2. Interview, Madame Sandrine (Toulouse).

PART TWO

Women's Lives after the Occupation,
1944–48: A Liberation?

CHAPTER SIX

Women and the Purges

As the Liberation approached, members of the *milice*, the PPF and their families, and others who had been closely associated with the Germans became aware that they were in danger. Some left with the German convoys, finding work and accommodation in Germany where they remained until the end of the war. Others tried to escape to Spain over the Pyrénées or to Switzerland. Most ultimately ended up in the courts on their return, and many of those accused of serious crimes were sentenced in their absence (*par contumace*).

The departure of the Germans and the arrival of the FFI or Allied troops was seen as cause for celebration across the country. People took to the streets with French flags and met in the main central squares to celebrate their newly-found freedom. At the same time, a wave of reprisals against those who had helped the Germans began almost immediately. The initial spontaneous movement, which became known as the 'wild purges' (*l'épuration sauvage*), was violent and motivated by revenge. Almost as soon as the prisons were emptied of Resisters, they were filled again with collaborators. Young men, often last-minute additions to the ranks of the Resistance, supposedly FFI, wandered around the towns and the countryside brandishing rifles, anxious to find victims to help prove their allegiance to the cause of Resistance. Arrest centres were established and in a matter of days the tables had been turned; the hunters became the hunted. Some of those who had helped the Germans and who had been directly implicated in battles that had taken place not long before lost their lives. From as early as July 1944, special military tribunals and courts martial were established particularly in areas where there was an intense *maquis* presence. Although these did not always have proper jurisdiction, they tried renowned collaborators on a local level. Many passed and carried out a series of death sentences.

Some of those executed were women. Commentators agree that there were considerable variations in the way collaborators were treated in the courts both over time and geographically. As Rousso has pointed out, regional differences could depend on factors like the presence or absence of *maquis* or Allied armies, the experiences of local populations during the war, and the extent of persecutions and massacres in specific areas.[1] Head-shaving was another aspect of the 'wild purges' which was designed to punish women who were thought to be guilty of 'horizontal collaboration'.

In the mean time, the provisional government organized structures designed to bring the 'wild purges' under control and to try those members of the population who were considered to be guilty of acts of collaboration. On 26 June 1944, a law had established Courts of Justice (*Cours de Justice*). These were designed to prevent hearings in the military tribunals, attempting to implement a uniform approach both to the definition of the crimes involved and to the sentencing of them. A magistrate sat in these courts accompanied by four jurors chosen by the departmental Liberation committee (CDL) from citizens who were considered to have 'proved their national sentiments'. These courts remained in session until 31 January 1951 and dealt with the most serious crimes associated with collaboration: crimes which indicated an active, conscious, military or economic involvement on the side of the Occupier, including belonging to the *milice*, LVF, Waffen SS or armed sections against the Resistance.[2] Those accused of political collaboration, who had been involved in activities which aided the Occupier, including denunciation and belonging to collaborationist groups, or who had participated in economic collaboration, a definition which encompassed all commerce with the enemy as well as voluntarily going to work in Germany, could be sanctioned with death sentences, forced labour, and prison, often combined with the confiscation of property and the payment of fines.

On 28 August 1944, a further law was passed to deal with what were seen as the less serious forms of collaboration, but which nonetheless needed to be sanctioned. Civic courts (*chambres civiques*) were established to judge whether individuals had behaved unpatriotically by displaying patterns of behaviour which indicated that they had been involved with the Vichy regime or, more importantly, supportive of the Germans. These people were not seen as having

1. Henri Rousso, 'L'Epuration en France, une histoire inachevée', *Vingtième Siècle* (Jan.–Mar. 1992), p. 81.
2. Ibid., p. 87.

committed a crime in the legal sense, but, if found guilty, were often fined and punished by being excluded from the workings of the nation through being deprived of their civic rights so that they could not vote or stand for election for the duration of their sentence. This punishment, known as *dégradation nationale*, also accompanied most of the more serious sentences passed in the Courts of Justice. Guilty parties were also often deprived of residence rights which meant that they were forced to move house. Those who had been members of pro-Pétain or pro-German organizations appeared in these civic courts, which had to evaluate the extent to which individuals had been involved in the different groups. Those who were discovered to have collaborated on a more serious level could then be referred on to the Courts of Justice.

In parallel, a series of purge committees (*commissions d'épuration*) were established to inspect the behaviour of people in various professions. Government administrations, for example, established their own committees to purge their offices of bureaucrats who were thought to have worked against the Resistance. However, the committees very quickly came up against the problem that some continuity of personnel was necessary to ensure the functioning of the state, and in this context allowances had to be made. Further committees were established to deal with economic collaboration to try those who had made illicit profits out of the Occupation. These committees were composed of senior and middle management, workers and state representatives, presided over by a magistrate.[3] They could deliver sentences of professional exclusion or deprive individuals of their civic rights in cases where they had not already been sanctioned in other courts. Sentencing could often depend on the personality of individual judges and the atmosphere of the times. After the return of the deportees, when the true nature of their experiences was revealed, collaborators tended to be treated much more harshly. Furthermore, many of those who had returned were then able to testify in person as witnesses against certain individuals.

Despite extensive historical debate about the exact figures involved, Rousso estimates that the purges (both 'wild' and 'legal') between them led to about 10,000 deaths, of which 8,000–9,000 were 'illegal' and 1,600 were carried out as the result of court sentences.[4] The number of dossiers sent to the Courts of Justice was 311,263, of which 124,613 were judged and 76.5 per cent given sentences: 44,000 went to prison, more than 55,000 people lost their civic rights and

---

between 22,000 and 28,000 state employees were sanctioned. Generally speaking, the punishments became less severe with time as the cases dragged on into the late 1940s. Most of those who were sentenced in 1944–48 were amnestied by de Gaulle in the 1950s.

Women were affected by the purges but not always in the same ways and to the same degree as men. Leclerc and Wending estimate that 20–30 per cent of those executed were women.[5] In Toulouse, for example, a 17-year-old girl who had been the mistress of the head of the local Gestapo had her head shaved, was paraded around the town with swastikas drawn on her chest and back and was later executed. These early executions were part of the 'wild purges'. Many women had their heads shaved, and those thought to be guilty of crimes related to collaboration were brought to appear in the courts, where they then had to undergo thorough and intimate public exposure of their lives. Judges in the courts and purge commissions were set up as moral arbiters in an atmosphere of moral collapse and a thirst for revenge. Thus, at the same time as women were gaining the right to vote, they were also being shown that their behaviour could have severe and damaging consequences for them should they have chosen the 'wrong' side. This chapter will argue that although the purges punished suspected collaborators of both sexes, they were also used as a way for men to express disapproval of women's wartime behaviour in a particularly gender-specific way. Women had to be made to understand that in cases where they had transgressed traditional gender roles, roles which had to some extent been extended and redefined by the war, as was shown in Part One, they now had to return to the home and re-embrace the accepted prewar notions of what they should do and how they should behave.

Femmes tondues

The image of a woman with her head shaved or shorn is a lasting and pervasive memory of the events of the Liberation in France for most French people.[6] The extent of head-shaving, which served to

5. Françoise Leclerc and Michèle Wending, 'La Répression des femmes coupables de la collaboration', in Françoise Thébaud (ed.), *Clio: histoire, femmes et sociétés, résistances et libérations* (Toulouse, 1995), p. 132.

6. For film see 'Le Chagrin et la pitié'; for photos see Alain Brossat, *Les Tondues: un carnaval moche* (Paris, 1992), p. 192; Corran Laurens, 'La Femme au turban: les femmes tondues', in H.R. Kedward and N. Wood (eds), *The Liberation of France: Image and Event* (London, 1995), pp. 159–73.

project women who had previously been more or less hidden from public view onto the centre of the public stage, was unforeseen. This chapter will show that head-shaving was an extremely complex phenomenon, loaded with a symbolic importance which functioned on several levels and that there were a number of interrelated reasons why it took place.

Almost as soon as the Germans moved out, and sometimes even before (there were instances as early as March 1944), a movement of head-shaving swept the country. Fabrice Virgili has found examples in most departments of France, as much in large towns as in rural areas.[7] Burrin puts the number of women affected at 100,000–300,000 and suggests that it was more widespread in rural areas where personal relations were more visible and little of what had happened during the Occupation was forgotten in the heated weeks of the Liberation.[8] The way the shearings were conducted tended to vary and the procedure could take on a more or less organized pattern. Most commonly, shearings took place in an outdoor public space, in town squares or market-places, often involving more than one woman at a time. Once their hair was cut off, women were undressed and marched around the locality or paraded on carts. Swastikas were sometimes painted on their chests and backs. The reactions of the crowd could be extreme and based on little evidence. Anger, frustration and a need to find a scapegoat might be vented on women who had very little observable contact with Germans, as the following witness described:

> I knew a woman in this area who made funeral wreaths. She worked near to the window for the light. Not far from her house there was a German post which patrolled the crossroads. One of these men went to speak to her in the evening, he stayed outside talking to her, he never went indoors. At the Liberation there was a furious crowd who went to this poor woman's house. They made her come out, they hit her, they knocked her down, they undressed her and they shaved her head. Then, they dragged her round the roads around the area with her daughter behind her who must have been about 14. Then, when they had had enough, she went home and did not dare to come out for weeks.[9]

Frequently, as in the above example, the women concerned were those who had had some direct involvement with the Germans

7. Fabrice Virgili, 'Les "Tondues" à la Libération: le corps des femmes, enjeu d'une réappropriation', in Thébaud (ed.), *Clio*, pp. 113–14.
8. Philippe Burrin, *La France à l'heure allemande 1940–1944* (Paris, 1995), p. 213.
9. Interview, Monsieur Alexandre (Toulouse).

and/or who were suspected of sexual collaboration. They could be prostitutes, women who had worked for the Germans, in France or in Germany, or the wives, daughters and sisters of those involved in the extreme collaboration groups like the *milice*. Women who were well dressed or who appeared to be well fed were easy targets at a time when food and clothing were so hard to come by. Jealousies and personal rivalries also played an important part. Although head-shaving normally involved women, this was not exclusively the case. Virgili has found evidence in seven departments of men whose heads were shaved, but male shearing was very rare by comparison with the number of women whose heads were shaved.[10]

The practice of shearing as a way of punishing women for sexual infidelity was not unprecedented: it was the traditional punishment for adulterous women. It was a symbolic act which forced repentance for past acts, and prisoners had their heads shaved before being guillotined. Shaving women's heads was therefore a symbolic process of purification dating back to the Bible, which attributed purifying virtues to it. Heretics whose heads were shaved underwent a kind of symbolic bereavement which after its completion offered them a new existence, making it possible for them to marry a Christian and start a new life.[11] Head-shaving was also designed to target the woman sinner who had sinned through seduction. For example, it is said that Marguerite de Bourgogne, Queen of France from 1290 to 1315, was shorn as an adulteress, repudiated and strangled on the orders of Louis X (although this may well be a myth).[12] This punishment was also adopted in the twentieth century. French women who consorted with the Germans in 1918 had their heads shaved, and during the Occupation of the Rhineland by French soldiers in the 1930s, German women's heads were shaved for sleeping with French soldiers. From 1940, the Nazi party shaved women's heads in public if they were found to have had relationships with foreign workers.[13] Thus, the shaving of women's heads in 1944 had a deep-rooted symbolic precedent.

In 1944, there was no law or national appeal from the government to shear women suspected of collaboration.[14] In some areas it was decreed by Resistance chiefs, or the local *Commissaire de la*

10. Fabrice Virgili, 'Les Tontes de la Libération en France', in François Rouquet and Danièle Voldman (eds), *Les Cahiers de l'IHTP*, 31 (1995), p. 65.

11. Yannick Ripa, 'La Tonte purificatrice des républicaines pendant la guerre civile espagnole', in Rouquet and Voldman (eds), *Les Cahiers de l'IHTP*, p. 44.

12. Lorrans, 'La Femme au turban', p. 156.

13. Burrin, *La France à l'heure allemande*, p. 212.

14. Virgili, 'Les Tontes de la Libération', p. 59.

République. The Departmental Liberation committee (CDL) in the Pyrénées-Orientales, for example, reminded the Prefect on 10 November 1944 of their decision to shear the heads of women involved in intimate relationships with Germans. Fortnightly medical visits were also imposed on them as if they were prostitutes.[15] Henri Rousso cites another example where head-shaving was organized with the agreement of the legal authorities. In Montpellier, at an FFI meeting, it was decided that 'women who had slept with Germans would be taken to the prostitution department; they would have their heads shaved and be given a card after being checked for venereal disease'.[16] Luc Capdevila also found that in Brittany head-shaving was not spontaneous but was orchestrated by the Resistance milieu, backed up by the state's anti-venereal disease controls.[17] Thus head-shaving was largely an initiative which originated with the Resistance authorities, and women who were suspected of 'horizontal collaboration' were immediately equated with prostitutes and treated accordingly.

In some circumstances, the local hairdresser might have been called upon to carry out the practice. However, most of those responsible for shearing were men, often young *maquisards* who were anxious to prove their allegiance to the Resistance. One witness suggested that:

> There were those who did it out of personal revenge, a large number of them . . . and those who wanted to cleanse themselves politically, who had reasons for reproaching themselves, who had had more or less collaborationist relations and shaved the heads of other women in order to prove that they were patriots.[18]

However, men were not always so keen to carry out the procedure, and in one village in the Pyrénées 'the heads of several women were shaved but a number of men refused to take the scissors, in the end a Spanish FFI took charge'.[19]

It was not unknown for women to shave the heads of other women. For the women of the *Union des Femmes Françaises* in Indre it was seen as a way of redressing the balance against those women who had escaped suffering during the war. They described 25 August 1944 as

15. Danielle Costa and Jocelyne Joussemet, 'Femmes des Pyrénées Orientales', unpublished Mémoire de Maîtrise (University of Toulouse, 1981), p. 150.

16. Rousso, 'L'Epuration', p. 84.

17. Luc Capdevila, 'La "Collaboration sentimentale": antipatriotisme ou sexualité hors-normes?', in Rouquet and Voldman (eds), *Les Cahiers de l'IHTP*, p. 81.

18. Interview, Madame Antoinette (Toulouse).

19. Costa and Joussemet, 'Femmes des Pyrénées Orientales', p. 156.

a jubilant day in Châteauroux, a day when women had their revenge. The lovely hair of some women was lost to them. So much the better, now it's their turn to tremble . . . the schemes of these miserable and infamous creatures, dishonoured and corrupted by the enemy, represented a challenge to the sacrifice tolerated by French women.[20]

On the other hand, oral sources have brought to light some rather different evidence about this issue. The behaviour of the women of Châteaulin (Finistère) offers an interesting example of female solidarity.[21] In reaction to the head-shaving of two of the women in the town, the entire female population decided to wear headscarves for the time that it took for the shaved heads of the women to regrow. It is evidently difficult to generalize from this one incident and I have not come across evidence that this happened elsewhere, but it does indicate the presence of a very strong feeling that head-shaving was unjust. Those women who donned the headscarves felt that the singling out of the two individuals concerned was arbitrary; it could just have easily been any of them. Women certainly tended to express disapproval of head-shaving as an extremely personal and violent attack; many also articulated the feeling that the punishment was more severe than the crime. Madame Delphine, for example, who was asked to join her factory Liberation committee at Dewoitine in Toulouse, explained that when it was discussed at a meeting, 'I tried to avoid the shaving of women's heads. As a woman I felt that we had to try and preserve a woman's dignity. If you had been in Germany, I told them, you would have done the same thing.'[22] Indeed, it is known that many men did become involved with local German women: some even married and stayed on in Germany after the war.[23] Thus, women who had slept with Germans provoked intense public anger whereas male prisoners-of-war, who were in a parallel but not identical situation, and who had consorted with German women in Germany, were not condemned as being collaborators upon their return some months later. Indeed, their arrival seems to have passed without any particular public interest. In June 1945, the female UFF delegate to the Toulouse local council asked: 'What position should the municipality take towards a French

20. Virgili, 'Les Tontes de la Libération', p. 60.
21. Interview, Madame Anna (Finistère).
22. Interview, Madame Delphine (Toulouse).
23. Azéma puts figures at 10,000 out of one-and-a-quarter million who elected to stay in Germany; Richard Cobb, *French and Germans, Germans and French: A Personal Interpretation of France and Two Occupations, 1914–1918/1940–1944* (Hanover, 1983), p. 66.

prisoner-of-war who returns accompanied by his German wife and child?' The committee responded without any interest whatsoever.[24] This suggests that head-shaving went beyond straight punishment. Not only were women victims of ingrained double standards, but they were also punished less for the actual crime they committed, in so far as there was a crime, and more for supposedly enjoying themselves at a time when, at worst, people were risking their lives and, at best, experiencing privation, separation and struggling to survive. Admittedly, there is also a difference between sleeping with the enemy on enemy soil, and consorting with them when your country is being invaded. However, women did undergo a gender-specific punishment which was largely imposed on them by men.

Furthermore, the physical nature of head-shaving was certainly an attempt to adapt the punishment to the crime. It was a way of attacking women's very sexual and seductive being. The female body was the location of the crime and it was this body which had to be punished, to be de-sexed (as Fabrice Virgili puts it).[25]

> It has to be said that if women's heads were shaved, men's were not, and this seems typical of the attitude the population had towards women, which is, I won't say as a sex object as that is not the language of the time, but the image of a seductive woman who had to be punished for what she represented for men, moreover to be punished publicly and humiliatingly.[26]

Indeed, the true horror of this punishment inflicted on women is difficult to comprehend. French women who experienced it will not speak of it openly, whereas Spanish Republican women whose heads were shaved by the Phalangists during the Spanish Civil War are able to discuss it more acceptably. Their testimonies indicate that losing their hair was the worst punishment to endure, worse even than rape, because if raped they could feel hatred towards someone, an individual with a face. But when their heads were sheared, they explained, there was only their own face to hate, and they were forced to confront their own shame.[27]

A long-standing interpretation of head-shearing has been that women were targeted because the population needed to find scapegoats who would take the blame and expiate the war from the

24. ADHG 1867/102, Délibérations CDL.
25. Virgili, 'Les "Tondues" à la Libération', pp. 119–20.
26. Intervention by Hélène Augot, Rolande Trempé (ed.), *La Libération dans le Midi de la France* (Toulouse, 1986), p. 400.
27. Ripa, 'La Tonte purificatrice des républicaines', p. 51.

community, allowing everyone to move into a phase of reconstruction and start to put the war behind them. Peter Novick suggests that women whose heads were shaved saved *miliciens* and other collaborators who would have died if these women had not served to appease the crowds.[28] The same position is taken by Lottman, who argues that without head-shaving there would have been worse anger and more blood might have been spilt.[29] According to this interpretation, shaved women symbolically represented the nation and thereby served to bear the brunt of all the collaborationist crimes, allowing the country to move towards retrieving its unity.[30] The public nature of the shearing ceremonies allowed everyone to participate directly in this process. Many could use these occasions to provide evidence of their allegiance to the Liberation and assert their position of support for those who were taking power. The parading of women in the streets also acted as a way of reappropriating public space which had been taken over by the Vichy regime and the Germans with their propaganda posters and posted commands to the population.[31]

As has already been seen, women who were thought to have been involved with the Germans were directly equated with prostitutes and head-shaving was therefore part of the cleansing process they had to undergo. Women were physically contaminated by their involvement with the Germans, and the process of shearing their hair served to 'decontaminate' them in an explicit way as if after an epidemic. The shaved head therefore became, Virgili argues, a 'positive' image of the purges, and the cutting of hair became a hygienic measure, necessary to clean up the country.[32] In this way, the country was symbolically cleansed of collaboration. By losing their hair, women became ugly and were thus excluded from the community. The concern of those involved was to destroy the image of the women who were seen to have collaborated, without actually destroying the image of a people liberating itself or occluding the importance of women's contribution to the Liberation through their part in the Resistance. (François Rouquet has described how some women teachers who were threatened with shearing took shelter in the local school.[33] It was as if, he suggests, the Republican legality represented by the

28. Peter Novick, *L'Epuration Française, 1944–1949* (Paris, 1985), p. 123.
29. Herbert Lottman, *L'Epuration 1943–1953* (Paris, 1986), p. 93.
30. Virgili, 'Les "Tondues" à la Libération', p. 126.
31. Virgili, 'Les Tontes de la Libération', p. 62.
32. Virgili, 'Les "Tondues" à la Libération', pp. 124–5.
33. François Rouquet, *L'Epuration dans l'administration* (Paris, 1994), p. 135.

school would discourage unreasonable purgers, one of whom waited at the school gates for several hours. For the women, their identification with the school may also have been an attempt to shake off the association with prostitution.)

A further level of interpretation is related to male sexual insecurity. During the Occupation, women had not hesitated to express their sexuality freely by choosing partners among the Germans. This, argues Mike Kelly, made French men feel emasculated. He maintains that masculine identity was one of the areas of French life which was most damaged by the war. The humiliation of the defeat, the failure of the men to defend France and protect their women and children, plunged French manhood into crisis. The fact that women had played a significant part in the economic activity of the country during the war, and were also involved in the Resistance, only served to compound the problem. Kelly sees the shearings as one of the ways that men were able to exorcize these feelings.[34]

I would argue that this interpretation could be taken a step further. By victimizing some women, men were endeavouring to reassert their dominance and control over them. Women had to be made to realize that the male patriarchal order was being re-established.[35] Hair was seen as the symbol of an active feminine sensuality, an instrument of seduction and therefore an element of power for women.[36] Raymond Frith has shown that cutting hair was a means of social control and that 'the loss of hair represented the destruction of personality, a lowering of status, a reduction of the individual to order in the name of a collectivity'.[37] Therefore, by depriving women of their hair, they were also being forced under the power of the men.

Thus, head-shearing episodes can be seen as a central part of the transition that France was undergoing in the Liberation period. They carried a powerful symbolic message, warning women that they should revert to their pre-established patriarchally defined roles. The public nature and the extensive presence of the image of women with shaved heads, widely reported in the newspapers, served to remind women that any diversion from their prescribed role could have serious and unpleasant consequences. The less frequent shaving of men, on the other hand, was probably not loaded with the

34. Mike Kelly, 'The Reconstruction of Masculinity at the Liberation', in Kedward and Wood (eds), *The Liberation of France*, pp. 117–19.

35. See also Laurens, 'La Femme au turban'.

36. Raymond Frith, *Symbols, Public and Private* (London, 1973), pp. 289–91.

37. Ibid., p. 291.

same symbolic significance, and was designed more to humiliate the men by assimilating them with head-shaved women.

Women in prison and in camps

Many of these women with shaved heads soon found themselves in prison or in one of the nearby internment camps, especially if they were suspected of other collaboration activities. In some cases, women were allowed to return home after the shearing but were soon re-arrested. Male and female collaboration suspects were normally taken to their local prison, or to local internment camps where they were often held for some weeks, even months, while they awaited trial. The authorities seem to have engaged in a kind of panic arrest in an attempt to respond to a popular need for alleged collaborators to be seen to be arrested during the 'wild purges'. Officials in both the Finistère and the Haute-Garonne testify that they did not always know why internees had been arrested and it took many weeks, sometimes months, for the administrators to work through the documentation related to the various cases. One member of the Toulouse Liberation committee pointed out on 12 September 1944 that in the camp of Noé near to Toulouse, there were 'women with shaved heads, members of the *milice* and poor souls who had been arrested for reasons that nobody really knew'.[38] If Berthe A.'s account of her experiences in Noé is to be believed, those in charge were overwhelmed by the number of arrests. One guard complained, 'It cannot go on . . . they have arrested far too many people. At least 70 per cent of those detained are going to have to be released.'[39] The Commissioner of Police at Drancy wrote in his report dated 9 October 1944, that after having been in post for 10 days: 'I found there were 3,500 people being held with no dossier, that is to say, no document proving any charges. . . . If these reports do not exist, it would seem that for the most part, the men who arrested them did so with no understanding of why.'[40]

One of the arguments offered by the authorities was that the individuals needed to be protected during the period of uncontrolled revenge attacks and purges that could turn very violent and nasty.[41] Bertaux, who was *Commissaire de la République* in Toulouse, declared that he saved the lives of thousands of people by putting

38. ADHG 1945/159, Délibérations CDL, 12 Sept. 1944.
39. AMT 4/1988 422–428 Berthe A., Unpublished diary, 'Ma Prison', p. 18.
40. ALP 1027W Art. 13 Libération.
41. Jean-Pierre Rioux, *La France de la 4e République* (Paris, 1980), p. 55.

them in prison or by holding them in camps and thereby protecting them from public anger.[42] This seems convincing, particularly since others have confirmed the protective role played by the camps.[43]

However, when questions were asked about the presence of certain individuals in the camps, the police were anxious to justify their internment. The records on women held in Noé, for example, show that most were suspected of collaboration with the Germans.[44] One report explained: 'This woman left to work in Germany as a volunteer and as soon as she returned to France, she formed relations with the Germans. Furthermore, she gave members of the *Wehrmacht* French lessons.' And another: 'it seems that Mlle B. did not avoid compromising herself with the Germans, to the contrary, perhaps her attitude was not such that she sought to harm the country, or the Resistance, but it is nonetheless true that she did not have the attitude that a true patriot should have . . . these precise grounds justify her provisional internment.'[45] Berthe A. described the human microcosm of her co-internees in hut 84, where she spent some of her time. 'They ranged from the aristocrat to the prostitute, and included the factory worker, the office worker, and the bourgeois; from the young girl to the 50-year-old woman.'[46]

After the surrender of Germany, and the return of French nationals who were found on German soil, further numbers were added to those interned. From May 1945, as French workers returned from Germany they were automatically put into the camps unless they were carrying cards handed out by the Allies which proved that they had been deported. Needless to say, many tried to pass themselves off as deportees. In the Finistère, for example, internment camps became overcrowded after the arrest of women workers returning from employment in Germany. In one camp, at Pont-du-Buis, the female population rose from 25 on 15 June 1945, to 87 on 13 July. To deal with this dramatic increase in numbers, women were transferred into the men's compound as this was larger, and three supplementary female wardens had to be recruited.[47]

42. Pierre Bertaux, *La Libération de Toulouse et sa région* (Paris, 1973).

43. Charles Louis Foulon, *Le Pouvoir en Province à la Libération: les commissaires de la République* (Paris, 1975), p. 140.

44. Eric Malo, 'De Vichy à la Quatrième République: le camp de Noé (1943–45)', *Les Annales du Midi*, 199–200 (July–Dec. 1992), p. 451.

45. ADHG 1831/44, Epuration, Oct. 1944.

46. AMT, Berthe A., Unpublished diary, 'Mes Barbèles', p. 242.

47. ADF 31W313; see also Karen Adler, 'Reading National Identity: Gender and "Prostitution" during the Occupation', in Hanna Diamond and Claire Gorrara (eds), *Modern and Contemporary France, Special Issue: Gendering the Occupation of France* (Feb. 1999), pp. 47–57.

Women were numerous among those detained under suspicion of various forms of collaboration, both because they were suspected of collaboration in their own right, and because of the activities of family members. Thus, in the camps, women who had been seen with the Germans mingled with the wives, sisters and mothers of male members of the various collaborationist groups, many of whom could not be found because they had gone into hiding or had left with the Germans. One account explained:

> They stopped women whose role in the *milice* was just a charitable one, looking after the sick, organizing soup kitchens, crèches and nurseries. They arrested women whose fathers, sons, husbands or brothers were on the run, to get them to denounce where they were hidden.[48]

German women who had come to France during the Occupation and who had not managed to leave in time were also put in these camps.[49]

The large numbers involved posed problems of food supply, hygiene and accommodation for the authorities. The men's and women's quarters had to be patrolled in order to keep them separate, but officials often complained about what they described as 'poor moral conditions' in the camps.[50] Numerous reports recount problems with control of disease, lack of adequate water supplies for people to wash and keep their living areas clean, and lack of heating arrangements. Despite a general awareness that conditions were bad, there was a reluctance to make a public case drawing attention to the plight of internees, as the popular mood was against them. The prevailing view was that after their wartime behaviour, they deserved whatever treatment they received in the camps or prisons. The *Front National* (a communist-organized Resistance grouping) and the UFF came together to draw up a petition against the lax treatment afforded to those held in Drancy in 1944.

> This petition is to protest against the unjust and scandalously comfortable lot allocated to collaborators and others now interned in Drancy. We energetically call for them to suffer the material and moral life conditions established by former hosts at Drancy and all other prisons where their victims were interned.[51] [There followed 16 pages of signatures.]

48. Fabienne Freyssinnet, *Quatre saisons sous les geôles de la Quatrième République* (Monte Carlo, 1953), p. 20.
49. AN F7 14968 Inspections Générales des Camps d'Internement, Oct. 1944–Jan. 1946.
50. Ibid.   51. ALP Conseil de Paris, 1027W Art. 13 Libération.

There is no evidence to suggest that women were treated in any way that was particularly different from the men in the camps. Those whose heads had been shaved underwent discrimination from other internees. 'Women with shaved heads were not allowed to wear a turban, and all the other young people there laughed at them.'[52] There is no doubt however, that women had the disadvantage of being expected to pay for the misdeeds of their male family members, and it seems that they were not always deserving of this treatment. Many of those women who found themselves in internment camps in 1944 often remained there for many months, sometimes as long as a year, and then, when their case was finally heard, accusations against them might well be found to be ungrounded. Freyssinnet recounts the example of two primary school teachers who were sent to the camp of Noé because they were supposed to have encouraged the children in the school to salute Germans in the street. There were never any Germans in their village.[53] Berthe A. spent nearly a year in Noé only to be told at her trial that there were no accusations against her. Some judges doubtless took these long periods of waiting in camps or prison into consideration when sentences were passed, and despite the fact that most internees tried to avoid a court appearance, most were eventually called to court where their cases were heard in front of a judge and jury.

Women in court

Women who were accused of collaboration-related behaviour appeared in the courts, though in fewer numbers than men. The documentation relating to the postwar collaboration trials suggests, however, that women were treated rather differently from men. The main focus of discussions in court, whatever the accusations involved, tended to be on the moral behaviour of the women as compared with the men. Furthermore, sexual collaboration was a 'crime' which only concerned women, and each court set its own barometer as to how it should be sanctioned.[54] In some areas of France it was defined as punishable in itself, whereas other courts used alternative, less direct ways of punishing this crime. Thus some courts defined it as a crime of intelligence with the enemy, punishable with sentences of forced labour and imprisonment, whereas

---

52. AMT, Berthe A., Unpublished diary, 'Mes Barbèles', p. 62.
53. Freyssinnet, *Quatre saisons dans les géoles*, p. 119.
54. Leclerc and Wending, 'La Répression des femmes', pp. 137–9.

others only saw fit to deprive women found guilty of their civic rights. Luc Capdevila's study of women who were condemned for sexual collaboration in Lorient is fascinating in this context. He describes how the judge literally 'created' a crime of 'sentimental collaboration' when in most other areas of France women were charged under other counts such as the denunciation of patriots, the traffic of foodstuffs, acts of betrayal or economic collaboration.[55] Legally speaking, sexual collaboration in itself was not enough to condemn women, but the accusation often served to aggravate or reinforce other charges of behaviour perceived as anti-national. In Capdevila's case study of women in the Lorient, many worked for the Germans as well as being mistresses to them, but their professional activities, most of which corresponded to a form of economic collaboration, were put in second place to their sexual activities, which were seen to have been their 'real' crime.[56]

Many of those who found themselves in the courts or in front of purge commissions were there on the basis of a denunciation, and this tended to weigh particularly heavily against women. Evidence presented in court was often a police report put together from interviews with the friends and neighbours of the accused who had been asked to comment on the 'moral behaviour' of the women. In the Finistère, the authorities concluded that:

> Nothing has been as difficult to judge as the trials in the civic courts because of the absence of established facts. The members of the jury have found themselves divided between fear of believing false accusations made through revenge or based on appearances, and the fear of allowing themselves to be influenced by the enormous number of accounts given in the interests of their defence through friendship or fear.[57]

Giacomina E., for example, was sentenced to 6 months in prison with a 20,000 fr fine for passing on intelligence to the enemy in the form of denunciation. Her lawyer attempted to argue that it was really 'a woman's quarrel between tenant and landlord, the origin of which lay in eviction procedures'. But the police report gave a rather different picture:

> According to information collected in the neighbourhood, it seems she had Germans in her home and appeared to revel in their company. She eulogized German soldiers and criticized American

55. Capdevila, 'La "Collaboration sentimentale"', pp. 68–9.
56. Ibid., p. 75.   57. ADF 31W313, Epuration.

troops. She is badly thought of by her entourage, known as a nasty woman always looking for trouble with her tenants even for the most futile of reasons and is considered to have collaborated during the Occupation.[58]

On the other hand, Renée P., a chambermaid, was accused of having had intimate relations with the Germans. She was said to have 'assiduously frequented German soldiers' and spent time with them in a totally carefree fashion. 'She even took them to her sister's home at all hours of the night and the neighbours frequently saw soldiers leaving the house in the early hours.' But, apart from her 'bad behaviour', no one was able to report any anti-national attitudes or denunciations, so she was acquitted.[59]

During the trials, women frequently denied accusations completely. In cases where they admitted that there was some degree of truth to accusations, special pleading was common. A frequent argument was that they joined groups because they were pushed into it by male family members, and never became involved with their activities. The courts were sometimes sympathetic to these wives who claimed that they had simply been enrolled by their husbands and attempted to deflect charges against them by arguing that they were victims of their husbands' politics. One woman made the following claim in her defence at her trial: 'My husband joined the *milice* right at the beginning of 1943. He made me a member too without asking my opinion. One day he came home and presented me with my membership card.'[60] But other witnesses at her trial saw things differently:

> Zuick affirms that the wife . . . during interviews with Stotz was even more enraged than her husband in the denunciation of patriots and members of the *maquis*. . . . this woman was one of the most active agents of the German police. I consider her husband to have been no more than a simple associate.[61]

If women who had joined groups as part of a family commitment were treated by some judges with more leniency, those who joined groups of their own volition were less well thought of. This was the experience described by Fabienne Freyssinet, who knowingly joined the *milice* and admitted it in court. In her memoirs, which are a lengthy apology for the *milice,* she explained that her membership of the *Parti Social Français* in 1936 led her naturally to join the *milice*

58. AN Z6 213, dossier 2613.   59. AN Z5 120, dossier 5615.
60. ADHG 3808/6, Cours de Justice de Toulouse, 1945, no. 2540/62.
61. Ibid.

in 1944. When her lawyer extolled her education and cultural background in her defence:

> The government Commissioner retorted that because of the cultivated milieu I had been brought up in, as well as my cultural background, I was more guilty than other women; most women who had joined the *milice* had signed in obedience to their father or their husband, or out of a sense of solidarity, whereas my membership was voluntary and thought out. As a consequence, he called for me to lose my civic rights for life, a 20 years banning order to prevent me from residing in my department and the confiscation of my property.[62]

In fact, the rest of the court did not completely agree with the judge's sentence and decided only to deprive her of her civic rights for life, abandoning the banning order and the property confiscation. She rather provocatively recounts that 'I do not have a profession which is affected by this penalty. I am therefore not bothered in the slightest, although I know that this sentence impoverished a large number of my friends by preventing them from returning to their jobs.'[63]

In some cases whole families appeared in court. In La Rochelle, for example, a case was heard where the husband was a member of the collaborationist group *Francisme* and was said to be Darnaud's right-hand man; his three sons were *miliciens* and the wife/mother had no obvious activity except that she was a member of *Francisme* like her husband. Her husband was given the death penalty, her sons sentences of five to ten years' forced labour, and she had her civic rights revoked for ten years.[64]

Another argument made by women was that a party card helped them in dealings with the Occupier.[65] 'I joined the *Légion des Combattants* because my mother insisted that I need to do so in order to obtain a good position after the war. I never went to any meetings during the year that I was a member.'[66] Even if women recognized the truth of the accusations made against them, they would come up with a number of arguments in their defence. Some claimed that they had been forced to behave in certain ways or that they had believed that they were working for the Resistance. Others tried to transfer responsibility onto the Vichy government. Berthe A., for example, argued quite convincingly that she had joined the group *Collaboration* to obey the requests of the government authorities

---

62. Freyssinnet, *Quatre saisons sous les geôles*, p. 127.   63. Ibid.
64. *Combat*, 6 Jan. 1946.   65. Burrin, *La France à l'heure allemande*, p. 437.
66. ADHG 1831/44, Epuration.

of the time and that she should not therefore be punished simply because she had done what she was told.[67]

In some cases, women attempted to justify themselves in political terms, but, as Leclerc and Wending point out, this may have been because they believed that this would minimize their responsibility rather than indicating a real political commitment. YT, aged 36, was a member of the *Jeunesses du Maréchal*, then joined the RNP and finally became an intelligence agent for the *milice*. She declared:

> I acted through political passion . . . I did not like the Germans, but after Montoire, I had the impression that we could come to an agreement with them to avoid future wars . . . I followed this political direction because it was supported by Marshal Pétain.[68]

Other women were accused of having demonstrated their political conviction by their behaviour, as this police report describes:

> after the Armistice, [Mlle X] entered the German placement office as a typist where she displayed collaborationist sentiments. She was not afraid to carry on openly in town with the Germans, talking to them in their language. . . . She was blatantly pro-German, accused of favouring deportation, not attempting to hide her affection for the Nazi regime, only having confidence in the Germans.

She joined the group *Collaboration* and came to their meetings regularly.[69]

Those accused of sexual collaboration, whether explicitly or implicitly, had the most difficulty defending themselves. When they appeared before the purge committees, women might emphasize the anti-Nazi opinions of their lover, or their Austrian rather than German origins. They did not associate themselves with a regime or a system, but described their partners as normal men who came close to those being occupied because of their situation. Some were just looking for solace in difficult times. Marguerite, for example, was not unaware of the political implications of her situation, but had no regrets: 'I considered that I had done nothing wrong in associating with the Germans. During the Occupation, I worked for the Germans and I had a German lover, but that does not prove that I was pro-German.'[70] Capdevila rightly points out similarities with Arletty's stand when she claimed when accused of having consorted

67. AMT, Berthe A., Unpublished diary, 'Mes Barbèles', p. 139.
68. Leclerc and Wending, 'La Répression des femmes', p. 146.
69. ADHG 3808/6, Cours de Justice de Toulouse, 1945, no. 2540/60.
70. Capdevila, 'La "Collaboration sentimentale"', p. 79.

with German officers that 'Mon cœur appartient à la France, mais mon cul est international'.[71]

Women who were involved in the entertainment industry were particularly susceptible to accusations of collaboration. The actresses and singers who went on tour in Germany or worked for the propagandist Radio-Paris all appeared before a commission which was designed especially to deal with them.[72] Everyone could be called to appear, from top ballerinas, actresses and opera singers to the ushers in the theatre. Obviously, those women who were in the least prestigious jobs were the most easily pushed out. Several were given six to eighteen months' unpaid suspensions. Denunciations were prolific, reflecting the professional rivalry between those in this milieu. Lawyers' defences often revolved around the impossibility of actually proving the accusations, and cases where denunciations could not be proved one way or another often ended in acquittal. Those who had been involved in musical and theatrical sessions for the collaborationist Radio-Paris had little defence, particularly if they had been well paid. Madeleine, for example, was given three months' suspension because she played on Radio-Paris 61 times and appeared in three propaganda films.[73] She explained in her defence that women's roles were insignificant, but the commission felt that she had to realize that the films had been designed to maintain or arouse French animosity towards England and that she should have had no part in them. But the commission was sensitive to the difference between the true propagandists who had written lengthy passages in support of the Germans and those who were session musicians and singers simply trying to make a living. Ninette, a solo pianist at Radio-Paris, was suspended for two years because it was felt that she had fully participated in German radio programmes without being obliged to do so.[74] Most importantly, she had also made material gains from them, and it was public knowledge that she was politically close to Laval's cabinet as she had tried to convert people to Vichy. However, she did have some extenuating circumstances in that she had enabled several musicians to escape the labour draft to Germany and had protected a number of Jews.

Judges were able to be more lenient where women could prove that they had also been involved in some way with 'patriotic acts', even if only through family relations. One actress was accused of

71. This might be loosely translated as 'My heart belongs to France, but my arse is international'.

72. See AN F21 8085–8126, Comité d'Epuration du Spectacle.

73. AN F21 8108, dossier 3.   74. AN F21 8107, dossier 2.

having been on very good terms with the Germans, but she was able to prove that while in Germany she distributed and collected a number of letters for prisoners and their wives. A member of the Prisoners-of-War association wrote in her defence explaining that 'the many letters from wives of prisoners-of-war testify to the fact that they were able to have news of their husbands, thanks to her help'.[75] The actress Arletty, who was also accused of having had relationships with Germans, demonstrated to the commission that with Sacha Guitry she had been responsible for helping a number of Jews to escape arrest.[76] Overall, the sanctions do not seem to have been too severe. Women were only sacked in extreme cases, when their dossiers were also passed on to the Courts of Justice which then conducted a more thorough examination of their behaviour.

The purging of administration also involved a considerable number of women since, as was shown in Chapter 2, women were recruited into the sector in large numbers. Once again, the recommendations of the administrative purge committee in Finistère (Quimper and Châteaulin) offer an interesting example of the moral tone adopted and the criteria used to judge women.[77] Several of those who appeared before the commission were teachers, and most were accused of having intimate relations with the enemy. Mlle C, for example,

> far from keeping her distance from the Germans, displaying the dignity one would expect from a French primary school teacher, scandalous scenes were produced daily during the holidays between a group of young teachers, of which she was one, and enemy soldiers (playing games together, swimming and sunbathing whilst engaging in intimate conversation with the Germans); these scenes took place on a very busy beach under the eyes of the local population whose indignation one can imagine. . . . The attitude of Mlle C. discredited the teaching profession in the area, stimulated protests from the population and complaints from the parents of the pupils who threatened to withdraw their children from the school.[78]

The commission recommended that she should be demoted along with three other teachers who were part of the same crowd. However, a certain Mlle S. dared to answer back to the commission explaining that the Germans were 'correct and courteous, perfect partners for games'. This attitude apparently indicated to the commission that she was unworthy to work in French education and it proposed that

75. AN F21 8109, dossier 4.   76. AN F21 8106, dossier 1.
77. ADF 31W391, 25 Aug. 1944–28 Feb. 1945.   78. Ibid.

she should immediately be dismissed without a pension. Another teacher from Concarneau was also to provoke the disapproval of the commission.

> Mlle B., although quite a good teacher, looked after the children on the beach in the company of German soldiers. She behaved very badly . . . and pushed her love of the New Order as far as introducing it into her bed by taking an officer as her lover. Considering that she has not lost any of her arrogance, despite the fact that her head has been shaved, she is to be dismissed without pension and will be arrested and questioned about her wartime activities.[79]

So it would seem that women were not only punished for their wartime behaviour, but that sentencing was often centred around their lack of remorse and failure to see the error of their ways. Generally speaking, the tone of the reports was very patronizing towards the women, although if an excuse could be found in their defence (a son in the Resistance or excessive loneliness) this counted in their favour. Some were sent to internment camps to 'teach them a lesson', some more serious cases were passed on the local Prefect. Where no solid evidence emerged or if the evidence seemed conflicting, the commission recommended a change of institution in the interests both of the individual and of the institution concerned. The commission also reinstated a number of women who had been forced to take early retirement under the Vichy laws and reviewed the case of women who had been promoted for their 'good Pétainist ideas'.

François Rouquet has conducted a detailed study of the purges in administration.[80] He found that a large number of the young women who had been taken on as auxiliaries during the war were accused of associating with or having had intimate relations with the enemy, and that there was a strong degree of bias in the way they were treated. In cases where there was some element of doubt, the extent of the attempts to establish the facts varied according to the status of the person under examination. As in the courts, the accusations could depend on the reputation of the accused, and the rumours surrounding them. In this way, women were more likely to be victims of unjust accusations and would be more seriously investigated if they were the wives or mothers of renowned political collaborators. Their sex was therefore a serious handicap, and, for Rouquet, men and women were not equal in the face of the purges.

79. Ibid.   80. Rouquet, *L'Épuration dans l'administration*.

Women, who made up a quarter of those purged, accounted for 40 per cent of the guilty verdicts. He sees this as directly related to the fact that, by 1945, the administrations were grossly overstaffed and needed to find some way of ridding themselves of the women auxiliaries who had been recruited to replace the absent men. Their sometimes dubious behaviour and attitudes gave the administrative authorities a pretext to get rid of them, and many lost their jobs subsequent to their appearance at commissions.[81]

This chapter has demonstrated the various ways that the purges explicitly affected women. Undeniably some women were collaborators and deserved to be found guilty and punished for their crimes. The evidence does however suggest that women were disadvantaged on occasion, although there were doubtless times when justice was not always fair to men as well as women. It would seem, however, that men's moral conduct was not mobilized as a subject of public scrutiny to the same degree. The sense of independence and freedom experienced by some women which was articulated at the end of the first part of the book, and which often came to light in the courts, was apparently seen to be quite threatening. Women had often demonstrated a considerable degree of initiative at a time when the men were lacking in self-esteem because they had lost the war and left their women in the hands of a foreign army. The purges can therefore be seen as part of a process used by men to try and regain their lost self-respect. Women's arguments that they should be allowed to choose their sexual partners and have the freedom to express their feelings and the use of their bodies could not have much impact in the atmosphere of the time, when these relationships were seen as shocking public statements of independence, and when, unfortunately, their partners were the enemy. In many areas of France, women may have spent time with the Germans because there were no other young men available. Nonetheless, their behaviour was almost universally taken as a demonstration of a lack of interest in 'public' affairs. Thence many were punished by being deprived of their civic rights and underwent a public exposure of their intimate lives which was designed to teach them humility. This need to ensure that women make way for the men was further articulated in the desire to exclude them from the labour market which is explored in the next chapter. As Rouquet has found in administration, women's sexual infidelity and the so-called collaboration which accompanied it was often taken as an excuse to exclude them from jobs. The desire

81. Ibid., p. 90.

for women to stay in the home was also expressed through the ongoing repression of abortion, the closing of the brothels and the emphasis placed on the importance of marriage and having children. All of these policies had some continuity with the prewar period, and were continued into the postwar period, as is discussed further in the next chapter.

CHAPTER SEVEN

Everyday Life and Paid Employment 1944–48

Despite the departure of the Germans and the drama of the events of the Liberation, women experienced little material change in terms of their daily life conditions in the immediate postwar years. For most women, the war only really ended with the return of the men and it was this, more than anything, which had the most impact on their daily lives. This chapter argues that despite the changes adopted during the war years, after the end of hostilities, for the most part, women returned to their traditional roles as wives and mothers in the home, and appear to have been happy to do so. Pressure was placed upon them both through the experience of the purges and through the measures that were passed by the postwar governments to ensure that they did indeed return to their prewar roles; however, the evidence also indicates that the situation and experience of women after the war was sometimes more complicated and nuanced than traditional interpretations suggest.

Everyday life

In the short term, apart from the obvious release from the constraints of the Occupation, the Liberation brought little change to daily life. The problems of reconstruction were acute, and locally based problems depended on the extent of the damage that had been inflicted during the Occupation and Liberation. Three inter-related problems of transport, energy and food supply preoccupied the population. The last was exacerbated by the black market and inflation, with the addition of the irritations and rivalries created by the purges. By comparison with the Occupation period, conditions were, if anything, worse rather then better. Departmental Liberation committees (CDL) took measures to try and alleviate problems of food supply as soon as they took over, but queuing and rationing remained a crucial part of people's lives. The problems of survival described in Chapter 3 continued for several years. Moreover, heightened expectations made continuing food shortages even more difficult to bear. As Georgette Elgey pointed out, 'the victory did not lift the constraints of the shortages, it just made them more difficult to put up with'.[1] The population of France was hungry. In March 1945, 70 per cent of men and 55 per cent of women had lost weight. One in three children had growth problems due to undernourishment.[2] The national figures for infant mortality were 66 per 1,000 in 1943 and went up to 100.5 per 1,000 in 1945 – figures that were worse than at any time during the Occupation.[3] Families continued to depend on the networks and relations which had been carefully built up during the war. The black market increased and barter remained a common way of obtaining food. Factories complained of high absenteeism as people took days off to search for food or dig their gardens. The situation only started to improve considerably in 1948, when food deliveries became more reliable and regular as roads, transport and communications had been repaired. By December 1948 a number of products were no longer rationed, but throughout 1950, in some areas, shops still only opened on three or four days a week. The patterns of women's everyday lives in the immediate postwar years therefore remained the same as before; housewives' lives continued to be dominated by the search for food supplies, and many hours were spent queuing and juggling the budget or the ration books.

However, there was a group of women who did experience dramatic change in their lives immediately after the Germans had left. Many of the men who were members of the FFI left their homes in the weeks after the Liberation to join the Allies at the Front when the FFI was dissolved by decree on 19 September 1944.[4] These families were therefore again disrupted and became dependent on the family benefits which were provided by the government. From 1 October 1944, wives of members of the FFI received sums according to the number of children and the military grade of their husband.[5]

1. Georgette Elgey, *La République des illusions* (Paris, 1969), p. 56.
2. Jean-Pierre Rioux, *La France de la Quatrième République. 1944–1952* (Paris, 1980), p. 32.
3. Elgey, *La République des illusions*, p. 57; also quoted in Alfred Sauvy, *La Vie economique des Français 1939–45* (Paris, 1978), p. 225.
4. Rioux, *La France de la Quatrième République*, p. 23.
5. ADHG M1940(14), CDL, Affaires économiques et sociales.

The apparent generosity of these benefits in comparison with those awarded to the wives of prisoners-of-war provoked some comment. The *Commissaire de la République* in Toulouse wrote to the Ministry of the Interior on 30 October 1944 warning that these measures might provoke some reaction from the wives of prisoners-of-war.[6] But the provisional government had already planned a number of measures to help these families too, and on 1 November 1944 the daily allocation for the wives of prisoners-of-war at last increased by 90–96 per cent.[7]

RETURN OF THE ABSENT MEN

The wives and families of prisoners, drafted workers and those deported to Germany or who had gone to fight with the Allies had to wait for some months after the liberation of France from the Germans before their men returned. The long-awaited prisoners-of-war started to arrive in March 1945, at first slowly and then in larger numbers by May. Their return was the subject of much government speculation and discussion.[8] Plans for their arrival had been laid by regional delegates of the Ministry for Prisoners-of-War. Significant numbers of them were expected to be weak and ill. Various women's groups and the Red Cross set up reception committees at the stations to welcome the prisoners and help sustain them during their first days. For many families, the return of the prisoners brought varying degrees of disruption. Wives who had taken on a new role and adapted the household to the circumstances of war had to reintegrate their men who had often been away for as long as five years. Some were able to slip back into the patterns of their prewar marital lives, while others found it more difficult to readapt to married lives with husbands who had become virtual strangers.

By July 1945, the bulk of the men had returned. Their health and state of mind depended on where they had come from and their problems of readaption corresponded to their own experience of the war. The deported men tended to have the most severe health problems. If they were not hospitalized, they often needed nursing care from their wives or families.[9] Marguerite Duras' autobiographical account of waiting for the return of her husband from a concentration camp and the subsequent efforts she put into nursing him

6. Ibid.   7. ADHG M1913(9), Allocations aux femmes de prisonniers.
8. Christophe Lewin, *Le Retour de prisonniers de guerre français* (Paris, 1986), pp. 60–95.
9. Interview, Madame Juliette (Toulouse).

back to health makes horrifying, but compelling, reading.[10] Although
prisoners-of-war tended to be in better health, they faced different
problems of readjustment in the sense that they were more likely to
have been absent for a full five years and therefore had little understanding of what had happened to those they left behind. Many had
a distorted view of what life had been like for those who remained
in France. Claire Chevrillon observed this attitude in her brother-
in-law, who, like other prisoners, took a while to realize that civilians
had also been through a bitter struggle.[11] Their food parcels had
often led them to believe that circumstances had not been too bad,
and few realized that their families had always saved the best of
what they had to send to them. As Christophe Lewin put it, 'the
repatriated prisoner made contact with daily life again. He soon
realized that behind a decor which sometimes seemed familiar, a
totally unknown reality was hidden.'[12] In some cases it even emerged
that prisoners had suffered less in terms of everyday life and that
they had consistently been better fed than their families in France.

> Many of them [women] were able to cope while their husbands
> were in Germany, while they thought of him as a victim and a sad
> unhappy person. But when they came home they said, 'But I lived
> on a farm in Germany, I had all the milk I wanted and the farmer's
> wife was pretty.' The newly returned husband was on magnificent
> form, he had not suffered at all. He came back to his farm in the
> south of France and found that his machinery was inadequate. In
> these cases, the women found it difficult to accept their husband's
> reproaches because they had been obliged to destroy the horse for
> example.[13]

Therefore, despite the euphoric feelings experienced by some
wives of prisoners-of-war when their husbands returned, many found
that the gap of five years was difficult to bridge. The Associations of
Prisoner-of-War Wives had been very concerned to help prepare for
the return, which everyone feared would be difficult. Married couples
found it hard to take up where they had left off: the personalities of
the separated individuals had evolved independently of one another,
some had changed, and both parties were embarrassed when they
found themselves confronted with a virtual stranger. One woman
recounted the following story:

10. Marguerite Duras, *La Douleur* (Paris, 1985).
11. Claire Chevrillon, *Code Name Christiane Clouet* (Texas, 1995), p. 42.
12. Lewin, *Le Retour des prisonniers de guerre français*, p. 67.
13. Interview, Madame Chloé (Toulouse).

A woman went to the station to wait for her husband. She recognized him, but he was in such a state . . . she did not know whether she should kiss him or not, she did not dare to kiss him. It was after five years. For her, it was an ordeal to be with her husband again, he was unrecognizable . . . at first there were those who hesitated to live with them again, sadly there were those who didn't want to.[14]

Yves Durand has shown that over half the prisoners were married and that they were young: nearly 90 per cent were under 36 in 1940.[15] Therefore, most of the married men who returned in 1945 had experienced a short married life followed by a very long separation.

The return of my husband did not bring me the great joy that I had hoped for. I had married a boy who was too young and had no job . . . I was twenty and I believed in love. My son helped us all to overcome the difficulties of the moment.[16]

But children could also be an added strain to a couple struggling to get to know each other again. Husbands returned to find children considerably older than when they left, and those who had been very young at the beginning of the war had sometimes forgotten their fathers so that when they came home they did not always recognize them. In some cases, husbands even returned to find that there was a new baby in the household. Some were able to accept this, understandably others were not.

This difficult situation forced some wives seriously to reassess the quality of their married lives. Finding themselves in the roles of head of the household, organizing and supervising the children's education, mistress of the farm, manager of a small business, women had learnt to deal with responsibility, going to work, taking decisions and resolving material and administrative problems. Some of the men were prepared to adapt to these changes in their home lives and accepted that their wives had changed. 'My husband would have preferred to find his home as it was before. His good little wife waiting for him. It was difficult at first, moreover, I was earning more than him.'[17] Other women found that they had to sacrifice their new role to save their marriages.

14. Interview, Madame Fleur (Toulouse).
15. Yves Durand, *La Captivité: histoire des prisonniers de guerre français 1939–45* (Paris, 1980), pp. 26–7.
16. Nelly, in Jacqueline Deroy (ed.), *Celles qui attendaient* (Melun, 1985), p. 14.
17. Interview, Madame Delphine (Toulouse).

He idealized family life in his dreams. I had matured. I had become more independent. He came back nervous and irritable, sometimes even brutal. I had got into the habit of not letting anyone walk all over me. I had lost the habit of letting go to my feelings, to my sexuality. I finally decided that the best thing to do was to efface myself to him to facilitate his adaptation.[18]

Sarah Fishman concludes that this was the decision taken by the majority of the wives of prisoners-of-war.[19] However, a significant number of women found that their lives had so much changed for the better whilst their husbands were away that they were not prepared to take up the pattern of their old marital lives. In this context, it is perhaps not surprising that many marriages broke down. Both women and men found that the changes they had experienced were too great and were unable to reconstitute their former households. Some women even left home before their husbands returned. The *Jugements Civils* for the department of the Haute-Garonne bear witness to a number of cases which involved couples where the husband was a prisoner-of-war. The following are two examples:

he was in captivity until July, and on his return he hoped to find his home life as he had left it, but his wife, as soon as she knew that he was going to arrive, wrote to him on 25 July 1945 to inform him of her intention not to take up their common life, wishing to conserve a 'liberty' that she had appreciated and that she did not want to 'renounce' and that it would be a waste of time for him to try and do anything to try and find her.[20]

this demand . . . is the result of . . . the long trial of captivity. Raymond, far from finding that his wife was giving him the affection that he was within his rights to expect, was met with coolness and distrust. . . . She reproached her husband with being authoritarian and overbearing at his return.[21]

The figures in the table show clearly that divorce increased significantly, even dramatically, after the war. Admittedly, it is difficult to evaluate exactly how many of these divorces actually concerned prisoners-of-war.[22] Durand's estimation that about one in ten prisoners-of-war divorced seems the most plausible suggestion, a figure which was considerably less than the 25 per cent that certain

18. Gisèle, in Deroy (ed.), *Celles qui attendaient*, p. 34.
19. Sarah Fishman, *We Will Wait! The Wives of French Prisoners of War, 1940–45* (New Haven, 1991), pp. 165–7.
20. ADHG 1033 w 160, Jugements Civils, Jan. 1946.   21. Ibid.
22. Durand, *La Captivité*, p. 519; Lewin, *Le Retour des prisonniers de guerre français*, p. 71; Fishman, *We Will Wait!*, pp. 156–62.

Divorce in France 1936–50

Year	Total number of divorces
1936	25,100*
1937	25,000*
1938	26,300*
1939	n.a.
1940	13,500
1941	17,000
1942	28,166
1943	31,976
1944	21,544
1945	37,718
1946	64,064
1947	56,292
1948	45,903
1949	40,335
1950	34,633

* = estimated figures
Source: Louis Roussel, 'Les Divorces et
les séparations des corps en France
(1936–1967)', *Population*, 25/2 (1970)

government agencies had feared.[23] The figures are also perhaps
less surprising in view of the fact that Vichy had made divorce very
difficult and that many couples may have decided to divorce once
these laws had been relaxed. It may also have been the case that,
as in Germany, where divorce rates also increased after the war, the
marriages which broke down were those which were hastily con-
tracted during the war and did not survive the burdens and deprivations of the peace.[24] Indeed, the circumstances of wartime France
must surely have had much to do with the increased postwar divorce
rate. However, the importance of these divorces should not be
overstated, as the vast majority of families were reconstituted. It is
also true that wives who succeeded in keeping their home intact
experienced a great sense of achievement. Wives who lived in rural
areas tended to be particularly relieved when their husbands returned. They were no longer responsible for the running of the
farm and their work load was considerably decreased. However, the
evidence also suggests that there were women who had enjoyed

23. Lewin, *Le Retour des prisonniers de guerre français*, p. 71.
24. Ute Frevert, *Women in German History* (London, 1990), p. 262.

a certain independence and satisfaction from the new roles and opportunities presented to them during the war, and many were loath to give them up.

MARRIAGE AND MOTHERHOOD

Young, single women were also affected by the return of the men, and the figures for the immediate postwar years show a substantial increase in the number of marriages. The parallel rise in the birthrate also suggests that women were having babies both from new marriages and from re-established ones. It is hard to imagine that women were not affected at least to some degree by the propaganda which had been present throughout the Vichy government and which in no way diminished after the war. The postwar governments continued to emphasize the importance of motherhood and the need for a high birthrate. De Gaulle himself declared that he wanted 12 million bouncing babies to help in the reconstruction of France. Women's groups and political parties echoed the call for women to have children; even communist delegates at the UFF conference of June 1945 exclaimed that 'France needs children'.[25]

This discourse was backed with family policies which reinforced economic incentives to have children. The Germans had not allowed the Vichy authorities to increase the departmental reference salaries (see p. 24) upon which family benefits were calculated throughout the Occupation, so benefits had dropped considerably in value in real terms. As early as March 1944, the National Resistance Council in Algiers had formulated a programme on family policies. An initial *Ordonnance* was passed on 17 October 1944, and subsequently a law on 22 August 1946 introduced a number of measures increasing reference salaries and the basic rates for the second child from 10 to 20 per cent and for the third or subsequent child from 20 to 30 per cent.[26] The terms of the Social Security system established in November 1945 also increased maternity leave to six weeks before and six weeks after the baby was born. Finally, changes in taxation known as the *quotient familial* favoured families with children. Despite these measures, contemporary research shows that family benefits did little to offset the extra expenses incurred by children in families with one breadwinner and more than two children. Where the

25. Bibliothèque de Documentation Internationale Contemporaine, UFF Congrès National Paris, 1945.

26. Pierre Laroque, *L'Evolution de la politique familiale en France* (Paris, 1985), p. 15.

government had more success in helping larger families was through the improved system of rationing which continued until 1948 and which enabled them to buy products of high nutritional value, like milk, more cheaply.[27] Women tended to stop working with the second child, so the household lost a salary and benefits failed to compensate for this loss.

The postwar government also sought to take advantage of some of the more propagandist measures introduced by the previous regime. For example, in May 1945, the Minister of the Interior wrote to all the Prefects in the country underlining the importance of the Mother's Day ceremony (which had been revived by Vichy). These days became a local event sometimes combining medal-awarding ceremonies with sports demonstrations and tea-parties for children.[28] Medals were allocated to the mothers of the most prolific families, and if reports on their 'moral behaviour' proved acceptable they could win considerable extra supplies. In 1946, for example, a gold medal, awarded for ten or more children, was worth a pair of sheets for a double bed, 3 kilos of sugar, 2,500g chocolate, 900g soap, 2kg jam, 1kg butter, 8 litres of wine and 500kg coal.[29] The occasion was also a glorious opportunity for pro-natalists to express themselves. In May 1946, the Secretary of the Finisterian section of the Union of Large Families, an invited speaker at the Mother's Day festivities in Quimper, demanded more substantial family benefits and declared, 'Women have hands not to make machines work, but to bring up children.' He went on to suggest a complete revolution in women's education, which currently 'prepares brains not mothers'. This approach was then taken up by the Prefect, who in much the same tone complained that the decline in the birthrate in the country was one of the reasons why economic improvement remained slow.[30]

Another more serious example may also be indicative of the extent of the obsession with the birthrate in these postwar years, and also demonstrates the belief that having babies was thought to be a general cure-all for women and the nation. Madame Cécile, who was deported to Germany for her resistance activities, like others in her situation experienced severe problems of readaptation when she returned to France. After an extended illness, she was advised that the only way for her to recover fully would be to have a baby.

27. Alain Girard and Albert Michot, 'Les Conditions d'existence des familles', *Population*, 4 (Oct.–Dec. 1947).
28. ADF 31W311.   29. ADF 31W51.
30. Ibid.

They told us that the only thing that could put us right and clean us up, was a child. . . . You know that we did not have any periods all the time in captivity? What did they do to us? We had a medical inspection by a woman military officer, she put her hand into me, and then my periods stopped. It was a good thing in the end, because where would we have found sanitary towels? So when I came back there was all that to deal with, all that dirtiness. Moreover, I had a terrible birth, the midwife said, 'It's terrible. It smells of rotten cabbage. There's loads of dirt.' We had to clean it all up and my baby just escaped being blind.[31]

The events of the Occupation had led to a widespread concern that women should understand that their place was as wives and mothers in the home. The political parties were also united in the encouragement they gave women to respect marriage and have children. Marriage and motherhood were therefore reinforced in ways not dissimilar to those used by the prewar governments and the Vichy regime. In the same way, abortion and prostitution were taken as a serious threat to these institutions and therefore had to be controlled.

Abortion

In the postwar years, although women no longer risked the death penalty, abortion was almost as severely repressed as it had been during the war. The abortion law reverted to the old 1920 law which remained in vigour until 1975. This moved cases back to the magistrate's court (*tribunal correctionnelle*). But magistrates continued to sentence women to three to four years in prison for abortion, and such cases were heard in the courts on a very regular basis. Annette Lieris, who became governor of the women's prison in Hagenau in 1945, witnessed the sad results of a policy which prevented women from having control over their own bodies. Half the women who were in her prison in the immediate postwar period were there for abortion-related crimes, serving prison sentences of three to ten years.[32] She recounts the experiences of some of her prisoners.[32] One worked in a textile factory which had to be kept hot and humid for the treatment of the wool, so women worked in their blouses and underclothes. The men took advantage of their state of undress and women 'became' pregnant against their will. Other women, who knew how to deal with this 'problem', would carry out spontaneous abortions in the water of the mill. Sometimes the abortion worked, at other times it was not so successful and could lead to serious illness. If the aborted woman died, the woman who had conducted the abortion

31. Interview, Madame Cécile (Finistère).   32. AN 2A 544–548, Annette Lieris.

was arrested and sentenced to prison. Lieris argues that their punishment was extremely severe in relation to the crime. Indeed, if we go by the registers of women entering Fresnes and La Petite Roquette, women's prisons in Paris, during these immediate postwar years, their sentences do seem heavy when compared with those for other crimes. The magistrate's courts had the authority to pass sentences of six days to five years, and for abortion they regularly gave the maximum sentence.[33] Although some women took money for their services, most just wanted to help out other women workers. Another related group was that of women who were convicted of infanticide. This was of course a phenomenon which had existed throughout the nineteenth century, but Lieris indicates that she had enormous respect for these women who had been forced to hide their pregnancies at work, carrying on until the last minute. They then gave birth all alone, returning to work immediately afterwards. Many were hardworking but illiterate *bretonnes*, working in the textile industry, who became pregnant but were too ashamed to be single mothers in their village, where such a situation was unacceptable. When they were caught they were given a four-to-five-year prison sentence.[34]

The figures confirm this dreary picture. The Fresnes prison records give a consistent picture of women admitted for sentences of considerable length both during the war and in the immediate postwar period. The severity of this sentencing seems only to have tailed off in the latter 1940s, and only by the 1960s did the magistrates become more indulgent, perhaps because of the overall atmosphere of prosperity and the feeling that the birthrate was no longer such a serious issue.

Prostitution

Vichy measures to control prostitution were described in Chapter 2. The increase in prostitution during the war was followed by a further upsurge during the Liberation when the presence of the Allied soldiers followed by returned prisoners-of-war provided prostitutes with an ongoing clientele. This increase in prostitution was widely thought to be proof of the failure of Vichy policy to keep it under control. Indeed, a total of 12,000 women were stopped for soliciting in Paris in 1945.[35] Vichy regulation, it was felt, could not

33. ALP, Fresnes Prison, Registres d'écrou 1–3003, 26 Apr. 1946–1 Oct. 1948; La Petite Roquette, Audiencier, 7 Nov. 1946–23 Sept. 1948.

34. AN 2A 544–548, Annette Lieris.

35. Alain Corbin, *Les Filles de noce: misère sexuelle et prostitution aux 19e et 20e siècles* (Paris, 1978), p. 505.

control prostitution, which had reached unacceptable levels. Abolitionists argued that brothels were immoral and that in tolerating them the state revealed itself to be a party to prostitution: they made slaves of prostitutes, encouraging the white slave trade, and only gave illusory guarantees of sanitary cleanliness. The further argument that the brothels had been closely associated with the Gestapo during the Occupation also carried considerable weight in the postwar atmosphere of the purges.

However, a police report devoted to the subject of prostitution, dated February 1946 and drafted by Georges Zanetti, Commissioner in Marseille, comes out strongly against abolition.[36] Taking each of the arguments of the abolitionists, Zanetti manages to destroy them one by one. For example, he explains that 'the abolitionists reproach regulation with only controlling a relatively small number of prostitutes. Even if this is true it does not seem to be a reason for abandoning medical controls altogether.' He argues that the figures advanced by the abolitionists estimating the number of clandestine prostitutes were an exaggeration. He claims that the Vichy policy of obliging prostitutes to carry cards was a much more effective means of enabling the authorities to control soliciting than they believed. While conceding that the pimps were often the major problem, he explained that the legislation was already in place for the police to clamp down on them, but that this had not really been applied either because those concerned had been under the protection of the Gestapo or because lack of staffing had not made it possible. He concluded that brothels are an important element of public safety which would be compromised if the women working within them had to solicit on the streets. 'The system though not perfect, offers the possibility of more control and therefore less risk than other systems of prostitution: shutting them down would not diminish the problem but just displace it. Therefore, regulation should be maintained.' Despite the fact that these arguments seem compelling and that abolition seemed to have little to recommend it in practical terms, the so-called Marthe Richard law was able to gain an enormous amount of sympathy and was passed in April 1946. According to this law, the 1,500 official brothels were banned throughout France (177 of them were in Paris).[37] They were given one month's notice in small communes, three months for larger ones and six months

36. ADBduR 23J3, Georges Zanetti, Report on Prostitution, 8 Feb. 1945.
37. Claudine Legardinier, 'La Longue Histoire d'un enfermement', *Prostitution et Société* (Jan., Feb., Mar. 1996), p. 27.

in large towns and cities. The records at Fresnes indicate that the law was applied immediately, and between 26 April 1946 and 13 February 1948 a total of 2,106 women were imprisoned there for anything from one week, one month or more for crimes of prostitution and soliciting. More women were imprisoned in Fresnes at this time for this crime than for any other.[38]

The law was criticized almost as soon as it was imposed. Indeed, it effectively made prostitutes' lives even more miserable by pushing them out of a situation where they operated within some kind of structure into an even worse clandestine existence. With the advent of antibiotics, venereal disease was treatable, once it had been located, but the location of those infected was much more unlikely under the terms of the 1946 law, which actually reduced the existing hygiene controls; therefore, closure led to an increase in venereal disease.[39] Other commentators have observed that closure was difficult to enforce in reality and that the daily lives of prostitutes probably changed very little in practice.[40] The legislators and their supporters perhaps somehow imagined that abolition would be as good as its word, and that prostitution would disappear. For Corbin, this legislation followed on from the prohibitionist movement, which had already gained some momentum between the wars, and must be seen as that movement coming to fruition.[41] It also appears more as a measure which reflected the atmosphere of the purges than as a serious attempt to address the problem. Indeed, prohibition represented yet another manifestation of the pervasive ideology of pro-natalism which found extensive expression in the postwar years, strengthened by the Christian wing behind the new political grouping, the MRP.

Women in paid employment after the Occupation

Chapter 2 showed that the war brought women into the labour market, but did this have any lasting effects which changed women's situation in paid employment in the longer term? Did it create any openings which continued into the postwar period? Did the fact that women had worked during the war lead to more acceptance

---

38. ALP, Fresnes Prison, Registres d'écrou 1–2106, 26 Apr. 1946–13 Feb. 1948.
39. Alphonse Boudard, *La Fermature 13 avril 1946: la fin des maisons closes* (Paris, 1986), p. 120.
40. Colette Villey, '1946–1996, la fermature des maisons closes: l'efficacité d'une décision historique', *Prostitution et Société* (Apr., May, June 1996), pp. 23–8.
41. Corbin, *Les Filles du noce*, p. 506.

that women should work, and were there any structural changes for women in relation to prewar and wartime paid employment?

Generally speaking, the accepted interpretation of women in employment at this time is that they were pushed out of the labour market in 1944–45 as they were in 1919, and that this push came very strongly from government. Indeed, the overall figures for the rates of women's paid employment in France indicate a decline, with the exception of the two wars, at least until the 1960s. It therefore seems reasonable to assume that women who worked during the war through financial necessity and who responded to the wartime demands for labour left their jobs when they were no longer needed and embraced their domestic roles as wives and childbearers when their husbands returned. However, the evidence collected below shows a rather more complicated picture.

After the Liberation and as the men returned, the overall trend was for men to move back into the jobs that women had occupied during the war. Women who were employed in factories were asked to leave in cases where they were no longer the main breadwinner. The figures for the Toulouse gunpowder factory show that from July 1944 onwards, more women lost their jobs than men, and this seems to have been a typical scenario.[42] As factories were repaired and post-war plans were laid, it was men, not women, who were of the most interest to employers. Across the nation there was a definite policy of employing men, particularly ex-prisoners, rather than women. Many returned prisoners-of-war were channelled into agriculture.

The sagas of the Morlaix tobacco factory give a good example of the recruitment expectations of the population at this time. In 1945, a major argument arose when it was announced that the factory was to implement a new manufacturing programme. This would involve the redundancies of forty or so male workers, who would be replaced with women, as the factory was to reorientate itself from the manufacture of cigarettes to cigars, requiring female rather than male labour. The announcement of these measures created considerable uneasiness in the region as the redundancies were to affect former members of the FFI as well as recently returned prisoners. Furthermore, according to a long-standing tradition of the factory, the recruitment of women would benefit family relations of those already working there, to the detriment of war widows who would only have access to a quarter of the available posts.[43] The

42. Centre d'Archives de l'Armement, Ministère de la Défense, Chatellerault.
43. ADF 31W220.

Association of War Widows demanded that more jobs be reserved for them, complaining that widows' pensions were too low for them to have a decent existence, particularly if they had children. Eventually, the Prefect of the Finistère was moved to intervene by approaching the Ministry of Finance responsible for the factory, pleading the case that there was little industry in Morlaix and that a large number of prisoners-of-war, deportees and FFI soldiers had counted on a job in this factory and would therefore be bitterly disappointed. The Ministry was unhelpful, explaining that it was too late to change the policy.[44]

Although labour shortages for skilled workers continued to be a problem throughout the immediate postwar years, women were not encouraged to work as they had been during the war. The exceptional measures of employing women were not thought to be appropriate to peacetime and employers preferred to take advantage of the available immigrant labour force. Women were laid off in sectors where their labour had been seen as a stop-gap measure in the absence of the men and in industries which were wound down in the transition from a wartime to a peacetime economy. Parallel to this, there was less job availability in the sectors that had specifically catered for women before the war. Textile manufacturing, for example, traditionally a significant employer of women, especially as homeworkers, who were often married mothers and wives of factory workers, was particularly hard hit by the postwar shortages of raw materials. By 1946, the textile industry, which had employed half of the women in paid employment in the Toulouse region, had lost 41.4 per cent of its labour.[45]

All this would suggest a picture of massive women's unemployment. In the Finistère, in February 1945, it was reported that problems of men's unemployment were beginning to resolve, but there were very few openings for women.[46] By December, women were seen as particular victims of unemployment in this region.[47] Yet, paradoxically, Anne-Louise Moreau found that in the department of the Loire Atlantique, the move to normality after the war was accompanied by a surge in employment of untrained women who had not worked during the war, many of whom found domestic employment, whereas those who had worked during the war left

---

44. ADF 31W132/3.
45. Rolande Trempé. 'La Région économique de Toulouse aux lendemains de la Libération', in Gérard Cholvy (ed.), *Histoire du Languedoc de 1900 à nos jours* (Toulouse, 1980), p. 74.
46. ADF 31W250.   47. ADF 31W220.

their jobs.[48] The 1946 national census, though notoriously unreliable, shows that in the Haute-Garonne, for example, there was no change in the percentage of women in the non-agricultural labour force between 1936 and 1946, although the overall number of working women kept up with the overall increase in the labour force.[49] But, unfortunately, postwar figures for unemployment from the *Institut National de la Statistique et des Etudes Economiques* do not have a gender breakdown, so although some local figures exist it is difficult to gain a sense of the national picture and available national figures appear equally inconsistent. One study published in 1947 suggests that women who wanted work may have found it in sectors other than those where they were traditionally employed. Although there were fewer women in textile and clothing manufacture, there was an increase in the number of women who worked in the food industry, chemical production, metal work, leather and skinning, banking and commerce.[50] Jean Daric, in a study of the professional activity of French women published in 1947 by the *Institut National des Etudes Démographiques*, established that the number of working women across all the professions increased from 34.2 per 100 women in the population in 1936 to 36.7 in 1946. Even if women in agriculture are excluded, the figures still indicate a slight increase from 20.5 in 1936 to 21.8 in 1946. For Daric, the increase in marriages 'did not bring any real modification in the activity rates of married women in the total population'. But he noted a trend of more married women working and moving towards 'stable and sedentary employment'.[51] Another study, also published in 1947, indicates a similar slight increase of 2 per cent in the number of working women.[52] A later article by Jean Fourastié claims that there was a clear increase in the number of women working outside agriculture between 1936 and 1946, and he argues that female employment rates increased from 206 per thousand in 1936 to 220 in 1946. 'Women replaced men during the war and they continued to work after the end of hostilities.'[53]

48. Anne-Louise Moreau, 'La Traversée de la guerre et ses effets sur les itinéraires professionnels d'une cohorte de retraités et retraitées nés en 1919 et résident en Loire Atlantique', in Denis Peschanski and Jean-Louis Robert (eds), *Les Ouvriers en France pendant la seconde guerre mondiale* (Paris, 1992), pp. 48–50.

49. INSEE Recensement 1946.

50. Geneviève Vaillaud, *Le Travail des femmes* (Paris, 1947), p. 18.

51. Jean Daric, *L'Activité professionelle des femmes en France* (Paris, 1947), pp. 84–93.

52. Vaillaud, *Le Travail des femmes*, p. 8.

53. Jean Fourastié, 'La Population active française pendant la seconde guerre mondiale', *Revue de l'histoire de la deuxième guerre mondiale* (Jan. 1965), p. 8.

The evidence is so unreliable that it is difficult to know where the truth lies, and employment was closely linked to local circumstances. In her recent study of female Parisian factory workers, Catherine Omnès concludes that women gained nothing in terms of employment as a result of the Second World War. Far from promoting women in the growth sectors, as was the case in the First World War, she sees the Second World War as braking the feminization of industry which had temporarily been reactivated during the industrial mobilization of 1939–40.[54]

Still, the existing national figures certainly appear to suggest a general trend towards an overall increase in the number of women in the workforce, and it is therefore obviously not the case that all married women moved out of the workplace *en masse* and back into the home. A woman's decision to work or to continue to work depended on a number of factors: personal family circumstances, whether or not she had children, financial resources and her wartime work experience, as well as local economic factors. Some married women were very happy to leave jobs they had taken on for purely financial reasons in the absence of a husband, whereas other women found a certain satisfaction not only in the job they were doing but also in the quality of life it offered them, and they continued to work after the return of their husbands. Single women who had worked during the war and perhaps had access to some new opportunities did not unconditionally stop working after their marriages, and some even continued working after starting families despite the limited resources for childcare.

Denise Riley's research on wartime childcare provision in England has shown how extra childcare facilities were organized to deal with the influx of many married women into the labour force, and that this provision was largely withdrawn afterwards.[55] The provision created in France does not appear to have conformed to this pattern. Some degree of childcare was organized in public administration and in certain companies where there was a high concentration of married women. The evidence available suggests that this provision was not withdrawn after the war, at least not in the public sector. Crèches were gaining increasing acceptance with mothers and were beginning to be recognized by the authorities. Siân Reynolds has described how by 1948 crèches had become increasingly popular as

54. Catherine Omnès, *Ouvrières parisiennes: marchés du travail et trajectoires professionnelles au 20e siècle* (Paris, 1997), p. 239.
55. Denise Riley, *The War in the Nursery: Theories of the Child and Mother* (London, 1983).

a way of dealing with the problem of childcare in France.[56] An enquiry carried out by Alain Girard, published in 1948, concluded that crèches, as opposed to part-time work, were the best solution for working mothers, although there were not enough of them.[57] A further enquiry published in 1950 came to much the same conclusions: 69 per cent of those interviewed preferred crèches.[58] The increasing concern about the lack of childcare provision suggests that there was a growing acceptance that married women should be able to work, and indeed implies that many married women were already working. Despite this, childcare facilities remained limited in the immediate postwar period, and mothers who wanted to work were often still dependent on family or friends to look after their children.

Did women, then, benefit from the absence of men during the war years to gain education and training, and did they pursue this after the war, or were they generally pushed out by the men? Some women, particularly those who were students or in training during the war, found that they were offered unprecedented career opportunities, like the witness quoted below.

> I know personally several women of about my age who, thanks to the Occupation, were able to have a career afterwards. These women, who I got to know since the Occupation, and who started working during the Occupation, became directors of the department stores in Toulouse, and got jobs in management in the private sector and at the town hall.[59]

It seems that the absence of the men during the war years enabled some women to benefit from education and openings that were not previously accessible to them. Indeed, the figures indicate that more women were present at the University of Toulouse during the war years than afterwards, when their numbers declined. Numbers of female students at the universities and at the law and medical schools increased during the war but dropped afterwards except in law and pharmacy where their number remained high.[60] In industry, despite the fact that some women were trained in skilled jobs to

56. Siân Reynolds, 'Who Wanted the Crèches? Working Mothers and the Birth-Rate in France 1900–1950', *Continuity and Change*, 2 (1990), p. 190.

57. Alain Girard, 'Une enquête sur l'aide aux mères de famille, extension des crèches, travail à temps partiel', *Population*, 3 (1948), pp. 539–43.

58. G. Jacquemins, *Le Travail de la femme hors du foyer: un sondage d'opinion publique au sujet de sa rémunération et de son organization* (Brussels, 1950), p. 82.

59. Interview, Madame Simone (Toulouse).

60. Ministère de l'Education Nationale (Facultés), INSEE Toulouse 1947.

replace the men during the war, they were still confined to unskilled, repetitive, monotonous, and badly paid jobs. This was not because, as some contemporaries claimed, they wanted to centre their interests on the home, but because there were no other possible openings for them.[61] In the Post Office, the numerous women who had been taken on were relegated to the posts which had been available to them before 1939, despite the fact that many of them had held positions of responsibility during the war and had proved their capabilities.[62] On the other hand, there was a feeling that women should not have to be obliged to go out to work. In June 1945, for example, eight hundred people met with the CLL of Landivisiau to draw up their list of grievances. Therein they demanded that there should be a salary for women at home or that working men should earn enough to feed their wives and children without obliging wives to work. The state, they felt, was failing in its duty and should offer an example in this matter.[63]

GOVERNMENT LAWS AND DIRECTIVES

Jane Jenson has argued that the laws introduced in 1945–47 relating to women's employment represented a major breakthrough for women.[64] The postwar governments responded to a discourse of universal rights based on equality and also reacted against the Vichy legislation which had excluded married women from working. For Jenson, this legislation reflected a commitment on the part of the French Left to integrate women into the labour force, but only in ways that would not represent any kind of threat to men's wages and employment. Indeed, measures related to women's employment included the 1946 *Statut des Fonctionnaires* which stipulated in article 36 that 'women have access to posts in public employment where their presence in the administration is justified by the interests of the department'.[65] Women's rights were completely recognized when they were written into the Constitution of 1946, which claimed that 'the law guarantees women equal rights to men in all areas'. The

61. Vaillaud, *Le Travail des femmes*, p. 18.
62. François Rouquet, *L'Epuration dans l'Administration* (Paris, 1992), p. 500.
63. AN 72AJ 123.
64. Jane Jenson, 'The Liberation and New Rights for French Women', in M.R. Higonnet, J. Jenson, S. Michel and M.C. Weitz (eds), *Behind the Lines: Gender and the Two World Wars* (New Haven, 1989), p. 277.
65. Guy Thuillier, *Les Femmes dans l'administration depuis 1900* (Paris, 1988), p. 76. In 1946 there were only 50 women *chefs du bureau* in public administration; Andrée Lehmann, *Le Rôle de la femme française au milieu du vingtième siècle* (Paris, 1960), p. 39.

historian is tempted to conclude that this was compelling rhetoric that reflected the attitudes of the time but was not really put into practice in the immediate postwar years.

Several important measures were passed which gave women access to jobs, particularly in the realms of administration and the law, but the impact of these measures was slow. The *Ecole Nationale d'Administration* (ENA) was created by decree in October 1945 and from the outset it was decided that 'women can present themselves for competitive entrance exams in the same way as men'.[66] However, throughout its existence, few women have graduated from there.[67] Women were already allowed to go to law school, and postwar legislation was passed which allowed them to become magistrates. The law of 5 August 1946 gave women access to all judicial functions.[68] During the war, the number of women at law school in Toulouse increased from 15 per cent in 1942–43 to 27 per cent in 1944–45 and then dropped back to 23 per cent in 1946–47.[69] In his 1944–45 annual report, the Director of the Faculty accounted for the increasing number of women by explaining that most professions were soon to be open to women, including those in the law. He saw their 'access to public functions from which they had been excluded until then as the corollary of the access to public rights'.[70] Although he put the 1945–46 drop in women students down to the return of the men, he expressed real disappointment when the numbers continued to drop in 1946–47, and concern that women might be discouraged by the difficult nature of the training for jobs in the legal profession.[71] This promising trend appears to have fallen away nationally after the war. Andrée Lehmann claims that women had little or no impact on the law courts in the 1940s and only began to do so in the 1950s.[72] In 1957, out of 3,712 magistrates, only 150 were women.[73]

Legislation passed in relation to women's salaries was also of major importance, but, again, it would seem that this was more so in theory than in actual practice. The Toulouse *arrêté* passed in September 1944 relating to salaries stipulated that 'women's salaries are identical to men's in all circumstances where women do the

66. AN F60 2804, Administration Française.
67. See Thuillier, *Les Femmes dans l'administration*, for figures.
68. AN F60 1035, L'accession de la femme aux fonctions du magistrat.
69. ADHG 3807/199, Rapports Annuels de la Faculté de Droit de Toulouse, 1942–54.
70. Ibid., 1944–45.   71. Ibid., 1946–47.
72. Lehmann, *Le Rôle de la femme française*, p. 21.
73. Andrée Michel and Geneviève Texier, *La Condition de la femme française d'aujourd'hui* (Paris, 1964), p. 142.

same work with the same efficiency'.[74] This was progress because women's wages had previously been fixed at 20 per cent less than men's wages. But the *arrêté* was not applied automatically. At the aeronautics factories in Toulouse, it was established that where women were doing exactly the same jobs as men they would receive the same salaries. But where women were involved with work which was exclusively 'feminine' they should expect to receive at least 20 per cent less.[75] In January 1945, when most salaries were undergoing considerable revisions, a note written into the ministerial documents explained that in land transportation industries in the department of the Finistère, the salary of female employees should correspond to 80 per cent of that of male employees.[76] Although these represent just a couple of examples from across the country, they offer evidence of the lack of impact of this measure, and it was perhaps because of this that further legislation was introduced in relation to equal pay. A law passed on 15 March 1945 stipulated equal pay for the same jobs, and this was underlined by the equal rights declaration in the Constitution of the Fourth Republic. Yet, on the whole, despite these laws, women's salaries remained considerably inferior to men's. A study published in 1947 pointed out that men and women were rarely doing identical work and therefore women were generally paid less. The percentage of the female labour force was greatest in the lowest paid professional sectors, doubtless because the low salaries prevented men from taking the jobs.[77] The figures in the table show this quite clearly. The importance of the legislation cannot therefore be taken at face value. There was some progress embodied in the laws, and, as Jenson and other commentators have pointed out, there was a pervasive discourse that 'to participate in economic life had become a "right" for women'.[78] But significant inequalities between men and women's paid employment remained. Indeed, Louise Samoneau noted, perhaps rather naively, writing in 1947, that the right to work for women was 'not yet solidly established absolutely everywhere'.[79]

74. *Vaincre*, 8 Oct. 1944.
75. Céline Desmoulin, 'A l'Aérospatiale: perspective d'égalité des valeurs humaines', *L'Amicaliste: amicale des retraités de l'aérospatiale de Toulouse*, 16 (June 1985), pp. 3–4.
76. ADF 200W281.   77. Vaillaud, *Le Travail des femmes*, p. 20.
78. Agnès Denis-Morillon, 'Les Femmes et le syndicalisme dans La Fédération C.G.T. de l'habillement 1936–46', unpublished Mémoire de Maîtrise (University of Paris, 1981), p. 191.
79. Louise Samoneau, 'Du droit de travail des femmes', Propagande et Documentation pour l'Etude et la Solution des Questions concernant la Femme, l'Enfant et la Race, 6 (Paris, 1947), p. 3.

Annual Salaries by Department and by Sex in Industry and Business, 1947

	Average annual salaries (millions of francs)		
	Masculine	*Feminine*	*Both*
Haute-Garonne	106	75	101
Tarn	120	76	108
France	129	82	117

Source: INSEE, Bulletin de la Statistique Générale de la France, July–Sept. 1949.

There were important changes embodied in the laws passed in the immediate postwar period, but, as Jenson has shown, they were slow to take effect. What seems to be more significant about this period is the fact that there was an increasing acceptance that women, whether married or single, had a right to work. This was significant change compared with prewar and wartime attitudes. It is demonstrated not only by legislation for equal pay, but also by the fact that there were attempts to urge the creation of structures like childcare provision, necessary if married women were to be able to work. Yet, even if it appeared to have become more acceptable for women to work in a general way, there was also concern that they should not represent a direct challenge to men's work. This fear had also been very present during the war.

The end of the war did not represent a return to 1939, nor did it represent a repeat of 1919. The everyday lives of women between 1945 and 1948 had much continuity with the wartime years. Queuing, rationing and the obsession with obtaining food remained a major feature of women's lives until well after the war. Despite the lack of conclusive evidence about women's employment, it is clear that many married women who had worked during the war continued to do so afterwards, often for the same reasons of financial necessity. For these women, the end of the war did not represent any particular watershed. On the other hand, it is true that some women did experience dramatic change in their lives. This was particularly the case for women whose lives were disrupted by the return of absent men, or women who moved out of the labour market and into the home in 1945, or women who married after the war and started families.

As far as 'liberation' is concerned, if women experienced any of this at the Liberation it was only in the physical sense, from the Germans. There is very little in their lives to suggest that they experienced any kind of personal liberation in 1944–48. As has been seen, the conditions of everyday life remained difficult. Married women often found the return of the men oppressive, and many had to give up positions of responsibility and return to their prewar role in the household. For women, any kind of 'liberating' experience was more likely to have taken place during the war. As was suggested at the end of Part One, many discovered that their experience of running the household and going out to work brought them increased confidence:

> The Occupation was the step which allowed many women to find within themselves the necessary effort to overcome their problems. And afterwards they said to themselves, I overcame that, why shouldn't I overcome more, and they launched themselves into paid employment.[80]

> After the war, there were changes for women. They had evolved a lot, they had made themselves known, they had shown that they were courageous. There were many like me who did not work before the war, and who started to work during the war and continued afterwards.[81]

It would therefore seem that the postwar picture of women's lives was complex and fragmented, making it difficult to make generalizations.

80. Interview, Madame Sandrine (Toulouse).
81. Interview, Madame Flore (Toulouse).

CHAPTER EIGHT

Women Gain New Rights and Become Citizens

The impact and importance of women's political experience during the war cannot be properly situated without examining their reaction to the re-establishment of peace and the re-emergence of party politics. Paradoxically, at the same time as some women were being punished during the purges, legislation was being passed which was to enable women to become citizens and to participate fully in the democratic processes for the first time; universal suffrage had at last arrived. The acquisition of this right, along with their wartime involvement in the Resistance, an involvement which had become to some extent apparent during the events of the Liberation, seemed to herald a promising new direction in terms of women's political participation. At a time when women represented more than half of the population of France, it would seem not unreasonable for contemporaries to have anticipated that their vote might bring major change to the dominant French political culture (although this had not been the case elsewhere in Europe). Indeed, one police report asked whether women were going to push France into a new political era.[1] However, the author of this report was not articulating a concern that preoccupied the majority of the French people, not least women themselves. Despite the initial promising signs, this chapter will argue that women did not find gaining the vote to be particularly empowering, that little was made of it in French society, and that then, as now, few political parties made a serious attempt to court their vote and women made only limited impact on the immediate postwar political scene.

---

1. AN F7 15588, Les femmes et les problèmes politiques à la veille des elections, Direction Générale de la Sûreté Nationale, p. 1.

Universal suffrage is passed

During the events that were leading up to the Liberation on mainland France, debates were taking place in Algiers which were to lead to women gaining the right to vote. Women's groups had been pressing for this right since the early 1900s, and by 1914 the campaign had taken on serious momentum and was gaining a wider audience among those who mattered, namely parliamentary representatives. When the First World War was declared, the women involved in the suffragist movement agreed to set aside their demands for the vote and offered their services to the greater needs of the country. But, after the hostilities were over, women hoped that their contribution would be rewarded. Indeed, in May 1919, a bill giving women full political rights was passed by a large majority in the *Chambre des Députés*, where it was approved by 359 to 95, but it was subsequently delayed and then defeated by the Senate. Further bills met the same fate throughout the 1930s. Once passed in the lower chamber they were always delayed, then blocked, by the Senate, where the anti-clerical Radical caucus feared that giving women the vote would be to give a vote to the Church and therefore to the right and threaten the Republic.[2] When the Popular Front came to power in 1936, despite not having the vote, three women were appointed by Léon Blum as junior ministers in his cabinet, Irène Joliot-Curie, Suzanne Lacore and Cécile Brunschvicg.[3] Women had gained the vote elsewhere in Europe – was this to be the propitious time for French women? Women's historians have recently given much thought to why this was not the case. Christine Bard in her brilliant analysis of feminist movements in France between the wars has shown that they were extremely active, and, as Paul Smith has pointed out, women's enfranchisement was rarely off the political agenda throughout the period.[4] But continuing opposition from the Radicals, the gravity of the national economic situation and the looming dangers presented by Nazism and Fascism all served to push women's enfranchisement into the background.

Surprisingly, Pétain accepted the principle that women should vote, but since there were no elections from 1940 to 1944 the

2. The debates are detailed in Steven Hause and Anne Kenney, *Women's Suffrage and Social Politics in the French Third Republic* (Princeton, 1984).

3. Siân Reynolds, *France between the Wars: Gender and Politics* (London, 1996), pp. 159–62.

4. Christine Bard, *Les Filles de Marianne: histoire des féminismes 1914–1940* (Paris, 1995); Paul Smith, *Feminism and the Third Republic* (Oxford, 1995).

principle was never put into practice. Working parties were established to study the drawing up of a new Constitution for France, and although this Constitution never saw the light of day, it was the first text to anticipate real universal suffrage. Pétain was no doubt aware of the 'inevitable consequences of giving women the vote, that they would vote less for the Left than men'.[5] However, his acceptance of women's political involvement did have some impact on the law when in November 1940 'women could be named in the same capacity as men to sit on local councils' and it was established that each local council should have a 'qualified woman' representative to deal with charitable and social services issues. This law represented something of a watershed and as a result of it several women came into local government for the first time. Feminists greeted this measure as bringing real progress. This 'small revolution' made it possible for many members of the UNF (*Union National des Femmes*), for example, to be named as municipal councillors, according to Edmée de la Rochefoucault.[6] The Catholic family movements were particularly active and supplied many women: for example, as many as 150 members of the UFCS (*Union Feminine Civique et Sociale*) became local councillors in 1942.[7] Madame Beret, councillor in Vichy, was the first woman to conduct a wedding.[8]

Women's suffrage re-emerged as a subject for debate in January 1944, when the Consultative Assembly at Algiers discussed the organization of public powers after the Liberation. The generally accepted interpretation of events has been that women were 'granted' the right to vote by de Gaulle and this was written into the *Ordonnance* of October 1944, as a 'reward' for their participation in Resistance and recognition of their political involvement. Women had proved themselves to be worthy of citizenship and had shown that they could be trusted to vote. This was the argument used by the communist Fernand Grenier when he presented his amendment providing for women's suffrage to the Provisional Assembly in Algiers in 1944. He described not only the heroism of certain individual women in the Resistance, but also made reference to 'several million women whose husbands were prisoners-of-war or interned or deported or fighting in the *maquis*, [who] showed courage on a daily basis to take responsibility for bringing up the children, the management of the farm or the small business in the absence of the father

5. Raymond Huard, *Le Suffrage universel en France 1848–1946* (Paris, 1991), p. 359.

6. Bard, *Les Filles de Marianne*, p. 445.   7. AN F7 15588, p. 12.

8. Bard, *Les Filles de Marianne*, p. 446.

etc.'[9] This argument must certainly have influenced those who voted on the amendment. Indeed, its apparent logic was extremely powerful, and women's suffrage was voted for by 51 to 16. The position of the Radicals had not changed, but the composition of the Provisional Assembly with a predominant left wing and considerably weakened Radical party meant that, despite the reticence of the latter, female suffrage was passed.

This argument, that women's wartime bravery was the reason why they got the vote when they did, has been largely accepted and internalized by French women and men alike. One oral witness articulated this interpretation in the following terms: 'It was the Général de Gaulle who asked for women to have the right to vote. The Général de Gaulle thought that if women had participated in the Liberation of France, they should participate in the restoration of France.'[10] That de Gaulle was in favour of women's enfranchisement there seems little doubt, and his message to the Resistance on 23 June 1942 is normally taken as evidence of this: 'Once the enemy is driven from our land, all French men and women will elect a National Assembly which in the full exercise of its sovereignty will determine the country's destiny.'[11] Nonetheless, he was not directly involved in the debates around women's suffrage in Algiers, leaving them to other members of the commission, and his own rather laconic record of events, published in 1956, suggests that he did not attribute enormous importance to it. 'in addition, voting rights and eligibility were attributed to women. The *Ordonnance* of 21 April 1944 realized this huge reform ending 50 years of controversy.'[12] Nor does women's enfranchisement appear to have arisen directly out of the Resistance movement. Evidence is scarce to suggest that there was widespread discussion of the vote during the war within Resistance circles. Marie-France Brive found that the issue of women's suffrage was never seriously evoked as a question meriting attention and analysis by the Resistance press.[13] Indeed, the clandestine press which was disseminated, in the Haute-Garonne in any case, contained little reference to female suffrage. Only the paper of the socialist Resistance group *Libérer et Fédérer*, based in Toulouse, carried

9. Fernand Grenier, 'La Résistance et le droit de vote des femmes', in UFF, *Les Femmes dans la Résistance* (Paris, 1977), p. 261.

10. Interview, Madame Saskia (Toulouse).

11. De Gaulle, *Mémoires* (Paris, 1954), Vol. 1, p. 430.

12. De Gaulle, *Mémoires de Guerre: l'unité 1942–44* (Paris, 1956), p. 157.

13. Marie-France Brive, 'L'Image des femmes à la Libération', in Rolande Trempé (ed.), *La Libération dans le Midi de la France* (Toulouse, 1986), p. 391.

an article dated January 1944, entitled 'For women's access to political life', explaining how

> the considerable role played by women in the Resistance had the effect of breaking down old prejudices. By showing that they knew how to fight and die for their ideal as well as if not better than men, women have convinced even the most sceptical of their aptitude to participate in political life.[14]

The clandestine journal *Défense de la France* also advocated the vote for women in January 1944, explaining that 'their absence in elections prevents [French] suffrage from being truly universal'.[15] Although the *Union des Femmes Françaises* claims to have started to demand women's suffrage by 1944, I could find no evidence of this in the tracts, brochures and clandestine press in existing collections.

The debates at the meetings of the various bodies established during the Occupation to work out the future basis of French government are also interesting in this context. They indicate that women's suffrage was passed almost by accident and certainly not in an atmosphere of unanimous agreement. The *Comité Général d'Etudes*, established in July 1942 to put together the judicial framework for the country, had no real plans for a proper universal suffrage at the outset.[16] The committee asked for various Resistance groups to offer suggestions of what they would like to see in the future constitution; their replies made no mention of women's suffrage. The recommendations of the committee, which were sent to Algiers in September 1943, mentioned female suffrage as a possibility, but only as a point of detail, giving it little emphasis. The CGE seemed more attracted by the idea of a family vote, offering supplementary votes to the (male) head of family on the basis of the number of children. The final programme adopted on 15 March 1944 did not include women's suffrage. So, contrary to what was claimed afterwards, women's suffrage was not instigated at the request of the Resistance.[17]

Subsequently, in the meetings of the Algiers Assembly, which met 27 times between 23 December 1943 and 24 March 1944, William Gueraiche records that women's suffrage was raised at least ten

14. *Libérer et Fédérer*, 15 (Jan. 1944). Personal collection, Monsieur Danial Latapie.

15. Margaret Collins Weitz, *Sisters in the Resistance: How Women Fought to Free France* (New York, 1995), p. 72.

16. Ibid.

17. Albert and Nicole Du Roy, *Citoyennes! Il y a cinquante ans le vote des femmes* (Paris, 1994), p. 238.

times.[18] Some of the arguments that had surfaced in prewar parliamentary debates came to the fore again, but the absence of the men, 'natural educators', was seen as a major stumbling-block. Although the principle of women's vote was generally agreed, it was felt that the final decision should await the return of the men, as 'the absence of a very large part of the masculine element would bring too great a disequilibrium in the composition of the electorate'.[19] Much the same words had been used in the post-First World War debates. But eventually, despite the outspoken opposition of the Radical, Giacobbi, and thanks to the support of a few key individuals, opposition fell away and Fernand Grenier, the communist, was able to have his amendment adopted; his arguments were apparently inspired by Lenin's orders that 'Every housewife should learn to govern the country'.

In fact, these debates indicate that discussion of women's participation in the Resistance was a minor concern, since the number of women involved was relatively small and the true scale of their contribution was certainly unknown to those in Algiers.[20] De Gaulle and his entourage knew that women were likely to support him in the postwar elections, and this is a much more convincing reason why he and his supporters were prepared to support women's enfranchisement. Some credit should also be given to the French suffrage movement, which, as Andrée Lehman has pointed out, had already laid the groundwork so that women's contribution to the Resistance was seen as a decisive factor.[21] It seems reasonable to assume that the prewar suffrage campaigns did much to prepare the way for a *mentalité* of acceptance that women should vote, and the numerous prewar debates must have influenced the men at Algiers at least to some degree.

Even if the popular interpretation that suffrage was a reward for women's participation in the Resistance clouded the real reasons for women gaining suffrage rights in October 1944, it certainly served to enhance the reputation of de Gaulle and has augmented the myth that surrounded him. It has been an added factor in helping to gloss over the awkward reality of how few French men and women were

18. William Gueraiche, 'Les Femmes politiques de 1944 à 1947', in Françoise Thébaud (ed.), *Clio: histoire, femmes et sociétés, résistances et libérations* (Toulouse, 1995), p. 169.

19. Du Roy, *Citoyennes!*, p. 252.

20. Siân Reynolds, 'Marianne's Citizens? Women, the Republic and Universal Suffrage in France', in Siân Reynolds (ed.), *Women, State and Revolution* (Brighton, 1986).

21. Andrée Lehmann, *Le Rôle de la femme française au milieu du xxème siècle* (Paris, 1960), p. 7.

involved in Resistance, and has contributed to the creating of a climate during the postwar period in which it was assumed that most French people were involved in the Resistance in some way, reinforcing the Gaullist myth of a 'nation of resisters'. It ignores the fact that the majority of women were often doing no more than struggling to keep themselves and their families adequately fed and housed, and conveniently overlooks the behaviour of women who committed themselves politically to non-Resistance activities by explicitly supporting Vichy or collaborating, as was described in Chapter 4. There was little recognition of the fact that women were at last attaining a right which was theirs and which until then had been unreasonably denied to them and of course, as Siân Reynolds has forcefully argued, that universal suffrage which until then had not been universal at all since only men could vote, had finally arrived.[22]

But how did women themselves react to the gaining of this new and important right? Little was made of this enormous step towards democracy. Locally, at least, it was not heralded in the Toulouse press of the time as a major event. In October 1944, it was reported in very dry and formal terms in small letters and rarely made the front page: for example, *La Victoire* reported on 7 October 1944, that 'for the first time women will be eligible as candidates and will have the right to vote'. This is confirmed by other studies: for example, Marianne Leuilliez, who has worked on the Hérault, found that 'the great novelty which was the women's vote was accepted as a *fait accompli* without arousing any particular interest or emotion.'[23] In this context it is hardly surprising that many women did not perceive the event as being a particular watershed for them.

Women who were young adults in 1945, looking back on these years from the 1980s, appear to have seen the gaining of the vote as an obvious and inevitable result of the war, though it was also certainly seen as an important recognition of their worth. They did not express any sense of having been directly involved with it. It was something which was awarded to them outside their influence.

> The right to vote seemed very natural to us, it seemed the right moment . . . like a ripe fruit which had become ready quite naturally. I don't know whether we thought about it much at the time, especially in rural circles . . . We did not really make any demands, it

22. Siân Reynolds, *France between the Wars: Gender and Politics* (London, 1996), ch. 9: 'Rights and the Republic', pp. 204–21.
23. Marianne Leuilliez, 'Avril 1945, le premier vote des femmes. Etude de cas héraultais', *Bulletin du Centre d'Histoire Contemporaine du Languedoc*, 46 (Apr. 1990), pp. 3–12.

did not seem to us that with the right to vote we would be able to obtain anything directly. It's only afterwards that we participated gladly and easily.[24]

Oral evidence rarely shows that women experienced gaining the vote as an important event. The following woman was a major exception:

> For young women of my generation the right to vote represented a certain recognition . . . Really for me it was terribly humiliating, knowing that we could not vote. I belonged to a family of women, four women, all with political positions and beliefs, with our personal commitments, and we could not express ourselves with the ballot paper. My sister felt the same. She said that the imbecile walking down the road totally drunk has the right to vote because he is male and Madame Curie did not have it.[25]

Preparing women to vote

In the three years immediately after the war, French people were called upon to vote a total of nine times, so women were to have numerous opportunities to exercise their new right. Despite the rather muted pronouncements about the women's vote in the press in October 1944, a little more attention was paid to women when voting was in prospect and there was much more discussion about it when actual elections became a reality. The general anxiety was that women would abstain in droves because they would not know what to do or would not be interested in voting; some concern was also expressed as to their voting preferences. 'The women's vote is the great unknown of the forthcoming elections', asserted one police report.[26] Would the anti-clericals of the Third Republic be proved right? Would the women's vote precipitate a right-wing shift in government? To what extent would the clergy influence the women's vote?

Despite these concerns, little publicity was devoted to encouraging women to enrol on election lists. Some initiatives were taken by the UFCS, but little was done by the main political parties except for the communists and the UFF, which carried out a concerted campaign to inform women about what they should do. Telegrams were sent to Prefects in November 1944, asking them to encourage women to come forward to enrol on the electoral lists; the authorities were quick to criticize women for any lack of enthusiasm. In

24. Interview, Madame Margaux (Toulouse).
25. Interview, Madame Chloé (Toulouse).   26. AN F7 15588.

Toulouse, women were more prompt than men to enrol, but when 4,000 women had failed to enrol in the neighbouring Gers, it was reported that: 'It can be seen that straight away they are not very interested in accomplishing their civic duties. . . . the women's vote can only have an influence the day that women really interest themselves in political questions. . . . It seems that the moment has not yet arrived.'[27] In many areas women failed to register on the electoral lists, and the authorities were forced to transpose their names from the existing ration lists, the only reliable record of the local population. One police report recalled:

> The enrolment of women started very slowly . . . it transpired that women did not demonstrate the same eagerness everywhere to enrol . . . because this was indicated in the statistics, the government decided to adopt the lists used for the issuing of ration-cards, leaving it to commissions to summon the women concerned if they had any queries.[28]

By 1 January 1945, election lists had been drawn up to include women. Enrolment was higher in villages, where about 80 per cent of women registered to vote, whereas the percentage was lower in towns.[29] In most constituencies women outnumbered men, by as much as a third in some places.[30]

Police reports closely followed the attempts to educate women politically at this time. One report in particular is an extremely valuable source. Dated 24 April 1945, entitled 'Women and political problems on the eve of the elections', it offers an extremely detailed and valuable overview of women's political involvement, incorporating material from local reports around the country.[31] According to this report, it was the women's associations and groupings, rather than the political parties, that were the most effective at educating and mobilizing women. Ironically, groups like the *Union Nationale des Femmes*, which had been intensely involved in fighting for women's suffrage between the wars, were unable to adapt to the new situation; whereas the Christian groups, some of which had previously been sceptical or overtly against the vote, rapidly organized themselves, realizing that there was a great deal at stake. Thus, the *Union Féminine Civique et Sociale* was able to quadruple its prewar membership of 17,000 to 80,000 in 1945. Although it declared a non-party affiliation,

27. ADHG M1914/14, Les Femmes et le problème politique à la veille des élections; ADHG M2277, RG.

28. AN F1A 3216.   29. Huard, *Le Suffrage universel*, p. 371.

30. AN F7 15588, p. 39.

31. AN F7 15588, Les Femmes et les problèmes politiques à la veille des élections, Direction Générale de la Sûreté Nationale, pp. 1–41.

it participated in a major campaign for the elections. Tracts were distributed for the municipal elections underlining the importance of women voting.

> I will vote because as a woman, I want security for my home but I also want the freedom to bring up my children, as a worker I want what is in the interests of my profession, as a French woman I want prosperity and order for my country.
>
> All good French women must vote, abstaining would be equivalent to desertion.[32]

The *Ligue Féminine d'Action Catholique* also had a strong following in Catholic areas, notably in the Vendée and the Vosges, working beside the *Mouvement Populaire des Familles*. These associations encouraged women to vote for the newly-formed MRP, though they declared themselves to be apolitical. The MRP programme was very similar to that of the major Catholic movements. The MRP itself produced propaganda outlining aspects of its programme which they considered could be of interest to women. These included equal pay, protection of the family and free schooling. Their meetings all over France were well attended.

The communist-affiliated UFF explicitly sought out women's allegiance and targeted tracts and propaganda directly at them. The UFF paper, the *Appel des Femmes*, was widely distributed, and women were strongly encouraged to convince other women to join. It published a newspaper, *Femme Française*, which reached a national circulation of 170,000 in 1947.[33] Local publications included *Mariannes* in the north, with a circulation of 4,000, and *Amies en Gironde*, with a circulation of 15,000. The UFF aimed to reconstruct France, according to the joint resistance programme of the CNR (*Conseil National de la Résistance*) with no specific policies for women. Numerous information meetings were held across the country and attendance was high. Whilst playing on their Resistance past, the UFF also emphasized their immediate material achievements, making much of the countless demonstrations they had successfully organized across the country against insufficient food supplies and incompetent administration. For example, they rallied 500 women in Arras, 400 in Versailles, and on 19 March 1945, 3,000 women went to the Hôtel de Ville in Paris. Picking up on the same triangular structures they had used effectively during the Occupation, they worked towards raising

32. AN F7 15588, p. 13.
33. Marie-Thérèse Carbognani, 'Les Communistes et l'émancipation de la femme 1945–49', unpublished Mémoire de Maîtrise (University of Paris, 1975), p. 39.

women's consciousness of their political and civic duties. This continued emphasis on local concerns was effective in enabling women to feel directly involved with local politics. In this way the UFF effectively confronted the immediate problems faced by women, unlike any other political party.

Although other parties targeted women they did not do so with the same efficiency or success.[34] The police report noted that in spite of the alleged apolitical status of the Christian women's associations, these and the UFF had the most impact on women. The Catholics and communists therefore took the most interest in the women's vote, targeting them most forcefully. Priests urged women to perform their civic duties. In Toulouse, Archbishop Saliège actively encouraged the women's vote, and in the Finistère the clergy also went out of their way to influence the population, urging the people to vote for certain candidates.[35] On 22 September 1945, just before the general elections, *Ouest-France*, the popular Catholic daily paper in Brittany, explained that 'there is no worse negligence than abstention . . . it is because she is supposed to be more "conscious" than men of the decisions that weigh on the family that women are encouraged to accomplish their civic duty'.[36] The police report concluded by predicting that women would probably use their vote, and, particularly in the towns, most would use it to express their irritation about living conditions and would vote for those who offered the most convincing policies to remedy the situation.[37]

Women vote

Municipal elections were held on 29 April 1945, when women voted for the first time amidst controversy that the elections would not be representative because prisoners and deportees had not yet returned (in fact there were 2.5 million men missing).[38] In some areas, elections were even boycotted because it was thought that without the men they would not be representative.[39] However, the main concern was that women should vote, and, despite the worries of the authorities, the turn-out for the municipal elections was even

34. Claire Duchen, *Women's Rights and Women's Lives in France* (London, 1994), pp. 46–9.
35. ADF 31W250.   36. Du Roy, *Citoyennes!*, p. 272.
37. AN F7 15588.
38. AN F1A 3219 Participation des Electeurs au Scrutin, 22 June 1945.
39. Ibid.

slightly higher for women than for men. General elections to a Constituent Assembly were held a few months later when most of the men had returned. The results of these suggest that the number of women abstaining increased, since the overall abstention rate rose by a quarter in 1945 by comparison with 1936. The impact of the MRP was felt immediately. Although the communist party became the strongest political party with 26 per cent of the vote, the MRP came in a close second and the socialists took third position. As the elections progressed, the socialists gradually gained less votes and the MRP increased its support, gaining first place in June 1946. Despite a relatively high turn-out for these elections to the second Constituent Assembly, abstention rates had reached record levels by November 1946. But the high figures cannot be solely explained by women failing to vote. By 1946, French people were surely experiencing a certain election fatigue and perhaps beginning to become disenchanted with the postwar political scene. Fears of a dramatic right-wing governmental shift did not materialize. Women certainly supported the MRP, but they also voted on the Left, and left-wing parties, particularly the communists, remained strong nationally. Yet, overall, the impact of the women's vote does not appear to have been very great. In the Finistère, in any case, the Prefect was able to report in June 1949 that the women's vote had in no way modified the previous political dynamics of the department.[40] It seemed that the major political forces in the country had not been shaken by comparison with the prewar period.

The elections provided much terrain for discussion by political scientists who were concerned to explore the women's vote. In the early 1950s, a number of studies were carried out to examine women's voting patterns. The existence of a specifically female vote was difficult to establish as it was against the law to separate ballot boxes according to gender. It was, however, permitted in an experimental capacity in Vienne, Grenoble and Belfort, where women and men voted in different polling stations throughout the postwar period.[41] The results of these studies concur with others published at the same time. Women tended to vote for the MRP because it was supported by the Church and women were influenced by this.[42] Maurice Duverger, and Dogan and Narbonne continued

40. ADF 31W413.

41. Nouvelles Etudes de la Sociologie Electorale, 'Pour qui votent les femmes', in *Partis et Elections*, 60, Cahier de la Fondation Nationale des Sciences Politiques (Paris, 1954), pp. 185–95.

42. Ibid.

these attempts to establish women's voting patterns as distinct from men's.[43] They came to the conclusion that women were more conservative, less firmly opinionated than men and would therefore vote for the personality of a politician, i.e. de Gaulle, but that in general women from a certain socio-economic class tended to vote in the same way as men of that class.[44]

The problem with these analyses is that because the vote was granted to all women, the commentator immediately slips into the trap of referring to women as if they were one category, a homogenous group with particular voting characteristics. But, in reality, the generation of women who voted in 1945–48 was relatively old as the population was such that in the late 1940s there were more older than younger women in France. Elderly women tend to be conservative in the same way as elderly men. The age of the female voting population may go some way to explaining why 'women' tended to be more conservative. Furthermore, they often had much less education than men of the same generation, as some had not benefited from secondary school, and very few had attended university. Some older women were not well informed, few read newspapers and they rarely took an interest in world news. Marie-Thérèse Renaud has argued that it was women's socialization which prevented them from participating fully. They were conditioned to accept the traditional conception of women's role in society which did not include having and using political rights. But the most important factor for Renaud was women's lack of education and their indifference to the problems of the nation.[45]

Women in political parties

Most political parties established internal women's groups or sections, although the percentage of women members was often very small. The main responsibility of these groups was to organize propaganda directed at women. Inevitably, the battle for women to join parties closely resembled the battle for votes – thus in the immediate postwar period the main struggle was between the MRP and the communist party.

43. Maurice Duverger, *La Participation des Françaises à la vie politique* (Paris, 1955); M. Dogan and J. Narbonne, *Les Françaises face à la politique* (Paris, 1955).

44. Albert Brimo, *Les Femmes françaises face au pouvoir* (Paris, 1975).

45. Marie-Thérèse Renaud, *La Participation des femmes à la vie civique* (Paris, 1965), pp. 146–7.

The Radical party was the least successful of all the parties in attracting women voters. In April 1945 they still had not reacted to the fact that women could now vote. No women's sections were created, despite the presence of women like Cécile Brunschvicg and Marianne Verger in the hierarchy of the party. All the indications were that the party had been caught unaware by women's suffrage, and admittedly it had always been opposed to it.

The socialist party had little more success with women, as Philip M. Williams indicates in his study of the Fourth Republic. The socialists shared the traditional Radical empathy to women in politics.[46] Indeed, socialists were not always comfortable with the granting of the vote for women, as the secretary of the socialist section of Peyrestortes wrote in the *Cri socialiste* on 16 December 1944: 'So women are going to vote? Allow me to indicate that this is not an opportune time . . .'[47] Some attempt to interest and improve female membership was made through party propaganda. The initial suggestion was that existing married male members should enrol their wives and persuade them to come to meetings. 'What kind of impact can our propaganda have on other women, if the wives of our own members are uninterested in the party?'[48] A certain number of women had been involved with the party for some time. But the party failed to win many new members except in the north of the country. Lille, for example, boasted 400 women members, a quarter of the total membership for the town. But in other parts of the country membership was low, with just 12 women members in Angers, 50 in Rennes and 30 in Nancy. The female membership was incorporated into existing male sections, and women were often given responsibility for questions which were thought to be of particular interest to them, namely health, education and social services. As the socialist vote became weaker and weaker, it became apparent that the socialists had totally failed to gain female interest. In 1946, only three socialist women *députées* were elected. The women's commissions in the party complained that the electoral campaigns had been conducted without enough thought to the concerns of the female electorate. The socialists were particularly weak in the face of the propaganda onslaught women were experiencing from communist and MRP activists. Furthermore, women were rarely placed

46. Philip M. Williams, *Crisis and Compromise: Politics in the Fourth Republic* (New York, 1966).

47. Danielle Costa and Jocelyne Joussemet, 'Femmes des Pyrénées Orientales', unpublished Mémoire de Maîtrise (University of Toulouse, 1981), p. 131.

48. AN F7 15588, p. 21.

on the lists of socialist candidates, or, if they were, in positions which made it unlikely that they would be elected.[49] Ultimately, the socialists failed to attract the women's vote and women increasingly distanced themselves from the party, more or less disappearing from it until the 1970s. They were finally won over to voting socialist *en masse* by Mitterrand in 1981.[50]

Although no independent women's sections were formed in the MRP, women participated in the movement on the same terms as men, 'as their equals'. Some female commissions were created to study 'what were considered to be feminine' questions like food supply and issues relating to women's work. These commissions were organized on a local level with a national commission presided over by Mme Rollin, one of the vice-presidents of the movement. In their propaganda, the MRP claimed: 'We want women to be present in Assemblies and organizations where the interests of families, women and children are at stake.'[51] The MRP was keen, not just that women should vote, but also that they should stand for election. Nationally, female membership was not very high, except in the department of the Nord, where women represented 30 per cent of membership, and in l'Isère, Angers and Nevers. But even if actual membership was low, the party seemed to be very popular among women, and women certainly gave it widespread support in the elections.

The communist party, however, did more than any of the others to encourage women's involvement. For example, at a regional Conference in Toulouse in April 1945, it was proclaimed that 'Women have a place in our party. They should come and gain an education here and try to catch up on the delay created by our lack of democracy.'[52] Communists were aware of the importance of the role women were going to have in the democratic process. 'At the moment, the role of women in the great battle for the organization of the victory is most important.'[53] 'Women's grievances are numerous, they must be popularized with tracts and colourful posters and applied to local circumstances.'[54] The tried and tested methods of the UFF, which acted more like an association in its rallying methods, brought the communists mass female support. The *Union des Femmes Françaises* became official on 15 April 1945 with its role as 'the defence of the

49. Gueraiche, 'Les Femmes politiques', p. 184.
50. Jane Jenson and Mariette Sineau, *Mitterrand et les femmes: un rendez-vous manqué* (Paris, 1995).
51. AN F7 15588, p. 23.
52. Institut Marxiste de Toulouse, PCF Conférence Régionale, Toulouse, 7–8 Apr. 1945.
53. AN F7 15588, p. 20.   54. Ibid.

family, the liberation and reconstruction of France and the defence of women's political, social and civic rights'. Its aim was to attract the largest number of women of all possible political and religious confessions and to defend the rights of women as mothers and workers. Although it declared itself to be apolitical, preoccupied solely with social concerns, it was openly organized by the communists. All activist communist women were enrolled in the UFF, where they followed the directives of the party hierarchy. The UFF nonetheless managed to rally women from diverse political horizons, the nature of which varied across the country. In Rennes, for example, of 700 members of the UFF, 100 were also enrolled in the communist party, whereas in Lyon members of the UFF were more moderate, and in Chalons-sur-Marne no members of the UFF were members of the communist party. Some UFF sections even appeared to be predominantly socialist. By April 1945, the UFF had an estimated membership of 200,000 women of all political, philosophical and religious backgrounds.[55]

Finally, there was just one political party which was the exclusive domain of women. The *Fédération Nationale des Femmes* was founded in 1938, less to join the battle to demand female suffrage than to help women to gain a full awareness and understanding of their civic rights once they had them. In 1945, its time had come. It aimed to inform women of national and international problems and social issues and to provide them with education and advice during elections. This strictly female political party considered that it was of utmost importance for women to acquire personal convictions, to become fully conscious of their responsibilities and develop their own initiative. It was felt that this was not possible for them in the traditional political parties where they inevitably played an auxiliary role. However, the predominantly bourgeois membership failed to attract women workers in the factories, where the UFF was already well implanted.[56]

Thus the real battle for women members was between the UFF and the MRP and sometimes this became quite explicit. For example, on 13 August 1946, *L'Aube*, an MRP daily newspaper, published an article accusing the UFF of buying members by distributing chocolate to them. The journalist explained that this kind of tactic reminded him of the methods used by the *milice*, who attempted to attract members by offering them ration supplements.[57] In July 1947,

55. AN F7 15588, p. 26.   56. Ibid.
57. ADF 31W414 RG Quimper, Articles de presse parus dans les quotidiens parisiens de tendance opposée, 16 Aug. 1946.

a police report in the Finistère noted that the UFF meetings were only well attended in cases when there were distributions of rare foodstuffs or material for making clothes.[58]

The main problem with the female groupings in the parties was that they had no autonomy or power. As Duverger later pointed out, there were female commissions, teams or sections in almost all political parties, but none of these had any real autonomy or any real influence inside the party.[59] André Michel went even further, explaining that the female commissions had two roles. On the one hand they allowed parties to sideline female demands seen as embarrassing to the party by isolating women into small groups and preventing their voices from being heard in the central organization of the party. On the other hand, they were asked to liaise and transmit decisions taken outside of their influence by the party hierarchy.[60] Only the MRP managed to sign up women in significant numbers. Communist women preferred to join the UFF and the number of activists involved in the party *per se* seems to have remained limited. Women responded better to the approach of the associations where their interest was attracted by the discussion of local issues. The UFF adopted the same methods as the associations and in this they were effective, but the separation of women from the main communist party also served to ghettoize them and isolate them from the hierarchy and the main power base of the party. Nonetheless, the communists were the most successful of all the parties at getting women into elected positions.

SELECTION OF CANDIDATES

The male hierarchy of the main political parties was responsible for the selection of candidates and most did not take women seriously. Some enjoyed using women with well-known surnames to electoral ends, as in the case of Mathilde Péri (communist) and Gilberte Brossolette (socialist).[61] On the Right, the wives of the men who had voted full powers to Pétain in 1940, and who were forbidden from standing for election, were allowed to stand, and many were used by parties in the same way, as in the case of Mme Etienne Flandrin.[62] Both Maurice Duverger and Andrée Michel affirm that the selection

58. ADF 31W414 RG Quimper, Activité de l'UFF, 21 July 1947.

59. Duverger, *La Participation des femmes à la vie politique*, p. 100.

60. Andrée Michel, 'Les Françaises et la politique', *Les Temps modernes*, 230 (July 1965), p. 65.

61. Gueraiche, 'Les Femmes politiques', p. 182.   62. AN F7 15588, p. 40.

procedures operated against women. At first, most political parties made great efforts to incorporate women onto their lists, if only to catch the eye of the women voters. But it was the position of women on these lists which demonstrated whether parties had a real commitment to getting women elected. The proportional representation system meant that only women at the head of a list had a real chance of election. In 1946, only 16 per cent of women candidates were in first or second place and only 7 per cent of these were elected.[63] Yet women's interest in local issues was reflected in their success in the municipal elections when more than six hundred women were voted onto local councils.[64] More women were present on the lists of the communist party and the Resistance (16–18 per cent of candidates), than those of the Radicals and socialists (10–11 per cent).[65] In the 1945 general elections, 10 per cent of candidates in the whole of France were women (281 of 2,912): 14.1 per cent communists, 9.2 per cent MRP, 9.2 per cent socialists, and 5.7 per cent Radicals. Of the 552 elected, 30 were women (16 communists, 7 MRP, 6 socialists, 1 Right and none from the Radicals). Unsurprisingly, the communist party was the most successful of all the parties at getting women elected. In 1946, 26 women were elected, and in both 1951 and 1956 there were 15 communist women *députées*. They consistently presented more women candidates than any of the other parties and put them higher on their lists. The percentage of women rose from 14 per cent in 1945 to 19.9 per cent in June 1946 and 20.1 per cent in November 1946.

However, overall, 1945–46 was to represent a peak in women's political participation and election to the Assembly. Afterwards the number of women in the National Assemblies fell, from 39 (5.4 per cent) in 1946, to 23 (3.6 per cent) in 1951, to 19 (3.1 per cent) in 1956.[66] There was a parallel drop in the number of women on municipal and regional councils at a local level. While they had made up 7.6 per cent of the membership of the Liberation committees, this figure had dropped to 0.2 per cent in 1952.[67] Despite a promising start to their political involvement, then, the number of women in elected political positions (though those on the

---

63. Duchen, *Women's Rights and Women's Lives*, p. 18.
64. Lehmann, *Le Rôle de la femme française*, p. 18.
65. Huard, *Le Suffrage universel*, p. 372.
66. Figures from Albert Brimo, *Les Femmes françaises face au pouvoir politique* (Paris, 1975), p. 86. For an analysis of the women deputies see Hilary Footitt, 'The First Women *Députés*: "les 33 Glorieuses"?', in H.R. Kedward and Nancy Wood (eds), *The Liberation of France: Image and Event* (London, 1995), pp. 129–41.
67. Gueraiche, 'Les Femmes politiques', p. 178.

Liberation committees had been nominated rather than elected) declined dramatically after an immediate postwar high. After a few years women withdrew from the political scene. How can this be explained?

Women's experience of politics

From 1944, most women performed their 'duty' as they put it, and went out to vote. Some women, particularly those who had been active in the Resistance, became members of the parties, attended political meetings and were named as candidates. Many had joined the transitory Liberation committees (CDL, CLL) as a natural continuation of their commitment to resistance and most of them conceptualized their political presence there in those terms, seeing themselves as 'resisters' rather than 'women politicians'. Some agreed to become candidates for the re-established parties, but still in their Resistance capacity, a terminology that was reinforced by the party propaganda which always emphasized the Resistance past of their candidates. But these women were increasingly called upon to define themselves politically in relation to the various formations that were emerging. Some, particularly those who had some prewar experience, were happy to identify themselves with the traditional party groupings. But, in the political tumult of the months that followed the Liberation, it is clear that many women had started to draw back. A large number of them became less and less prepared to be associated with the political debates and groups that were emerging. During the war, they had worked together for the common cause of ridding France of the Occupier, turning a blind eye to the politics behind their activity, as had all the members of the various Resistance groups both male and female. Most had been less concerned with the political affiliations of the groups within which they operated and more interested in the fact that they were acting against the Germans.

> I knew people on the left and people on the right, everyone was against the Occupier, against the Germans, against the invader. We gave each other a hand while still remaining from very different parties politically. There were people in the Resistance who had completely opposing ideas, however, who acted like *brothers*, they were together, hand in hand [emphasis added].[68]

68. Interview, Madame Sandrine (Toulouse).

An example of this uneasiness to identify themselves with political parties is demonstrated by the reluctance of some women who had worked with the UFF during the Occupation to affiliate themselves to it once its political nature and links with the communist party became more apparent. One Gaullist woman explained that she did not agree with the UFF because it was of communist leanings and therefore refused to join after the Liberation.[69] Another woman, who later became a socialist councillor, also highlighted the difference between working with the UFF during the war, when everyone was working for the same cause, and after the war, when it became clear that they were essentially a communist grouping, despite communist attempts to play this down.[70]

Furthermore, voting was one thing, but joining a political party and attending meetings was another. Most party meetings often took place in the evenings, so women whose husbands were politically motivated were expected to stay at home and look after the children, while the husband went out to the meeting for both of them. It is not therefore surprising that women who were unable to attend meetings often voted according to the influence of their husbands. This account of a communist party meeting in September 1945 is very telling:

> Once I arrived in a village, there were about 65 men, there was not one single woman. So my intervention was very simple: It started with 'You are married?' . . . 'Yes, yes.' . . . 'Where are your wives?' . . . 'At home.' . . . 'So how will they vote?' . . . 'They will vote how we tell them to . . .'[71]

Women did not consider party politics to be part of their culture. After all, women had been trained to believe that they were not part of French political culture and that their role was to bring up their sons to be good citizens. They found it difficult to maintain their interest in public matters. Re-establishing the home and having children took precedence. As Evelyn Sullerot, who was 20 in 1944, explained, 'It was a reflex against death. Our desire for life manifested itself more in a family commitment than a political one.'[72] Married women also had to face the hostility of returning men who were not always understanding about their new rights. 'Many women did not become involved in politics because the men

---

69. Interview, Madame Saskia (Toulouse).
70. Interview, Madame Juliette (Toulouse).
71. Interview, Madame Violette (Toulouse).
72. Bard, *Les Filles de Marianne*, p. 450.

who returned did not want them to participate in party politics', explained a witness.[73]

Women who were prepared to be involved had more of a tendency to do so on a local level, perhaps because local politics were closer to their daily concerns and they could engage with the needs of the community. One woman who was a local councillor explained: 'When I was a town councillor, women came to my house to ask for information. I had to obtain what they needed from the town hall. They needed enough chits to feed and clothe their children and to take them to clinics to make sure they were healthy.'[74]

Generally speaking, the political parties failed to address the area and subjects that really interested women despite the fact that they were becoming increasingly aware that the female vote was an important constituency for them. They simply failed to relate to women's issues so that women felt that their problems were not being addressed. Their failure to put together programmes for women was a serious oversight. Women could be mobilized by becoming interested in issues which directly affected them on a local level, in the ways most effectively used by the Christian associations and the UFF. Activist women who took politics seriously were most likely to belong to these groups.

However, even within the UFF, there was a tension for militant communist women, who sometimes preferred to distance themselves from this formation, which they saw as a 'mother's association rather than a women's association'.[75] The main party was not a forum where they could articulate their concerns, as the following witness described:

> if we met up between women communists . . . if we prepared an event, it was the women who had to make cakes. We all met up, on the one hand, there were women who had a militant commitment to the Party, but who were in a minority in the committee meetings where women's problems were never raised, and the other hand, women who never came to these meetings because it was their husbands who came. We were not together for five minutes before two problems were raised. Firstly, relations with their husbands, the fact that they let women do everything in the home. The second was the fear of getting pregnant. It always struck me that when women were alone

73. Interview, Madame Juliette (Toulouse).   74. Ibid.
75. Renée Rousseau, *Les Femmes rouges: chronique des années Vermeersch* (Paris, 1983), p. 86.

together, they talked about these problems, problems which were never discussed in committee meetings.[76]

Birth control was a subject of major concern to women, but, despite this, the communist party continued to campaign against it as the 'Malthusian enterprise of the bourgeoisie' and to support pro-natalist policies (see Chapter 7).[77]

Even for those women who were motivated, the political world was not an easy one and they could not be educated to become political animals overnight. Some parties had problems finding women who were prepared to come forward and speak at meetings and to publicly represent them. Gueraiche suspects that this was one of the reasons why the UFF, which made an organized effort to politicize and promote women, was so successful in getting women onto committees and lists of candidates. The lack of available women meant that the authorities were obliged to take on women who were prepared to stand and this often meant that they had to take those who were designated by organizations like the UFF.[78] A member of the socialist party in Toulouse complained that women were rarely selected because they did not have the necessary skills and they were not eloquent enough.[79] Women were themselves conscious of their lack of political training and knew that they needed experience to gain expertise. A circular of the *MNPDG-Amicale des Femmes* dated January–February 1945 emphasized that women who were to take their place in the economic and political life of the country needed to learn discipline in discussion, lamenting that women lacked experience in organizing and running committees.[80] Those women who did find themselves on the party political platforms sometimes found

76. 'si on se retrouvait entre femmes communistes . . . si on préparait une fête, c'était les femmes qui devaient faire les gâteaux. Là venaient, d'une part des femmes qui avaient une vie militante habituelle et qui en réunion des cellules étaient minoritaires par rapport aux hommes qui ne posaient jamais des problèmes de femmes, et d'autre part, les femmes qui ne venaient jamais à la cellule parce que c'était leurs maris qui y allaient. Et il n'y avait pas cinq minutes qu'on était entre femmes, que deux problèmes se posaient. Un, les relations avec le mari, le fait qu'il laissait la femme faire tout dans la maison. La deuxième était la peur de la grossesse. Ça m'avait toujours frappée que dès que les femmes étaient entre elles, elles parlaient de ces problèmes-là qui n'étaient jamais évoquées dans les cellules.' Interview, Madame Antoinette (Toulouse).

77. Rayna Kline, 'Partisans, Godmothers, Bicyclists and other Terrorists: Women in the French Resistance and under Vichy', *Proceedings of the Western Society for French History* (1977), p. 38.

78. Gueraiche, 'Les Femmes politiques', p. 179.

79. Interview, Monsieur David (Toulouse).   80. AN 72 AJ 2177.

that their reception was not always a very friendly one. One woman described her experience when she went to address an MRP meeting: 'I went to campaign at St-Marthurin, where I had tomatoes thrown in my face. I defended women and people said that I should go home and mend socks. . . . There were no women at this meeting, only men.'[81]

Women therefore had to be really committed in order to want to carry on being involved in politics. Most felt that the discourse that was being used in postwar politics remained an essentially male one which had no real relevance for the majority of them.

> Yes, at the Liberation the Assemblies included large numbers of women, this number diminished rapidly. The return to prewar political structures, the fastidious games of a formal and often fawning parliamentarianism, and – why not – the masculine atavism which returned to ways of thinking, distanced women from becoming representatives of the country.[82]

Some commentators have put women's failure to remain in politics down to a certain disappointment because the political parties themselves did not take them seriously. For Marthe Gouffe 'political parties . . . did not take up their concerns. Discouraged, large numbers of them lost interest in politics as it is currently conducted, which in no way means that they abstained from voting.'[83] Andrée Michel argued that women moved into activities outside party politics to express themselves: 'For women, excluded from political responsibility in the parties, it is to be expected that women would prefer to act outside parties according to a tradition dating from a time when parties did not exist and women did not have political rights.'[84] Albistur and Armogathe, in their history of the feminist movement, confirm this idea, explaining that disillusionment with party politics eventually led to the feminist movement. 'Treated as minors by the political parties, women who wanted to fulfil their political ambitions turned away from male political life and tried to create institutions and forms of specific action.'[85] Those who did adapt to formal postwar politics were often those who already had some political

81. Interview, Madame Sybille (Toulouse).

82. Lucie Aubrac, in UFF, *Les Femmes dans la Résistance* (Paris, 1977), p. 21.

83. Marthe Gouffe, 'La Promotion féminine en France depuis la Libération', undated typed manuscript from CEDIAS (Centre d'Etudes de Documentation, d'information et d'Action Sociales) No. 39355, p. 10.

84. Andrée Michel, 'Les Françaises et la politique', p. 62.

85. Maite Albistur and Daniel Armogathe, *Histoire du féminisme français*, 2 (Paris, 1977), p. 604.

education, who had perhaps gained political experience before the war. Some might have found their wartime activities a consciousness-raising experience, but it is difficult to discover the extent to which the experience of resistance fostered a kind of political consciousness in women.

By 1948, there was general disillusionment with party politics and the Fourth Republic. The government had shown itself to be unstable at home and ineffective abroad in the face of foreign policy issues like the Cold War and the problems of decolonization in Indo-China and Algeria. The extent of the drift away from politics on the part of women is demonstrated by this appeal to women in 1948 to return to the political arena on the part of the UFCS:

> Do not condemn politics out of hand, it is necessary; it is simply the art of running the country. It is a difficult and ungratifying task; certain women have had the courage to launch themselves into it, we should help and encourage them.[86]

How can the political activity of women during the Occupation with or against the Occupier be reconciled with the apparent failure of women to become actively involved in postwar politics? The Resistance generation of women were certainly more involved in party politics immediately after the war, but many subsequently dropped out. It seems that they found it difficult to make the transition to postwar party politics. They may well have been frightened away from party politics by their apparent inability to make any headway within the established male parties and by a political agenda which did not concern or interest them. There were also other pressures which drew them into the home, a perceived need to re-establish the household which encompassed the bringing up and care of children. There were therefore structural reasons which made it difficult for them to combine these concerns with political activity.

But there also seems to be a case for the argument that the politically inchoate world of the Occupation made it possible for women to make political choices and carry them out in a situation which directly concerned them and had a direct bearing on their lives. Chapters 4 and 5 showed how during the war women were able to behave politically both inside and outside the home, even if this political behaviour was not recognized as such by women. An analysis of the following quote clarifies the argument:

---

86. Geneviève d'Arcy, Politique et Action Sociale, *Notre Journal. UFCS* (Dec. 1948).

> After the war women became politicised. They made choices, if a woman became part of an association, she really committed herself. But during the war, that was her first involvement, but it was global. There were no politics in it, for some yes . . . but many of them were not politicized, we were against the Occupier. I could do it in the home and at the same time I was niggling the Occupier.[87]

Here 'politics' were thought to belong exclusively to the realm of 'party politics'. For this witness, and many like her, what she did during the war was not 'political' – 'there were no politics in it', she explained. Whereas, a woman who became involved in postwar politics, 'had chosen . . . she really made a commitment to it.' Party politics were put onto a completely different conceptual level from resistance activities during the Occupation.

In this way it can be seen that when, after the Liberation, politics moved back into the domain of male political parties, many women who had been politically active during the war felt unable to integrate themselves into the structures of established party politics despite the fact that they could vote. There was little on the political agenda that they could relate to in the way some had responded to the threat Nazism posed to their homes and families. The kinds of political choices that were demanded of them were quite different and much further removed from the realities of their everyday lives. The continuing difficulties of everyday life demanded that in order to protect or restore their homes they remain within the private sphere, where party politics had no place. Where the Resistance had provided them with outlets to become politically involved and active in ways that were often an extension of their normal daily tasks, postwar politics demanded a definite and regular commitment and precise skills like public speaking and organizational abilities. The large political parties organized action groups, or at least women's commissions, to co-ordinate election propaganda, but these groups were much less successful than the associations. Few women appeared to be interested in 'pure' politics. Furthermore, the politicians and the policy-makers in the postwar period did not direct themselves at women, and did little to encourage and motivate their new electors. Then, as now, none of the parties put together an election programme which was specifically directed at women. The political system remained extremely complex, and often proved most inaccessible to women, who had no time to attend political meetings and gain the necessary political education. Alienation from

---

87. Interview, Madame Sandrine (Toulouse).

the Fourth Republic came very quickly; for some it was the revolution that never happened. Women were an important part of this general alienation.

Furthermore, it seems possible that once the vote was gained, the organizations which had been involved in mobilizing women in the battle for suffrage were unable to adapt to the new situation. As Christine Bard has pointed out, the purely suffragist movements found it hard to survive their victory.[88] Perhaps women had found it easier to be politically involved and mobilized when they were fighting for this specific right. It is true that women have achieved considerable political victories by channelling all their resources into specific demands and this has been behind the successes of later feminism.

As far as the traditional structures of democracy are concerned, until very recently feminists had more or less given up on liberal democracy as a way of politicizing and involving women in politics. As Anne Philips put it, 'no feminist in her right mind would have thought that democracy could deliver the goods'.[89] However, the 1997 elections in both Britain and France have brought unprecedented numbers of women into parliament. The *parité* campaign in France has had some success, but whether the presence of women in the *Chambre des Députées* will bring any long-lasting change to the paradigms of male-dominated democracy still remains to be seen.

88. Bard, *Les Filles de Marianne*, p. 451.
89. Anne Philips, *Gendering Democracy* (London, 1991), p. 61.

Conclusion

This study shows how the Liberation was in no sense a 'liberation' for women. Women did not experience a 'liberation' in 1944–48, neither from the point of view of their everyday lives nor from the point of view of political suffrage. The Liberation emerges from this study as an experience which meant the removal of German domination but offered women no other kinds of liberation. The hardships of wartime everyday life continued into the postwar years and women were forced to pursue strategies they had developed. Generally speaking, in terms of women's daily lives, there was much continuity with what had gone before and most categories of women continued to be predominantly concerned with the problems of economic resources and physical survival. It could even be argued that women's lives were even more constrained after the war. The return of the men was experienced as oppressive by certain categories of women who had to give up their wartime responsibilities and their sense of autonomy. Many pressures operated which pushed them back into the home, and the ever-present pro-natalist discourse was particularly influential. As for legislation, the gaining of the vote was certainly a major new step for women and important laws were also passed in relation to women's work. But these laws cannot be seen as having brought major changes to women's lives. Most of the legislation concerning paid employment established a principle, but, initially at least, had little impact. Furthermore, as Jane Jenson has shown, legislation stopped short of granting women full civic rights by failing to consider them as individuals but rather as working women with equal rights to men, or as mothers whose place was in the home under the tutelage of their husbands.[1] Even after the social postwar

1. Jane Jenson, 'The Liberation and New Rights for French Women', in M.R. Higonnet, J. Jenson, S. Michel and M.C. Weitz (eds), *Behind the Lines: Gender and the Two World Wars* (New Haven and London, 1987).

legislation, women were still not equal partners: 'the husband . . . can prevent women from exercising a profession . . . he has all the household income'.[2] Only if the wife had a profession distinct from that of her husband was she allowed to dispose of her own income. Legislation which ensured full equality in a married couple came much later. Gaining the vote was not a liberating experience, and married women still lacked the civic rights necessary for them to be fully equal with men. For most women, particularly those who were trying to run a household, gaining the vote was not an important event. The whole issue was overshadowed by other problems: the events of the Liberation, the continuing problems of food supply and the prospect and reality of the return of their men.

In terms of paid employment, during the war women entered the labour market, although not on the same scale as during the First World War. Despite Vichy legislation in 1940 to prevent married women from working, this law had little impact in the face of German demands for labour, and married women who wanted to find employment were able to do so and the government was forced to change its policy. Moreover, the failure of the Vichy government to compensate households for the loss of their main wage-earner had the paradoxical effect of forcing many married women to find jobs. Women were able to move into jobs that were previously male-dominated and some certainly benefited from training opportunities that were not open to them before the war; such women often wanted to remain at work after the war. The postwar situation was therefore more complicated than the traditional picture of a simple move out of the labour force on the part of women to make way for the returned men, although it is true that married women often left jobs when their husbands returned. Postwar legislation passed in relation to women's employment was slow to take effect but did indicate an increasing acceptance that women should work, and it seems probable that single women who were married after the war were less likely to stop working than they would have been six years before.

Political choices did not occur in a vacuum nor were there such sharp distinctions between collaboration and resistance as has previously been assumed. Women could be involved in varying degrees of political activity. In both cases women did not participate on the same scale nor in the same ways as men, but were present as

2. Andrée Lehmann, *Le Rôle de la femme française au milieu du vingtième siècle* (Paris, 1960), p. 8.

members of resistance networks and collaborationist organizations. On the whole women tended to be more involved with less organized and unofficial forms of collaboration or resistance. Other commitments and household constraints meant that they concentrated on activities which could be combined with their everyday lives. The more constraints they had, the more of a tendency they had to conform to the existing situation. Those with fewer constraints, as in the case of single autonomous women, were much freer to become politically active. There were structural reasons which prevented women from being as involved as men. Women tended to be less politicized, fewer were employed and therefore had less access to contact networks. The structures that operated to push women one way or another were more likely to be related to family links. A certain element of chance also came into play, as in cases where women had husbands, brothers or fathers who were involved in specific organizations. There were, of course, women who made free choices based on their own political consciousness. But a certain number of these were pre-determined choices based on previous political experience.

Despite their political contribution during the war, many of those who found that the Occupation offered them the means to behave politically withdrew after the Liberation just at the time when their political rights were recognized officially. The ambient discourse claimed that women gained their political education in the Resistance, but very few women assimilated it in this way. Many were reluctant to associate their resistance activity with the political groups that emerged after the war. The re-emergence of the party political system therefore served to exclude many women who were unable to relate to the complicated political issues of the postwar years in the same way as they had responded to the threat posed by the Germans to their nation, to their freedom and to their homes. This is not say that women did not vote, but relatively few became involved in active politics.

The communist party emerges as having been the most effective of all the political parties in mobilizing women. With the UFF and its particularly local emphasis, the communists established effective structures which enabled them to rally women throughout this period. Women responded to their organizational methods and identified their demands with the problems of their everyday lives. Although some women withdrew from the UFF after the Liberation when its communist allegiance became more apparent, the communist party succeeded in keeping the support of the highest number of women who had gained a certain political consciousness from their wartime activities. Furthermore, during the postwar years it was the communists who did the most to explicitly seek out the women's vote and to promote women within the party as candidates for election.

The material collected here suggests a much more fragmented picture of women's experience than that contained in most postwar accounts. The fact that there was no spectacular change has made it possible for commentators to overlook the subtleties this study has brought to light. Although the end of the war cannot be seen as having brought a watershed for women generally, some felt that they made important personal gains from their experiences of the war, particularly in cases where they were obliged to take on responsibilities in the absence of their husbands. This sense that women made progress towards a new feeling of personal independence emerged forcefully from the oral evidence. Many women articulated the feeling that their experience of the war had led them to a more positive assessment of themselves and gave them an increased confidence to confront the inequalities that continued to exist within their marriages. For many, their experience of new roles and the changes they experienced led them to a new self-perception. Women expressed disappointment with the re-establishment of society in the immediate postwar years, as Celia Bertin has explained:

> After the Liberation, things were immediately so different from what we had hoped for. And how were we to make ourselves heard? It seemed as if no one wanted to listen to us any more. It just did not occur to us to get together to challenge this attitude towards us. . . .
>
> Women allowed themselves to slip back into their old habits, brought up to conform by so many centuries of Judaeo-Christian morality. They accepted the old norms of society, without even appearing to notice it . . . Most of them returned to being the second-class citizens they had been before the war both within their families and in society.[3]

Others, however, did begin to reconsider the validity of conventional gender divisions. The war and the Liberation marked for them the beginning of a long process which is still continuing, in France as elsewhere.

3. Celia Bertin, *Les Femmes sous l'Occupation* (Paris, 1993), p. 218.

Glossary

Abwehr	German airforce
allocations	financial benefits put aside by government to help those in need
arrête	a municipal law
ausweis	a document required by the German Occupying authorities to allow individuals to travel, particularly if the journey involved crossing from one zone to another
Combat	Resistance network founded by Henri Frenay in November 1941; it involved a number of Catholic democrats
délation	the writing of letters of denunciation, sometimes anonymously and sometimes for payment
ersatz	the replacement of normal goods by artificial ones, for example, coffee
Francisme	a Paris-based collaborationist group
Gestapo	German police
Groupe Collaboration	a Paris-based collaborationist group officially recognized in January 1943
Légion Française des Combattants	created by decree in August 1940, it was intended to be a single organization for French veterans of the First and Second World Wars to provide moral and patriotic support for the Vichy government. A special section was formed to cater for wives of members of the *Légion*. These groups were confined to the southern zone, where they were extremely popular with over 1.5 million women members in the middle of 1941

Libération	Resistance network which originated in the southern zone and which tended to attract prominent socialists
maquis	groups of young men, often *réfractaires* who escaped into the countryside and were organized by the Resistance to help fight the Germans
milice	On 30 January 1943, Darnaud transformed the SOL into the *milice* (militia), a paramilitary organization, the role of which was to help the French police (and the Germans) crack down on 'terrorists' and *réfractaires*
réfractaires	those who escaped the compulsory labour draft (STO) and went into hiding
Relève	in response to German demands for French labour, the *Relève* scheme was introduced in June 1942. This system was designed to encourage French workers to go to Germany and it allowed for the return of one French prisoner in exchange for the departure of three French volunteer specialist factory workers to work in Germany. Recruitment offices were established across the country. Some volunteers came forward, women as well as men, but the numbers were far from enough to satisfy the Germans. Among the prisoners-of-war selected to return home, priority was given to First World War veterans, fathers of four children and those in jobs 'necessary to France', but very few prisoners-of-war were actually repatriated. The low numbers coming forward were doubtless one of the reasons the measure failed so completely, along with a genuine reluctance to live and work in Germany. The failure of this policy led to the introduction of the compulsory labour draft (STO).
révolution nationale	the national revolution planned by Vichy to set France to rights after the Popular Front and the impact of its crushing defeat. It involved a desire to return to traditional values and a number of right-wing measures were implemented
Wehrmacht	German army soldiers

Bibliographical Essay

Not a great deal has been published about women during the war in France and interested scholars are obliged to consult a number of more general works in order to gain some knowledge. Cited below are the main secondary texts which were helpful in the writing of this book. Most are in French; few have been translated into English and, where possible, English alternatives are suggested.

There are a number of helpful general histories of the war and the Occupation in France which act as an introduction to anyone interested in the period. In English, H.R. Kedward's *Occupied France: Collaboration and Resistance 1940–1944* (Oxford, 1985) is a standard text. In French, Yves Durand's *La France dans la deuxième guerre mondiale 1939–1945* (Paris, 1989) or Henri Rousso, *Les Années noires, vivre sous l'Occupation* (Paris, 1992) are both very accessible. Some other books deal usefully with the everyday life aspect of the war. Alfred Sauvy's *La Vie economique des Français de 1939–1945* (Paris, 1978) is a classic source of information. Henri Amouroux has written a lengthy series of books, *La Vie quotidienne des Français sous l'Occupation* (Paris, 1977–97). More recently, *Vivre et survivre en France 1939–47* (Paris, 1995) by Dominique Veillon provides detailed information. However, there is virtually nothing in English and none of these books really give much sense of the extent to which the war was a gendered experience.

On the other hand, there is now an extensive literature about French women between the wars which serves as essential background to women's wartime experience. *France between the Wars: Gender and Politics* (London, 1996) by Siân Reynolds is a superb example of gender history. Other works focus particularly on feminist groups, the best of which is by Christine Bard, *Les Filles de Marianne: histoire des féminismes 1914–40* (Paris, 1995). In English, *Feminism and the*

Third Republic (Oxford, 1996) by Paul Smith covers much of the same ground and gives a detailed analysis of the different feminist groups and their activities.

There is now a growing body of literature specifically on the personal experiences of women in the Second World War. The best starting place is probably a chapter by Hélène Eck, 'Les Françaises sous Vichy: femmes du désastre – citoyennes par le désastre?' in Georges Duby and Michelle Perrot (eds), *Histoire des femmes le xxe siècle* (Paris, 1992), pp. 185–209. *Femmes sous l'Occupation*, by Celia Bertin (Paris, 1993), although a personalized account, covers most aspects of women's experience, as does *Femmes dans la guerre 1939–1945* (Paris, 1989) by Guylaine Guidez, which also includes an international perspective. In English, a now dated but immensely helpful article by Rayna Kline, 'Partisans, Godmothers, Bicyclists and other Terrorists: Women in the French Resistance and under Vichy', *Proceedings of the Western Society for French History* (1977), pp. 375–83 sets up many of the key issues. A special issue of *Modern and Contemporary France* (ed. 1999) edited by myself and Claire Gorrara entitled *Gendering the Occupation* covers a range of topics related to women's experience.

There has recently been an increasing level of interest in the intentions of the Vichy government towards women. *Vichy et l'éternel féminin* (Paris, 1996) by Francine Muel-Dreyfus, and Miranda Pollard's *Reign of Virtue: Mobilizing Gender in Vichy France* (Chicago, 1998), pull together the main debates and research on this subject. Francis Spinzer's *Une Affaire de femmes, Paris 1943, exécution d'une avorteuse* (Paris, 1986) tells the story of Marie-Louise Giraud, who was guillotined by Vichy for abortion-related crimes.

Paid employment of men and women during the war is still a relatively open field. The collection of essays of the conference held in 1992 on *Les Ouvriers en France pendant la deuxième guerre mondiale*, published in the same year as an edited collection by Denis Peschanski and Jean-Louis Robert, is really the only research available. Catherine Omnès' study of *Ouvrières parisiennes: marchés du travail et trajectoires professionnelles des parisiennes au 20 siècle* (Paris, 1997) focuses on women and is a most necessary addition to the existing material, but more research needs to be carried out.

Prisoners-of-war were the subject of Yves Durand's detailed study *La Captivité: histoire des prisonniers de guerre français 1939–45* (Paris, 1980). Christophe Lewin's thesis, published in French as *Le Retour des prisonniers de guerre* (Paris, 1986), explored the return of prisoners-of-war. But Sarah Fishman was the first to take the specific category of wives of prisoners-of-war and examine their experience in France during the war in *We Will Wait! The Wives of French Prisoners of War, 1940–45* (New Haven and London, 1991).

As concerns political activity during the Occupation, local studies have been very helpful in showing how collaboration and resistance were not clear-cut choices. Paul Jankowski, *Communism and Collaboration: Simon Sabani and Politics in Marseille, 1919–44* (London, 1984) and John Sweets, *Choices in Vichy France* (Oxford, 1986) are illuminating although they do not take any account of gender. Similarly, the more recent study by Robert Zaretsky, *Nîmes at War: Religion, Politics and Public Opinion in the Gard, 1938–44* (University Park, Pennsylvania State University Press, 1995), provides a great deal of local flavour.

There is, to date, no study devoted to women and collaboration, but a number of the general texts are helpful. Richard Cobb's rather maverick book, *French and Germans, Germans and French: A Personal Interpretation of France under Two Occupations 1914–1918/ 1940–1944* (Hanover, 1983) was the first to raise some important questions about women's involvement in collaboration. Many of these are taken up by Philippe Burrin in *La France à l'heure allemande* (Paris, 1995), translated as *Living with Defeat: France under the German Occupation 1940–44* (London, 1996). The most developed work on women is being conducted by Françoise Leclerc and Michèle Wending in their studies of the collaboration trials: see 'La Répression des femmes coupables de la collaboration', in Françoise Thébaud (ed.), *Clio: histoire, femmes et sociétés, résistances et libérations* (Toulouse, 1995), pp. 129–51. (Their thesis is due for publication on completion.) The collection of essays *Gender and Fascism in Modern France*, by Melame Hanthouse and Richard J. Golsan (Hanover and London, 1997), covers a literary range of subjects.

Henri Rousso's article 'L'Epuration en France, une histoire inachevée', in *Vingtième Siècle* (Jan.–Mar. 1992), summarized the existing research at that time. Since then there have been a number of publications on the punishment of women by head-shaving. Alain Brossat's book, *Les Tondues: un carnaval moche* (Paris, 1992), was a first extensive study of this. See also a chapter by Corran Laurens, 'La Femme au turban: les femmes tondues', in H.R. Kedward and N. Wood (eds), *The Liberation of France: Image and Event* (London, 1995), pp. 159–73. Fabrice Virgili has published a number of articles on this subject: 'Les "Tondues" à la Libération: le corps des femmes, enjeu d'une réappropriation', in Françoise Thébaud (ed.), *Clio*, pp. 111–27, and 'Les Tontes de la Libération en France', in

Françoise Rouquet and Danièle Voldman (eds), *Les Cahiers de l'IHTP*, 31 (1995), pp. 53–67. Luc Capdevila's work is also fascinating in this context: see 'La "Collaboration sentimentale": antipatriotisme ou sexualité hors-normes?', in Françoise Rouquet and Danièle Voldman (eds), *Les cahiers de l'IHTP*, 31 (1995), pp. 67–82, and his *Les Bretons au lendemain de l'Occupation: Imaginaires et comportements d'une sortie de guerre 1944–1945* (Rennes, 1999).

There have been a number of descriptive accounts of women's individual and collective experiences in the Resistance, the best of which is the collection by the UFF, *Les Femmes dans la Résistance* (Paris, 1977). The collective experience of women who were arrested by the Germans and deported comes across forcefully in *Les Françaises à Ravensbrück* (Paris, 1965). Frances Hamelin, *Femmes dans la nuit 1939–44* (Paris, 1988) discusses the experience of women who were imprisoned in France. There are a number of biographical and autobiographical accounts of women in the Resistance, some of which have been available for some time, while others are more recent or have been republished: Marie-Madeleine Fourcade, *L'Arche de Noé* (Paris, 1968/1989); Brigitte Friang, *Regarde-toi qui meurs* (Paris, 1970/1989); Elisabeth de Miribel, *La Liberté souffre violence* (1981/1989); Mireille Albrecht, *Berty* (Paris, 1986); Lise London, *La Mégère de la rue Daguerre* (Paris, 1995); Claire Chevrillon, *Code Name Christiane Clouet* (Texas, 1995); Marie Chamming, *J'ai choisi la tempête* (Paris, 1997). The best of these is Lucie Aubrac's *Ils partiront dans l'ivresse* (Paris, 1984), translated as *Outwitting the Gestapo* (Lincoln, NE, 1993). For a literary analysis of these accounts see Claire Gorrara, *Women's Representations of the Occupation in Post-68 France* (Macmillan, 1998).

As for historians of the Resistance, a series of descriptive collections provides valuable material about women's involvement but lacks any extensive scholarly analysis: Nicole Chatel, *Des femmes dans la Résistance* (Paris, 1972); Ania Francos, *Les Femmes dans la Résistance* (Paris, 1978); Marie-Claude Coudert, *Elles la Résistance* (Paris, 1983); Margaret Rossiter, *Women in the Resistance* (New York, 1986). The work by Pierre Laborie, *Résistants Vichyssois et autres* (Toulouse, 1980), and H.R. Kedward, *Resistance in Vichy France* (Oxford, 1985) and *In Search of the Maquis* (Oxford, 1993), opened the way for a more gendered reading of the situation. Recent sociologies of the Resistance: Jacqueline Sainclivier, *La Résistance en Ille et Vilaine 1940–1944* (Rennes, 1993); Olivier Wieviorka, *Une certaine idée de la Résistance: défense de la France 1940–49* (Paris, 1995), and Laurent Douzou, *La Désobéissance: historie du mouvement Libération-Sud* (Paris, 1995), provide valuable indications of women's participation in the various Resistance networks. Dominique Veillon in her article 'Résister au féminin', *Pénélope*, 12 (Spring 1985), called for a rewriting of the history of the Resistance to include women, and Paula Schwarz did this in two essays: first, 'Re-Defining Resistance', in M.R. Higonnet, J. Jenson, S. Michel and M.C. Weitz (eds), *Behind the Lines: Gender and the Two World Wars* (New Haven, 1987), and then *'Partisanes* and Gender Politics in Vichy France', *French Cultural Studies*, 16/1 (Spring 1989). More recently, Margaret Collins Weitz, *Sisters in the Resistance: How Women Fought to Free France* (New York, 1995), offers a helpful overview of women's activities in the Resistance using extensive oral sources, but fails to offer much analysis.

The impact of the Liberation on women, a major concern of this book, is also raised in several of the essays edited by Françoise Thébaud in *Clio: Histoire, Femmes et Sociétés, Résistances et Libérations* (Toulouse, 1995). There are also a number of interesting essays concerning gender in H.R. Kedward and N. Wood (eds), *The Liberation of France: Image and Event* (London, 1995).

For a general history of the Fourth Republic see Georgette Elgey, *La République des illusion* (Paris, 1969), or Jean-Pierre Rioux, *La France de la Quatrième République 1944–52* (Paris, 1980). The books in the Cursus series are also very clearly laid out: Jean-Jacques Becker, *Histoire politique de la France depuis 1945* (Paris, 1988), and Dominique Borne, *Histoire de la société française depuis 1945* (Paris, 1988). In English, Philip William's *Crisis and Compromise: Politics in the Fourth Republic* (New York, 1966) offers an overview of the political issues. Albert and Nicole Du Roy, *Citoyennes! Il y a cinquante ans le vote des femmes* (Paris, 1994) gives the most detailed account of the debates leading to women acquiring the right to vote. Claire Duchen's book, *Women's Rights and Women's Lives in France 1944–1968* (London, 1994), takes women's experience right through the postwar period to 1968 and the beginnings of second-wave feminism.

For a European perspective of women and the war, there are now a number of national studies. On the UK, Penny Summerfield's *Women Workers and the Second World War* (London, 1984/1989) and the more recent *Reconstructing Women's Wartime Lives* (Manchester, 1998), are most useful. In Italy, Perry Willson's *The Clockwork Factory* (Oxford, 1993) is a case study of women's work under fascism. Victoria de Grazia, *How Fascism Ruled Women: Italy 1922–45* (Berkeley, 1992), is a detailed analysis of the impact of fascism on women; and Jane Slaughter, *Women and the Italian Resistance 1943–1945* (Denver, 1997), is a recent account of women's wartime activism in Italy. Ute

Frevert, *Women in German History* (London, 1990), deals with German women's wartime experience, but the classic study of women under Nazism is Claudia Koonz, *Mothers in the Fatherland: Women, the Family and Nazi Politics* (London, 1987). Rita Thalmann's collection *Femmes et fascismes* (Paris, 1986) contains a number of helpful articles, as does the more recent *Féminismes et nazisme* (Paris, 1997), edited by Liliane Kandel. Books are also appearing about women's experience of the war in other European countries. See Shirley Mangini González, *Memoires of Resistance* (New Haven, 1995) on Spain, and Janet Hart, *New Voices in the Nation* (Ithaca, 1996) on Greece.

Chronology

1939

July	*Code de la Famille* for implementation 1 January 1940
1 Sept.	Germany invades Poland
3 Sept.	Great Britain and France declare war on Nazi Germany
26 Sept.	French communist party and its organizations dissolved
Sept. 1939–May 1940	Phoney war

1940

20 Mar.	Prime Minister Edouard Daladier resigns; Paul Reynaud forms a new government
10 May	German offensive begins
18 May	The exodus begins
end May/June	British and French troops evacuated from Dunkirk
10 June	French government leaves Paris for Bordeaux
14 June	Germans enter Paris, which is declared an open city
16 June	Pétain forms a new government and orders a ceasefire
17 June	Pétain makes speech to French people telling them that he is going to request armistice: 'We must stop the fighting'
18 June	Charles de Gaulle makes speech on BBC calling for continued resistance to the Germans

216

22 June	France and Germany sign an armistice which takes effect from 25 June
1 July	Government moves to Vichy
3 July	The British bomb the French navy at Mers El-Kébir
10 July	National Assembly at Vichy votes full powers to Pétain; the Vichy regime is established
mid-Aug.	Vichy dissolves trade unions and outlaws Freemasonry
13 Oct.	Married Women's Work act
18 Oct.	First Jewish statute
24 Oct.	Pétain and Hitler meet at Montoire and Pétain declares he is on 'the path of collaboration'
Nov.	Appearance of first clandestine newspapers

1941

2 June	Second Jewish statute: the statutes racially defined Jews in terms more restrictive than those of the Nazis
22 June	Germany invades Soviet Union, violating the pact and allowing French communists to engage freely in resistance activities
22 July	Law confiscating Jewish property

1942

Feb.	Creation of the *milice*
15 Feb.	Vichy declares abortion to be a treasonable crime against the state
Mar.	First Jews deported from France to concentration camps
7 June	Jews in Occupied zone have to wear the yellow star
22 June	The *Relève* is introduced. Laval broadcasts a speech saying 'I hope for a German victory'
16–17 July	Vel'd'Hiv round-ups which led to the deportation of 13,000 Jews (including women and children)
8 Nov.	Allied landings in Morocco and Algeria
11 Nov.	Germans occupy southern France (the Free zone)
27 Nov.	French scuttle their fleet in Toulon

1943

Jan.	*Mouvements Unis de la Résistance* (MUR) is formed
16 Feb.	*Service de Travail Obligatoire* (STO) is passed
Winter	*Maquis* start to form
May	*Conseil National de la Résistance* (CNR) is formed

1944

1 Jan.	Joseph Darnaud is appointed to head the Vichy police and organize the *milice*
23 Mar.	Consultative Assembly in Algeria decides in favour of the vote for women
21 Apr.	French Committee of National Liberation (CFLN) votes in favour of women's suffrage
6 June	D Day invasion of Normandy coast. Massacre at Oradour-sur-Glane (642 victims, including 445 women and children)
15 Aug.	Allied landings in southern France
25 Aug.	Liberation of Paris
Sept.–Nov.	De Gaulle visits key towns in France
Oct.	Women acquire the right to vote

1945

Mar.–May	The return of the prisoners, deportees and STO workers
Apr.–May	Municipal elections
7 May	Unconditional surrender of Germany
July	Trial of Pétain (death sentence commuted by de Gaulle)
Sept.	Regional elections
Oct.	Legislative elections to the First Constituent Assembly and referendum which established that the Assembly should draw up a new constitution

1946

May	Referendum: draft constitution rejected
June	Legislative election to Second Constituent Assembly to draft a further constitution

Oct.   Referendum: Constitution narrowly accepted

Nov.   Legislative elections to the First National Assembly of the Fourth Republic

Index